PLAIN
TALK
ON
Isaiah

PLAIN
TALK
ON
Isaiah

MANFORD GEORGE GUTZKE
PH.D.

 **ZONDERVAN PUBLISHING HOUSE** OF THE ZONDERVAN CORPORATION
GRAND RAPIDS, MICHIGAN 49506

PLAIN TALK ON ISAIAH
Copyright © 1977 by The Zondervan Corporation
Grand Rapids, Michigan

Fourth printing November 1980

Library of Congress Cataloging in Publication Data
Gutzke, Manford George.
 Plain talk on Isaiah.
  1. Bible. O.T. Isaiah—Commentaries. I. Title.
BS1515.2G87   224.'.1'07   76-53766
ISBN 0-310-25551-1

Scripture quotations are from the King James Version.

Printed in the United States of America

CONTENTS

Chapter 1

THE FUNCTION OF A PROPHET

Do you know what a prophet of God was supposed to do?

This study in the book of the prophet Isaiah is made from the standpoint of the New Testament. When I read the prophecy of Isaiah, I do so with complete confidence, since my interest in it centers in the viewpoint of the New Testament, which tells about Jesus Christ. Jesus of Nazareth talked about the Old Testament and used it. Paul said:

> Now all these things happened unto them for examples: and they are written for our admonition, upon whom the ends of the world are come (1 Cor. 10:11).

I want the power of God in Christ Jesus in my soul, and for that reason I consider the Book of Isaiah to be the book of Isaiah literally, as it is esteemed in the New Testament.

To understand this book we need to consider the function of a prophet. The Bible speaks of both prophets and apostles, the prophets being especially those of the Old Testament, and these are they of whom we shall be thinking. Who were these men? They were designated by the word *prophet* because of what they did. A doctor is a person who doctors, just as a farmer is one who farms. One who prophesies is, therefore, a prophet. The prophets ministered primarily to the people of Israel, just as the apostles, in their letters to the churches, functioned primarily for the church, the people who believe in the Lord Jesus Christ.

There is a word from God to be said to the world, and we find that Isaiah says some things to people outside Israel. What he said to people outside Israel differed from what he said to the people inside Israel. He told those on the outside they would do well to get right with God. To those on the inside he said

7

they should draw nearer to God. The same is true with the writings of the apostles in the New Testament.

Who are these people called Israel? The fact that they were descendants of Abraham, Isaac, and Jacob is not the important thing. The truth of primary importance is that these are people who, in the covenant with Abraham and afterwards in the Law, have yielded themselves to God to serve Him. They are the people who openly committed themselves to follow God's way. God made of them a special people to demonstrate to the rest of the world what godly living was like. Israel did not have a perfect score in their history, but their record is that they walked in the direction in which God led them. Thus, they illustrated even in their failings what happens to people when they walk with God. We call them "a covenant people." They had a promise from God and it was very simple: "Walk where I show you and I will bless you." And this is the promise of God right down to our day. When they asked the Lord Jesus Christ how they might work the works of God, He said:

> This is the work of God, that ye believe on him whom he hath sent (John 6:29).

And that is God's word even now to the whole wide world.

God deals with people who have never heard Him; He deals with people who disobey Him, and He deals with them according to the Law:

> . . . whatsoever a man soweth, that shall he also reap (Gal. 6:7).

Every man has sinned and stands condemned in the presence of God; this is the record of the human race. It was for that reason Christ Jesus came to save "whosoever believeth in Him." He did not come to condemn but to save. That does not mean everyone will be saved.

> He that believeth on him is not condemned: but he that believeth not is condemned already, because he hath not believed in the name of the only begotten Son of God (John 3:18).

The Israelites were committed to walk in the ways of God; they were different from other nations — a people led of the living God by their own consent. In this respect they were unique; no other nation could ever make that claim. They were a type of all godly people living on the face of the earth; their thinking and their decisions were in terms of obedience to the revealed will of God. They walked in faith.

In order to have faith in God, a person needs to know His Word. God will do what He has promised, and that is beyond our natural understanding.

> Eye hath not seen, nor ear heard, neither have entered into the heart of man, the things which God hath prepared for them that love him (1 Cor. 2:9).

God has revealed them to us by His Spirit, and as people hear and understand His Word, they can believe and be saved. But this requires interpretation. The Word of God must be ministered to the people by persons who, because they have been given special gifts, are qualified leaders. The one thing that made the Israelites the people of God was that they had God's Word and said they would follow it.

On occasion, we find some prophet saying in effect to the people: "God didn't choose you because you are many, or because you are good (because you are not; you are stiff-necked). God chose you because through you He wants to show His grace and mercy, the way a teacher will take one student before the whole class and put him through his exercises to show the rest of the class the way it should be done." The only reason Israel was chosen was that they might demonstrate to the whole world the truth of God. The gospel involves the Seed of David, the Seed of Abraham, the Son of God, and the Son of Man: the Lord Jesus Christ in Himself being the express image of God. Believers today are now the people of God.

The church today among the groups of persons in the world is like Israel in Old Testament days among the nations of the world that then was. We must never think of any modern nation being like Israel. Israel was a nation with earthly interests, with earthly destiny, with earthly blessings, but they belonged to God in a special way. They worshiped in the tabernacle and in the temple; whereas now we know where God is: He is not in the tabernacle or the temple, He is in the hearts of believers.

> Know ye not that your body is the temple of the Holy Ghost which is in you, which ye have of God, and ye are not your own? (1 Cor. 6:19).

Believers today do not use tent tabernacles made of skins, neither do they use temples and offer animal sacrifices in worship. God does not dwell in any temple made with hands but in the hearts of the people. Just as the heart of the believer today is the temple of God and not the temple in Jerusalem, so the church is the people of God, and not the nation Israel or any other nation on earth. Among societies in a community there are clubs of various sorts, but the church is different. The church has a peculiar relation to God because His name is there.

No one can guarantee any local church to be the true church of God. I often tell those who join the church under my leadership that this does not give any of them a ticket into heaven. The local church is an association of professing believers; but it is also true that among these members is the true, invisible church — the company of those who believe in the Lord Jesus Christ (only God knows who they are). So far as a group of people who has a church building is concerned, they would not last long as a church unless some real believers were among them. Any local church, if it is worth anything, belongs to God in a peculiar way, because it has persons in it who believe in the living Lord Jesus Christ and yield to the ministry of the Holy Spirit. No other organization can make that claim.

God's people need leadership. In Old Testament times that leadership was set forth in three main offices: those of priest, king, and prophet. The priest's function was to appear before God on behalf of man. When a human being — a sinner — wanted to approach God and did not know how to do it, a priest could intercede on his behalf. The priest knows the frailty of man and the ways of God, so he is sympathetic with man and obedient and reverent toward God. He brings the sinner into the presence of God according to God's way of doing. Protestants hold that every believer is a priest in Christ Jesus. God has made believers to be a kingdom of priests and each of them has a responsibility to take some other person by the hand and bring him to the Lord. If he cannot do that in teaching he can do it in praying. All who pray for others are serving in a priestly function: believers can talk to God about other people. They can ask God to be gracious according to the revealed Word, which they know in their hearts. That is the priestly function.

The king serves to coordinate the activities of people. Someone has to organize any group that is brought together if anything is ever to be done. Israel needed a coordinator. That coordinator was their king. Today we have church officers: elders, deacons, stewards, etc., whose function it is to coordinate the activities of the church. They do all this as undershepherds, because the Lord Himself is the Shepherd, the great High Priest and the King.

There is one other functionary — the person who, knowing the mind of God, teaches it to the people. This is the prophet. He stands between God and the people, facing the people. Knowing the heart and mind of God, he tells the people what he knows, he reveals God to them. (When the priest stands between the people and God, his face is toward God; and looking to God, he prays for the people.) In the Old Testament times the prophets were the preachers. The preacher may have a certain priestly function; when standing between the people and God, he turns to God and prays for his people. When he coordinates their activities, he is the king. But when he tells the people the mind of God, he is the prophet.

When they were teaching Israel, the prophets dealt with the national problems of Israel involving geographical situations, political circumstances, cultural affairs, and moral conditions. They interpreted to Israel the life of Israel in their earthly setting. Today preachers deal with the church and minister to God's people the universal truth of the gospel, the worldwide purpose of God, the spiritual customs of believers, walking with God, and the practices of a godly life. Every now and again there are some well-meaning men who are still talking in Old Testament terminology, dealing with their congregations as if they were supposed to deal with national, geographical, political, cultural, and moral circumstances. When that happens, the spiritual meaning of the gospel tends to be lost. The tragic fact is that if the gospel is not heard from the pulpit, people will not get much of it anywhere else.

We shall now think about Isaiah, the prophet. He was a preacher in Judah. His function was to interpret to Judah the truth that God wanted them to have. These people had a certain relationship with God that Isaiah interpreted for them. There were certain conditions under which God would deal with Judah. Isaiah interpreted, evaluated, appraised, and judged their conduct as he told them about their future. He told them what God would do, and often that was the only message they could understand.

When we study any of the prophets of the Old Testament, we are listening to a preacher dealing with his people. Actually, reading the prophecies of Isaiah, Jeremiah, and Ezekiel is very much like picking up preachers' sermon notes. These preachers seldom, if ever, urged, "You ought to be good for goodness' sake." These prophets said to their people, "God has called you to Himself. He has in mind to bless you. He promised your fathers He would bless you, but you are to do His will. If you do not walk in the ways of God, He will not bless you. He will curse you." They also told the people of Israel, "You are not like the other people around you. They do things in certain ways because they do not know better, but you do know better. More is expected of you because you belong to God."

Many times the prophets had harsh things to say. In some sense, they were like doctors. If you have ever been sick and gone to a doctor, he may have had a harsh word to say about your sickness, but not about you. Most doctors are very careful about that; they do not make you feel they are opposed to you. They are against your sickness, whatever that happens to be. That was the way the prophets were. They loved these people, but they saw the soul sickness among them; and they pointed out to them that unless they let the Lord God cure them, this sickness would bring about their undoing. This happened over and over again.

Chapter 2

THE LORD'S COMPLAINT AGAINST HIS PEOPLE

Do you know what was the basic fault of Israel in the sight of God?

The first five chapters in the Book of Isaiah can be taken as one unit. They constitute a description of the conditions that existed in Israel during the preaching of Isaiah. At the very outset there is a description of the conditions into which Isaiah was sent and the kind of thing he faced when he preached. In a sense, Isaiah presented the symptoms of the sickness that was in the nation. He was sent as a doctor to apply healing (therapy, if you will) to introduce measures that would help a sick people and deal with them in spiritual matters. A reading of those five chapters will give one a general grasp of the situation. We can understand what made Isaiah preach as he did and also to whom he was preaching.

The first verse tells about the time in which Isaiah preached:

> The vision of Isaiah the son of Amoz, which he saw concerning Judah and Jerusalem in the days of Uzziah, Jotham, Ahaz, and Hezekiah, kings of Judah.

"Judah" was the name of the country and of the nation. At that time the nation of Israel was divided into two parts: the northern part, which took the name "Israel"; and the southern part, which took the name "Judah." The southern part had two and a half tribes — Judah, half the tribe of Manasseh, and Benjamin — while nine and a half tribes were in the north. The north was much larger, richer, and stronger, in a military sense, while the south was smaller and poorer but more staunch. Over and over in battle Judah proved to be just as strong, often defeating the northern tribes. What made Judah so strong was the fact that the city of Jerusalem was there with the temple. This gave them the center of the original worship of God.

The naming of the four kings gives some idea of the time of Isaiah's ministry. Not all of the days of Uzziah's reign are included, because Isaiah received his call in the year King Uzziah died. I suspect the young Isaiah felt things about Israel and Judah before Uzziah died, because when a man receives his call to preach, he already has the whole grasp of his mission in his heart. That is why he was called. In any case, the days of Jotham, Ahaz, and Hezekiah taken together amount to sixty-one years, and this represents the time of this prophet's ministry. The conditions described in the first five chapters existed during these sixty-one years.

In verses 2 to 4 we read Isaiah presenting the complaint of the Lord against His people. Remember this is a message to the people of God about their relationship with Him. Thus, we can see that Isaiah was called when this nation was sick. It may be a good idea for us to keep in mind that many people today are sick in spiritual matters. Here is the complaint of God:

> Hear, O heavens, and give ear, O earth: for the Lord hath spoken, I have nourished and brought up children, and they have rebelled against me. The ox knoweth his owner, and the ass his master's crib: but Israel doth not know, my people doth not consider (Isa. 1:2,3).

"The ox knoweth his owner, and the ass his master's crib." If you are from the country, you will know what is meant by that. Farm animals know where they belong. During my boyhood days in Canada, there were times when I had to go out at night, riding a horse in a snowstorm when I was unable to see even the horse's head. Every country boy knows what to do: let the horse go. He will take you home. And that is what is said here. The ass knoweth his master's crib — that is where he is fed.

"But Israel doth not know. My people doth not consider." These are my people; I gave them my word and they will not even read it. They do not even come to me. That is the Lord's complaint. These are sinful people, a people laden with iniquity.

Today He would be sending this message to His church:

> Ah sinful nation, a people laden with iniquity, a seed of evil-doers, children that are corrupters: they have forsaken the

Lord, they have provoked the Holy One of Israel unto anger,
they are gone away backward (Isa. 1:4).

If a man felt led to preach this today, he would say to a group of
professing church members: "Ah, sinful congregation, a
people that is laden with iniquity, you have your sin with you
right while you are sitting in church. You are a seed of evil-
doers. You do things over and over that are not right. You are
children that are corrupters. You have forsaken the Lord." God
would say this to people who never pray, never read the Bible,
and are never concerned about God; who turn to everything
except to God, completely forsaking Him. They have provoked
the Holy One of Israel to anger, they are grieving the Holy
Spirit.

What I would say to you at the very outset is this: God is
concerned about my heart's attitude toward Him. If I let my
time be taken up with other things, and if I let my interests,
activities, and relationships be so filled with other things that I
do not have time to worship Him, to have communion with
Him and praise Him, God counts that my heart is cold and that
I do not love Him as I should. In the Book of Revelation is this
word to the Ephesian church: "Thou hast left thy first love"
(Rev. 2:4). That is what Isaiah is saying here and that is the
complaint of Almighty God about His people. God is entitled
to first consideration, and no business, social study, political
issue is so important that it deserves to have first place in our
minds. The important thing is that Christ Jesus died for us; we
belong to Him and we want to be well pleasing in His sight. We
do not know how many days we have here; we will be forever
— throughout eternity — with Him. God is more important
than anything or anybody; that is what Almighty God wants us
to remember at all times.

Isaiah then presents the plight of Israel: an almost poetic
description of the spiritual condition of these people.

Why should ye be stricken any more? ye will revolt more and
more: the whole head is sick, and the whole heart faint. From
the sole of the foot even unto the head there is no soundness in
it; but wounds, and bruises, and putrefying sores: they have not
been closed, neither bound up, neither mollified with ointment. Your country is desolate, your cities are burned with fire:
your land, strangers devour it in your presence, and it is desolate, as overthrown by strangers. And the daughter of Zion is left

as a cottage in a vineyard, as a lodge in a garden of cucumbers, as
a besieged city (Isa. 1:5-8).

Everything Israel had was to be ruined. While Isaiah was
saying this, Judah was prosperous and large crowds of people
were going into the temple. Judah had not yet been defeated in
war; but Isaiah, with the insight given to him, penetrated to
their heart and exposed them as paupers.

If any preacher would say these things today, what effect
would he have? Suppose a minister stood before his congregation and said, "What is the use of the Lord's punishing you any
more; you won't ever turn to Him. The whole head is sick and
the whole heart faint; you just do not have the inward strength
to turn to God." You can feel this sickness in many congregations; few have any interest in spiritual matters. Seldom do
church members get together to really pray seriously. I need to
remind myself just as I would say it to you who read these
words: How could you know if a person were sick? Would you
not look for symptoms? Then how would you know if a person
were spiritually dead? You would know it if there were no
evidence of life! How would you know a person has no interest
in God except by seeing that he never reads his Bible? How
would you know he has no interest in getting the help of God
except by seeing that he never prays?

I think of believers in this country, where we have churches,
and where we bring our young people up the way we do. We
send them to some university where instructors will teach
them things that will make them disbelieve what we believe.
By the time these young people are through with their courses
and come home, they will not go to church any more because
they think they have learned something better than they had at
home. Their parents paid their expenses for them to go and
they paid those professors, so actually they invited the whole
business to happen. There are people in this world who do not
believe in the Lord Jesus Christ and there are people who do
not believe in God. Such persons can get right in among us and
among our young people, and before we know it, we are not as
faithful to God as we once were. Strangers who do not even
believe in God come in and devour what we have, until we are
"left desolate." So the very things we have cherished can be
taken away from us.

This was the plight of Israel:

> Except the Lord of hosts had left unto us a very small remnant,
> we should have been as Sodom, and we should have been like
> unto Gomorrah (Isa. 1:9).

Here is the beginning of a little glimmer of light in the dark. All through the prophecy of Isaiah we must watch this "remnant," because here is an amazing thing. Though the night may settle all over, God made the stars. They shine at night. Though darkness may settle all over the land, God makes the sun rise. Never at one time will the darkness completely win out, though a generation may be lost. God will win out and He will bring His Word on through. Even in Israel's day it was not all the way of desolation. There are churches today where prayer meetings are not held, but in those churches there are people who pray. Many people do not pay special attention to Bible study, but there are those in every congregation who care about the Scriptures.

As we come to the close of this portion of Isaiah, let us now consider this: Suppose you have become conscious of the fact that in your family there are hearts that are filled with the things of the world; what can you do about it? If you have not found out already, you will find that you cannot talk about it all the time. And you certainly cannot tell them; they will not listen. But one thing you will find out and that is that you can talk to the Lord. You can call on Him. Let me assure you that the very fact that you notice it and are grieved about it is something the Lord God will notice and appreciate. That is what He wants, and He looks down upon us and He appreciates our concern.

In the Book of Malachi we read that those who feared the Lord often spoke with one another. And Almighty God heard what they said. They are the people God actually had His eye on. So far as you and I are concerned, even in our own hearts, even though we may be largely given over to the things of the day, there may be inside ourselves a small remnant — something that really belongs to God. Let us honor that because that is our hope for future blessing.

Chapter 3

THE LORD'S REJECTION OF
INSINCERE WORSHIP

What one aspect in Israel's religious practices was particularly obnoxious to the Lord?

During the time of Isaiah the daily life of the Jews was marked by much routine worship. Many came to the altar to confess their sins and to offer animals in sacrifice for the propitiation of their sins. The people observed sabbath days and fasts, as well as the annual feast days as set aside in their traditional calendar. At certain times they gathered in large assemblies to share in public worship. But the sensitive soul of the prophet was grieved to realize that despite this outward display of religious observance of prescribed practices, the people did not really in their heart seek the face of the Lord.

In poetic language Isaiah referred to the Jews, using the names of cities that had been destroyed by God in a classic demonstration of His judgment upon sin.

> Hear the word of the Lord, ye rulers of Sodom; give ear unto the
> law of our God, ye people of Gomorrah (Isa. 1:10).

By this the prophet was intimating that Judah and Jerusalem were in danger of being destroyed as Sodom and Gomorrah had been destroyed in the days of Abraham and for the same reason (Gen. 18:20,21). It is shocking to think that God would destroy people who have named His name and called Him their God, but this is the message that Isaiah was given to deliver to the Jews.

It is clear to see how John the Baptist would be strengthened to preach as he did when he called on the Jews to repent.

> But when he saw many of the Pharisees and Sadducees come to
> his baptism, he said unto them, O generation of vipers, who
> hath warned you to flee from the wrath to come? (Matt. 3:7).

It is impressive to remember that Jesus of Nazareth spoke even more directly when He said:

> Woe unto you, scribes and Pharisees, hypocrites! for ye are like unto whited sepulchres, which indeed appear beautiful outward, but are within full of dead men's bones, and of all uncleanness. Even so ye also outwardly appear righteous unto men, but within ye are full of hypocrisy and iniquity (Matt. 23:27,28).

We can be humbly aware that this is the judgment of God on all insincere worship. Going through the prescribed exercises is not sufficient. To attend worship services and even to partake of the sacrament of the Lord's Supper can only add to the condemnation of the worshiper if he is not sincere (1 Cor. 11:27-29).

At the time of Isaiah, Judah was experiencing a time of prosperity and affluence. Large numbers of people brought many sacrifices as they observed the routines of worship. No doubt, the outward appearance would suggest that all was well, but the prophet startled the people with a sharp criticism of their real attitude toward God. Isaiah revealed the Word of God as a direct challenge to their consciences:

> To what purpose is the multitude of your sacrifices unto me? saith the Lord: I am full of the burnt offerings of rams, and the fat of fed beasts; and I delight not in the blood of bullocks, or of lambs, or of he goats. When ye come to appear before me, who hath required this at your hand, to tread my courts? (Isa. 1:11,12).

Isaiah questioned their motives in their worship. He challenged them to reflect on their own attitudes and to ask themselves why they were coming to worship. This would be a pertinent challenge to many churchgoers today: Why are you going to church? Are you going to worship God? In that case, why don't you think about Him when you go?

The prophet then bluntly reveals that God is "fed up" with their superficial conduct in their worship practices. God is no fool. He is not impressed with their outward conduct while their hearts are not involved in what they are doing. David had realized this truth when he wrote:

> For thou desirest not sacrifice; else would I give it: thou delightest not in burnt offering. The sacrifices of God are a broken

> spirit: a broken and a contrite heart, O God, thou wilt not
> despise (Ps. 51:16,17).

There was certainly nothing wrong with bringing the offerings as specified in the regulations, but there was nothing right in bringing such offerings without heartfelt contrition about sin. The poet said it all when he wrote, "The gift without the giver is bare."

In modern times this is all too often the case. In church services Scripture is read without the consciousness that this is the Word of God, prayers are offered while minds are wandering with interest in personal, natural things and events, songs are sung with no thought about the meaning of the words, and sermons are preached and heard with no concern about souls that are lost. No matter how conventional all this may be, Isaiah and John the Baptist in their times would have condemned all such practices as utterly unworthy. And they are. "God looketh upon the heart." The angel warned the Laodicean church that being lukewarm was entirely unacceptable to the Lord:

> So then because thou art lukewarm, and neither cold nor hot, I
> will spew thee out of my mouth (Rev. 3:16).

In view of the trashy nature of their worship, Isaiah reveals the mind of God in admonishing the Jews to put an end to their worship activities:

> Bring no more vain oblations; incense is an abomination unto
> me; the new moons and sabbaths, the calling of assemblies, I
> cannot away with; it is iniquity, even the solemn meeting. Your
> new moons and your appointed feasts my soul hateth: they are a
> trouble unto me; I am weary to bear them (Isa. 1:13,14).

God has been revealed in His Word as a God of great patience "slow to anger, and plenteous in mercy." But the longsuffering of God can be exhausted. His patience can come to an end. When people show themselves to be incorrigible, having ignored His prophets and having stedfastly refused to heed His call, God can be provoked to judgment.

Jesus of Nazareth taught:

> Except your righteousness shall exceed the righteousness of the
> scribes and Pharisees, ye shall in no case enter into the kingdom
> of heaven (Matt. 5:20).

And He warned His disciples:

> Not every one that saith unto me, Lord, Lord, shall enter into
> the kingdom of heaven; but he that doeth the will of my Father
> which is in heaven (Matt. 7:21).

He used the parable of the ten virgins to illustrate the fact that
when He returns, there will be many who will have neglected
to be ready for Him. The five foolish virgins found they were
shut out from His presence. It may be hard to grasp but the
truth is that some people who actually think they are going to
heaven will find they are shut out because they failed to be
ready for His coming.

Even praise offered in a superficial fashion is actually offensive to God: "Incense is an abomination unto me." And so it
was with their special services. The ritual of Israel provided for
occasions when the people would hold special services of worship: "new moons and sabbaths" were the occasions for the
"calling of assemblies." There was also "the solemn meeting,"
very much the same as when we call for a special prayer
meeting or promote a season of fasting, as some communions
observe Lent. And when they followed the ritual to call for
seasons of praise, "new moons and . . . appointed feasts," their
exercises were actually disgusting to God.

Perhaps even more serious was the fact that such insincerity
made their praying useless.

> And when ye spread forth your hands, I will hide mine eyes from
> you: yea, when ye make many prayers, I will not hear: your
> hands are full of blood (Isa. 1:15).

It is shocking to think that there ever would be a time when
God would not listen to urgent praying, but this was actually
the message Isaiah had to bring to the people. Apparently God
had not yet shut the door. Isaiah could preach the call to
repentance, because there was yet hope; but it was his mission
to warn the Jews that such a final act by God was imminent.
They actually stood in jeopardy because with God they were
almost at the "point of no return." Isaiah urged the people to
repent and to turn to God in sincere confession of their sins,
while there was yet time.

It would be practically impossible to overemphasize the
importance of this message to the church today. There seems

to be a widespread opinion that the patience of God is limitless, as though His tolerance of evil insincerity is everlasting. But this is a grievous error.

> Be not deceived; God is not mocked: for whatsoever a man soweth, that shall he also reap. For he that soweth to his flesh shall of the flesh reap corruption; but he that soweth to the Spirit shall of the Spirit reap life everlasting (Gal. 6:7,8).

A sober warning has been written in Scripture:

> For we know him that hath said, Vengeance belongeth unto me, I will recompense, saith the Lord. And again, The Lord shall judge his people. It is a fearful thing to fall into the hands of the living God (Heb. 10:30,31).

Peter adds a solemn admonition:

> The Lord is not slack concerning his promise as some men count slackness; but is long-suffering to us-ward, not willing that any should perish, but that all should come to repentance. But the day of the Lord will come as a thief in the night . . . (2 Peter 3:9,10).

As surely as God will keep His word, just so surely will God judge His people. The Jews were obstinate and did not turn to God when Isaiah preached, and in due time Jerusalem was destroyed. Let us pray that our generation will respond to exhortation and turn to God in repentance while there is still time!

Chapter 4

THE LORD'S OFFER OF MERCY

Do you know what Isaiah called Judah to do in view of their peril?

Because he was a prophet of God, Isaiah not only revealed the judgment of God upon sin, but also what the sinner could do to come to God and what God would do in His mercy and grace. We have noted in our previous study how drastic the judgement of God is on any insincerity in the heart of the worshiper: we are now to see that God in His mercy is ready to receive any person who will come to Him in true repentance. It has been well said, "The light that reveals, is the light that heals." But such response to God's judgment must be genuine.

John the Baptist declared this truth plainly when he instructed his hearers:

> Bring forth therefore fruits worthy of repentance (Luke 3:8).

Isaiah makes it even more personal:

> Wash you, make you clean; put away the evil of your doings from before mine eyes; cease to do evil; learn to do well; seek judgment, relieve the oppressed, judge the fatherless, plead for the widow (Isa. 1:16,17).

Such actions on the part of anyone show a real desire to be pleasing in the sight of God. Here, as always, "actions speak louder than words."

The person who would come to the Lord must be willing to submit his manner of life to the judgment of the Word of God. Jesus of Nazareth told His disciples:

> Now ye are clean through the word which I have spoken unto you (John 15:3).

As the worshiper came to worship God in the ritual of the

tabernacle, he was to pass by the laver, where he would be washed from his sins. In the prescribed procedure for consecration of the priests, the first thing done with the candidates for this office was to wash them:

> And Aaron and his sons thou shalt bring unto the door of the tabernacle of the congregation, and shalt wash them with water (Exod. 29:4).

It should be noted that the detailed instruction given by Isaiah makes it clear that the worshiper is not to be passive while someone else washes away the filth of his sin. Not only does the prophet say, "Make you clean," but he goes on to amplify the imperative command to the worshiper by saying, "Put away the evil of your doings from before mine eyes." God will not look the other way while the cleansing is carried out. He sees the heart of the sinning person and His will is that the change of behavior is to be from the heart. The repentant soul is to be genuinely sincere. This will be demonstrated in the subsequent continuing action of the worshiper.

In a series of directives the prophet spells out plainly what acceptable conduct will include:

> Cease to do evil; learn to do well; seek judgment, relieve the oppressed, judge the fatherless, plead for the widow (Isa. 1:16,17).

There must be a definite putting away of evil habits and customs. The people had the law and the judgments of Moses. They would have no excuse such as claiming they were ignorant, as though they did not know what was wrong. Not only the law and the judgments of Moses, but also their own consciences would help them to know what was evil. But the prophet exhorted them to do more than refrain from evil.

"Learn to do well" implies they would not naturally know what to do to please God nor how to do it. This was something to be learned. As practical life situations confronted them, they were to follow the revealed Word of God and learn through actual experience what was really involved in obedience.

> Though he were a Son, yet learned he obedience by the things which he suffered (Heb. 5:8).

If Jesus of Nazareth "learned obedience" by His own participation in the problems of living, how much more necessary is it that sinful persons learn. by activating the will to obey God.

The prophet is then more specific in his analysis of what is involved in obedience to God.

> Seek judgment, relieve the oppressed, judge the fatherless, plead for the widow (Isa. 1:17).

The sincere repentant soul who desires to be well pleasing in the sight of God will exercise his judgment in honest factual appraisal of any situation he may face. In humility he will set aside personal preferences and arrive at conclusions on the basis of the actual facts involved. There will be no easy superficial assumption that all will be well and that anything will go as acceptable.

Such candid evaluation will reveal that some are being oppressed by others. In selfishness the strong are inclined to take advantage of the weak, even as the rich are inclined to oppress the poor. But to please God, one must do more than refrain from taking advantage of others. Actually, one must act to help the poor. It will require personal initiative on behalf of the weak to do the will of God in "relieving the oppressed." This is a form of behavior that must be learned through personal participation in such social situations.

In a similar way, the commandment of God to "judge the fatherless" calls upon the person to help children who have no parent to protect their rights. To be righteous, a person must not only refrain from taking advantage of children who are defenseless, but he must involve himself in helping such children by sponsoring them as a parent would do. Righteousness is not merely the absence of evil but it is also, and primarily, the performance of that which is good.

But children are not the only persons who are mistreated by evil persons; widows, who do not now have the natural protection a husband could give, are also liable to be exploited by unscrupulous, greedy persons. Here again is a situation that challenges the righteous person to become involved. Once more it can be noted a person must not only restrain himself from taking advantage of a widow, but he must stand ready to become involved so that when he sees any widow being unfairly treated, he will champion her rights.

In all of this it is obvious that God expects His people who are called by His name to judge themselves in repentance. Not only does He want them to repudiate insincerity in the worship of God, but He wants them to put away evil in their conduct and to embrace the situations in which they can actually perform the will of God in obedience.

After this is found one of the most wonderful promises in Scripture:

> Come now, and let us reason together, saith the Lord: though your sins be as scarlet, they shall be as white as snow; though they be red like crimson, they shall be as wool (Isa. 1:18).

Here is the call that is brought by the prophets to Israel. God knows His people will commit sin, but He is ready and willing to manifest His grace in forgiving their sin and cleansing them from it. This is the very essence of the gospel, which was revealed in the person and in the work of Jesus Christ.

The Old Testament prophets, such as Isaiah, could foresee that God would make salvation available to all men through His Son, Jesus Christ the Lord. But this truth was afterward made more clear through Jesus of Nazareth. Paul wrote:

> For ye know the grace of our Lord Jesus Christ, that, though he was rich, yet for your sakes he became poor, that ye through his poverty might be rich (2 Cor. 8:9).

It is important to notice that this cleansing from sin is not described as something the believer will do; rather, it is something that will be done to him, for him, and in him by the saving grace of God.

And this is a most important truth that must be believed by anyone who would understand and believe the gospel.

> Not by works of righteousness which we have done, but according to his mercy he saved us, by the washing of regeneration, and renewing of the Holy Ghost (Titus 3:5).

Chapter 5

APOSTASY CALLS FOR JUDGMENT

In the first chapter we have just looked at that wonderful eighteenth verse. After the prophet had spoken the word of the Lord to Israel, indicating that they had sinned against God and that the worst condition about them was their insincere worship, he speaks this marvelous word of promise that they can be cleansed. When Isaiah dealt with God's people, he put his finger on the crux of all delinquency in spiritual experience. When the Lord Jesus Christ was asked what is the greatest commandment, He said,

> Thou shalt love the Lord thy God with all thy heart, and with all thy soul, and with all thy mind, and with all thy strength (Mark 12:30).

It is in the believer's heart's attitude toward God that the victory is won or lost. That was where Israel went wrong. That is where any believer can go wrong today, in the attitude of his heart. The prophet put his finger on the hearts of believing persons and said to them, "You have unconfessed sin in yourselves of which you have not repented. Because of this you turn away from God."

The psalmist said, "Thy word have I hid in mine heart, that I might not sin against thee" (Ps. 119:11). And again: "If I regard iniquity in my heart, the Lord will not hear me" (Ps. 66:18). And here is a wonderful thing: no one can listen to the prophet bringing this charge of insincerity in worship without feeling in his or her own heart, "I too am guilty." But no matter how great that sense of wrongdoing, of sin and of guilt, there is in this passage this marvelous word: He will wash you and make you clean. Believers can be washed in the blood of the Lamb:

> Put away the evil of your doings from before mine eyes; cease to
> do evil; learn to do well; seek judgment, relieve the oppressed,
> judge the fatherless, plead for the widow (Isa. 1:16,17).

John the Baptist said in this connection:

> Then said he to the multitude that came forth to be baptized of
> him, O generation of vipers, who hath warned you to flee from
> the wrath to come? Bring forth therefore fruits worthy of repen-
> tance, and begin not to say within yourselves, We have Abra-
> ham to our father: for I say unto you, That God is able of these
> stones to raise up children unto Abraham. And now also the axe
> is laid unto the root of the trees: every tree therefore which
> bringeth not forth good fruit is hewn down, and cast into the fire.
> And the people asked him, saying, What shall we do then? He
> answereth and saith unto them, He that hath two coats, let him
> impart to him that hath none; and he that hath meat, let him do
> likewise. Then came also publicans to be baptized, and said unto
> him, Master, what shall we do? And he said unto them, Exact no
> more than that which is appointed you. And the soldiers
> likewise demanded of him, saying, And what shall we do? And
> he said unto them, Do violence to no man, neither accuse any
> falsely; and be content with your wages (Luke 3:7-14).

Some may think that he is telling the people to be good, but
we should look at it this way: he is laying upon them the call to
be different, to reverse their procedure. At once, some may
say, "Who can do that?" The simple fact is that this is done by
the grace of God, with the help of the Lord Jesus Christ.
Believers are not expected to do this in themselves. God gives
the grace to do it but the believer must be willing. It is basic
that he recognize the evil of his ways and confess; he must see
the will of God and strive to be of a humble and sincere heart.
"Though your sins be as scarlet, they shall be as white as snow."
Anyone with the gospel of Christ in his heart is to keep in mind
that the way he becomes white as snow is to be washed in the
blood of the Lamb.

> If ye be willing and obedient, ye shall eat the good of the land
> (Isa. 1:19).

To be willing and obedient does not mean specifically the
keeping of the Ten Commandments. It goes far beyond that.
Being willing and obedient means that the sinner receives the
Lord Jesus Christ. For those living in New Testament days that
includes everything the Ten Commandments had, and more.
When the Lord Jesus was here, people came to Him and asked,

"Master, what shall we do that we might work the works of God?" Jesus of Nazareth answered them by saying, "This is the work of God, that ye believe on Him whom He hath sent." Believing on Christ means that one yields himself into the will of the Lord. So this passage is saying if you want to have the will of God done in you and you are willing to yield yourself into God's hand, you shall eat of the good of the land. "If any man soweth to the spirit he shall of the spirit reap life everlasting." But if a person refuses the gospel call, he

> shall be devoured with the sword: for the mouth of the Lord hath spoken it (Isa. 1:20).

The prophet continues with more discussion. He presents a revelation of God's judgment about His people: "How is the faithful city become a harlot!" That language is used because of its rough implication. We would not use the word *harlot* or its modern equivalent without a shudder; we tend to shrink away from such terms. Why is it used here? Throughout the Bible the word *harlot* is used to refer to a heart that is not faithful; just as a heart that is faithful is spoken of as a "faithful wife," the "bride of Christ." The great difference is pictured in the Book of Revelation between the bride that comes down from heaven to meet the Son of God, and the great harlot that sits on a hilltop — that great harlot Babylon that was doomed to destruction. This symbolizes in a dramatic way that God sees the heart. He sees something acceptable in a faithful, committed person, but He sees something entirely unacceptable in any heart that is not faithful and that does not stay committed to Him.

In the Old Testament records there is an account of a graphic demonstration that all acquainted with the Old Testament know about. This is set forth in the book of Hosea, who, by the way, was a contemporary of Isaiah. Both prophets talked about the same country and the same people and they use the same figures. Hosea had a wife who lived with him for a time with all faithfulness. Then her heart was turned away to another and she left Hosea. God dealt with Hosea about this. Then something happened that throughout the ages some good men have never been able to fully accept as real: Hosea took his wife back after she had been utterly ruined, forsaken by the very persons with whom she had lived as a harlot. When she was a poor slave, a woman of the street suffering under the social condemnation of the worst kind, so that no one had pity on her, Hosea went to the marketplace and bought her like a common harlot and brought her home. His action shocked the Jewish people because Hosea was a prophet, a preacher. But some of the finest words we will ever read in the Old Testament concern God's love to His unfaithful people:

> I have loved thee with an everlasting love (Jer. 31:3).

Loving a person does not mean liking that person, because one cannot like such conduct as Judah was practicing. But we can be merciful and have compassion.

The darkest days of Israel were approaching. They had four of the greatest preachers who ever preached on this earth at one time — Isaiah, Hosea, Micah, and Amos. These all saw their country in exactly the same light and each put his finger on one thing: God's people were not faithful to Him. Calling Israel a harlot will remind us of these words:

> Ye adulterers and adulteresses, know ye not that the friendship of the world is enmity with God? (James 4:4).

The Jews were adulterers and adulteresses, not so much because they performed the physical acts of adultery, which they may have done. But this designation was made concerning the Old Testament prophets, implying that these people had not been faithful to God, who had betrothed Israel to Himself. The Jews were to be to God as a wife to her husband. But their hearts went out to other gods. That is the way God looks on my heart when I give it to anyone or anything other than God Himself. God feels that way toward any person who gives his heart to any other than the Lord Jesus Christ. The truth is, the Lord Jesus Christ died for me! He purchased me! I am going to heaven because of Him! And so He is worthy of all my love and devotion.

The apostle Paul said:

> If any man love not the Lord Jesus Christ, let him be Anathema Maranatha (1 Cor. 16:22).

All Bible interpreters should be careful to not water that down. That warning should stand right as it is; it is a warning to our hearts. Human hearts are wayward, and someone might say,

"But you can't help the human heart." The truth is that you can. You may not be able to change it but you can control it. The human heart may be wayward, but the believer will yield it to God. A person can come before God humbly and admit that he is not good, and so find out the amazing truth that God will receive him. God will never deal with the believer according to his past. It is to the glory of God that He will not deal with us according to our sins. God will deal with sinners in grace because He is a God of grace. One thing God wants is the person's sincere response. There is nothing that can take its place.

This is what Isaiah labored for in his day; and this is the way he described the will of God to them. Israel had started out walking with Him. They left Egypt walking with Him; they crossed the desert and eventually entered into the land walking with Him; and although they fell from time to time, they won victory after victory over the Canaanites, walking with Him. Israel had had faith, but now

> How is the faithful city become a harlot! it was full of judgment; righteousness lodged in it; but now murderers (Isa. 1:21).

That word *murderers* sounds like a rough word, but it does not imply physical murder on every occasion. The apostle John said any man who hates his brother is a murderer, because God looks on the heart. If I turn my back on the man in trouble, I have condemned him to his trouble. If I see a man in trouble and walk away, I am as bad as if I saw a man drowning in a canal, walked away, and let him drown. We cannot see a man's heart in his dealing with God, but we can see a man's heart in his dealing with his fellowman. The man who does not love God does not love his fellowmen.

If I do not treat others right, my neighbors know it. They know how I act toward the poor, the wayward. If my heart is right, I will care for the poor. If I do not care for the poor, my heart is not right; and if I do not care for the poor, I am like a murderer of them in God's sight. That is spelled out very carefully in John's first Epistle (1 John 3:15).

> Thy silver is become dross, thy wine mixed with water: thy princes are rebellious, and companions of thieves: every one loveth gifts, and followeth after rewards: they judge not the

> fatherless, neither doth the cause of the widow come unto them
> (Isa. 1:22,23).

James was writing of this when he said:

> Pure religion and undefiled before God and the Father is this,
> To visit the fatherless and widows in their affliction, and to keep
> himself unspotted from the world (James 1:27).

It is always helpful in reading the book of James to also read
the prophets. James was well acquainted with the prophets and
took much of his phraseology from them.

> Therefore saith the Lord, the Lord of hosts, the mighty One of
> Israel, Ah, I will ease me of mine adversaries, and avenge me of
> mine enemies (Isa. 1:24).

This is a way of saying that God is going to judge, and because
the people are wrong, He will chasten them by bringing misery
and trouble upon them.

> For whom the Lord loveth he chasteneth, and scourgeth every
> son whom he receiveth (Heb. 12:6).

There is a sober warning here: If you should see someone
suffering who has done wrong, you should keep your hand out
of it; stand back. Let God have His way. The fact that the
wrong doing person is suffering is not evidence that God is
malicious. God is faithful and in His faithfulness He will chasten His child. If you see someone suffering a great deal, you
could by the grace of God be able to say, "God must love that
soul very much."

Why does a person spend so much time cleaning the family
silver? Because he appreciates it. Why does he take so much
time trimming his rose bushes? Because he has pleasure in
them. Why does a woman scrub her floor? She wants it to be
clean. Every intelligent mother will require wholesomeness of
character because she loves her children. This is the common
experience of all who grow up in a family where parents are
faithful. This means that if any child did wrong, this brought
some kind of consequence so that the child would associate
misery with wrongdoing. To excuse a child who is disobedient
damages that child, because such slackness confirms his disobedience. It is sad to see children growing up without being
nurtured in the admonition of the Lord. This happens when

parents are lazy and indifferent; the easiest thing is to let the child get away with it. The only way to teach responsibility is to get into the mind of the child some notion that whatsoever a person sows, that will he also reap. God, in His faithfulness, will have to take up where many parents have let down. When we, as believing people, see others suffering, we should look up to Almighty God, keeping this in mind: God is not angry with anybody's soul. He gave His Son for sinners. He is angry with wickedness, and He will punish and destroy it. When God deals with anyone in severe fashion, we should remember that God loves that person and is giving him an opportunity to recognize his own limitations and weaknesses.

Believers who have a sincere attitude toward God will admit that when they have suffered the most, they have had the most heart-searching experiences. At times like that believers search themselves to find out in what way they have failed or come short. It is true that not all suffering occurs in this chastening fashion. Some suffering is due to other people. But God's Word reveals that it is the purpose of God to bless His people even in their afflictions:

> And I will turn my hand upon thee, and purely purge away thy dross, and take away all thy tin: and I will restore thy judges as at the first, and thy counsellors as at the beginning: afterward thou shalt be called, The city of righteousness, the faithful city (Isa. 1:25,26).

These judges and counselors are similar to revival preachers and evangelistic preachers of today. Every now and again a pastor will preach a revival message to his congregation. In such a message he will invariably urge his people to recognize their sin, confess it, and turn to God. That is always the way of blessing, and thank God, that way is open.

> If we confess our sins, he is faithful and just to forgive us our sins, and to cleanse us from all unrighteousness (1 John 1:9).

Chapter 6

GOD'S PLAN FOR DEALING WITH
HIS SINNING PEOPLE

The people of Israel were human beings like everybody else on earth, but God had promised to bless them if they would walk in His ways. This they had undertaken to do. They did not have a perfect record in their history, but God had. They were weak, but God was strong; they were wayward, but God was faithful. It belonged to the mercy, the grace, and the glory of God that even though they faltered, God did not falter. He went right along with them. The time came that these people, in spite of the fact that God had blessed them, were wayward to a point where it became serious and dangerous; because, though God is gracious and merciful, He is holy, righteous, and just. He will not clear the guilty, nor endorse anything that is unacceptable to Him. He will forgive anybody and He can cleanse every sin, but He will so operate in grace only with those people who put their trust in Him. His people do not have to promise Him that they will never do anything wrong; He knows better. But they must commit themselves to Him and they must put their hands in His to let Him lead them. For such people there are the promises of God that He gave to Abraham and to all of Abraham's children. And such are we as we believe in the Lord Jesus Christ. The promise is that if we walk with the Lord, God will bless us and keep us and do for us more than we can ask or think.

Israel was such a people. But they had become wayward. God's way of dealing with wayward people is to send them messengers to tell them about it. So Isaiah preached to the people of Israel, as we read in 1:25 – 2:5. This is a sketch of God's plan of dealing with His sinning people. There are two aspects: the first is one of judgment, and the second is one of

34

victory. God is going to see this thing through; I may falter, but He will not. He who has begun a good work in me will complete it. I can know His ways and facilitate His work by yielding to Him. If I am unwilling to respond to Him, He has to take other measures. The measures that God took with Israel are indicated in this book of the prophet Isaiah.

The historical fact is that Israel continued to disobey God; they continued to falter. They continued to turn away from God, until He finally had to deal with them. Because of their continued failure, God, through His prophets, told Israel He was going to do a new thing on the earth. He was going to deal with people differently in the future. God's way of dealing with Israel had been to show them what they should do. That was in the law. God promised them that if they would do His will, they would be blessed, and He warned them that if they did not, they would be cursed. If they would do His will, they would live; but if they would not do His will they would perish. Even with warning as clear as that, Israel failed. Human nature does not have sufficient inward grace: the human being isn't strong enough, even in the interest of the salvation of his soul, to walk the way of righteousness and truth.

So God said He would do something else. We now know the new thing God would do, viz., what He does in Christ Jesus. We will see this referred to in this prophecy from time to time. We who live on this side of Calvary, on this side of the Resurrection, in the day when God gives His Holy Spirit to those who believe in Him, have several advantages over those people. Those of us who believe in the Lord Jesus Christ actually have the evidence of being born again: a new thing is begun in us. By the grace of the Holy Spirit working in us, God works in us to will and to do of His good pleasure.

In the Old Testament times God put His law in Ten Words on tables of stone. These Words were set up before the people: the people looked at them and understood that if they walked that way, they would be blessed. But in the New Testament God works in the heart, and the prompting to walk in His ways comes from within. When we yield to the grace of God that is in the hearts of believers, we are carried along in the will of God. God shows us what He wants us to do by His Holy Spirit who dwells in us. It is our great advantage as believers in Christ.

Yet, the same principle holds true for believers now as was true for Israel in this: even with the Holy Spirit given to us and the grace of God being mediated to us in our spirit and soul by the Holy Spirit of God and by the intercessory work of the Lord Jesus Christ, believing people can falter. But they will not falter as badly as they would have; and when they do, the same principles of revival, of coming back to the Lord, are operative with believers as were operative with Israel.

God's plan for dealing with sinful people can be seen in the case of Israel as interpreted by Isaiah in this passage (Isa. 1:25-31). God's plan of dealing with believers today who are not walking in His way is similar; He will use judgment and chastisement as a corrective:

> For whom the Lord loveth he chasteneth, and scourgeth every son whom he receiveth (Heb. 12:6).

It is the mark of the faithfulness of God that when a believer wanders away from him, His way of working to keep him close is to let him have suffering, sorrow, and anguish.

> Now no chastening for the present seemeth to be joyous, but grievous: nevertheless afterward it yieldeth the peaceable fruit of righteousness unto them which are exercised thereby (Heb. 12:11).

When God chastens the believer, the thing for him to do is yield himself to God in complete confidence that He who began a good work in him will complete it.

God had said through the prophet:

> And I will turn my hand upon thee, and purely purge away thy dross, and take away all thy tin (Isa. 1:25).

Silver and other metals are refined by burning out the impurities. The trying of faith, "which is more precious than gold that perisheth," is the common experience of believing people. It is always true that God will chasten, but if the believer will yield to God, his suffering will not be in vain. God will actually rid him of the thing that is displeasing. Isn't that wonderful? If God were just getting even with the sinning soul, that would be punishment. But that would not be "of grace"; that would be "of law." When God deals with the believer in grace and mercy, the affliction that He brings has a result that is wholesome and healthy. We read about this from time to time throughout the Scripture.

> And I will restore thy judges as at the first, and thy counsellors as
> at the beginning: afterward thou shalt be called, The city of
> righteousness, the faithful city (Isa. 1:26).

God is talking to Israel and reminding them that in the days
after Moses and Joshua there were judges in the land who
taught the people what was right and what was wrong. Those
judges were not perfect. But our Great Judge is the Lord Jesus
Christ. Faithful pastors serve as "judges" in the church today.
Such are the evangelists, all of whom — if they have been
faithful — have talked to the people about their sins. Every
grace-filled heart yields to God, confesses sin, and is forgiven
and cleansed. The word *counselors* in the Book of Isaiah means
pretty much the same as it does today. The counselors referred
to in verse 26 have their counterpart in faithful pastors who
minister to their congregations in their trouble.

Isaiah was saying to Israel, "God is going to have to shake you
up. He will deal with you in chastisement, but He will work
through to your blessing."

> Zion shall be redeemed with judgment, and her converts with
> righteousness. And the destruction of the transgressors and of
> the sinners shall be together, and they that forsake the Lord
> shall be consumed (Isa. 1:27,28).

This message has an edge to it. God will deal with all His
people faithfully, showing them where they are wandering
away from Him. The ones who are willing and turn to Him will
be delivered. Those who do not turn will not be delivered; they
will be destroyed.

> For they shall be ashamed of the oaks which ye have desired,
> and ye shall be confounded for the gardens that ye have chosen
> (Isa. 1:29).

The oak was a tree that was used in pagan worship. The gardens
were places where they shared pagan pleasures. God takes
note that these people turned away from Him and accepted the
ideas and pleasures of the world. He links this together here
and says they will be ashamed and confounded because of these
things.

> For ye shall be as an oak whose leaf fadeth, and as a garden that
> hath no water. And the strong shall be as tow, and the maker of it
> as a spark, and they shall both burn together, and none shall
> quench them (Isa. 1:30,31).

The fading of the leaf and the wilting of a cut plant or of a dried-out garden is known all over the world. That will be the condition of people who in their hearts turn away from God. Jesus of Nazareth said that the worm will not die and the fire will not be quenched. He implied that the everlasting fire will destroy those who are disobedient to God. Here in Isaiah is an inkling of it, pointing in that direction. This is the first phase of what God will do. He will correct His people through chastisement. This chastisement will correct the willing people. Suffering will always benefit a person who humbly trusts in God. But suffering makes some people bitter, and in their unbelief and misery they turn away from God. That is like saying the fire that will refine the gold will burn the wood; the fire that will cleanse the silver will burn up the trash. Here is an amazing fact: if I, as a believer, will yield myself to God in suffering, it will turn out for good; but if I rebel against God the very suffering itself can make me more bitter and hardened.

In the second chapter of Isaiah we are told the second phase of the Lord's dealings with His people. After God has judged, chastised, and brought the consciousness of sin to their hearts with the result that they yield to God, repent, and trust themselves to Him, the second phase will work: the Lord's hosts will reign in triumph. That will come to pass through the rule of God. God's way of leading His people through to victory is not to show them where they should go and how fast they should run. No! Then they would be as bad off as they were before. When He has delivered them from their sins, the forgiven and cleansed persons, yielding to God, will find that God will work His rule in their souls.

Let me summarize it like this: when God has dealt with me and my sin, and through suffering and chastening has brought me to where I humbly confess and admit I am a wrongdoer, He graciously forgives me. But He does not leave me alone. He then comes in to rule in my life in the person of His Son, the Son of God, the King of kings, the Lord of all. I will know Him as Jesus Christ, who will rule in my soul. "Christ in you" is the hope of glory. Isaiah 2:1-5 is a description of the blessing that comes when God's law is taught to His people as a message directed to their souls.

Chapter 7

THE DAY OF THE LORD
WILL BRING JUDGMENT

In the second chapter of Isaiah there is a description of how God will judge His people. The Scriptures reveal that Almighty God in heaven watches His people, but the course of their lives is not always from better to better; it fluctuates. Sometimes they draw nigh to God; sometimes they wander away from Him. God does not change; it is to the glory of God that "he that hath begun a good work in you will perform it" (Phil. 1:6). He will complete His work, but you and I could falter with ours. And so God, in grace and mercy, speaks to us and teaches us in the Scriptures.

That which is written in the Old Testament by the prophets to Israel is for our learning (Rom. 15:4). The way God dealt with Israel is the way He will deal with us. Believers are to learn that as wayward as Israel was and as much as God would chasten them, this never resulted in His cutting them off, although He led them through severe chastening many times. Any believer is to understand as he studies this book that he does not need to fall as they fell (1 Cor. 10:1-12), but the Word of God will keep the obedient one close to the Lord. Our purpose as we study is to see these things so that we can be helped and spiritually blessed.

In Isaiah 2:10-22 there is a description of God chastening His people. This is the way the prophet foresaw God dealing with Judah. And this is the way the Holy Spirit would show me how God will deal with me in mercy when He chastens me, in order to turn me away from my waywardness and bring me closer to Him. Verses 12-17 can be read as one continuous thought. The expression "the day of the Lord" is used over and over again in the prophets. It is my belief this is the day when God will bring

His will to the surface and make it obvious; the day when God will take a hand in the affairs of His people to bring His will to pass.

> For the day of the Lord of hosts shall be upon every one that is proud and lofty, and upon every one that is lifted up; and he shall be brought low [God is going to cut the ground from under those who think highly of themselves]: and upon all the cedars of Lebanon, that are high and lifted up, and upon all the oaks of Bashan (Isa. 2:12,13).

This is figurative language. You will remember Lebanon was a mountainous country in which there were great cedar trees. King Hiram sent the cedar trees from Lebanon to Jerusalem for David, his friend, to use in building the temple, although it was Solomon who actually built the temple. God is using those cedar trees as a symbol of man's achievement in building his great structures that are high and lifted up; "and upon all the oaks of Bashan," an area that was the center of pagan worship. This whole statement refers to the achievements of man, whereby he has lifted himself up to rule over his brethren.

> And upon all the high mountains, and upon all the hills that are lifted up, and upon every high tower, and upon every fenced wall [the tower was for defense; it was like a fort], and upon all the ships of Tarshish [that referred to man's merchandise, his money-making schemes], and upon all pleasant pictures [the art of man] (Isa. 2:14-16).

There, put before us poetically, is the description of the loftiness and the haughtiness of man. In each of these symbolic references we see some aspect of human achievement that God is going to bring down, because God is going to humble man.

Ask yourself this question: "If God were going to deal with wayward men, how would He begin?" It is important to remember that the one reason a man goes wayward is that he is full of himself. The one reason anyone turns from God is that he has confidence in something or someone else. So the first thing God does is to smash the thing in which man has his confidence. We can humbly say to ourselves if we look back over our lives, that perhaps one of God's ways of dealing with us is to take away the very thing we may have centered our hearts upon, the very thing in which we have put our confidence.

How many human beings have had the dearest thing they ever knew taken from them! We should not question God about that. It may be beyond our understanding, but we can trust God. God is too interested in us to let us become fully and finally enamored with something else that will absorb all our interest apart from Him. God loves a humble heart. "A broken and a contrite heart, O God, thou wilt not despise" (Ps. 51:17). God loves us too much to let us become self-satisfied and self-sufficient.

"The day of the Lord" will bring down everything that is proud and lofty. Everyone that is lifted up will be brought low: "the cedars of Lebanon" — man's great building projects; "the oaks of Bashan" — man's great religious ideas; "the high mountains" — the governments in which we put our trust; "all the hills that are lifted up" — the little things in government in which we put our trust and confidence; "every high tower" — every kind of local material security we try to build ourselves. "Every fenced wall" — everything we thought we had really made safe and secure is going to be taken away. "All the ships of Tarshish" — all the merchandising and the making of money; and "all pleasant pictures" — all the art, whether it be painting or music or whatever it may be: on all of this God will lay a hand of judgment.

> And the loftiness of man shall be bowed down, and the haughtiness of men shall be made low: and the Lord alone shall be exalted in that day (Isa. 2:17).

Remember that He is talking about His people.

> And the idols he shall utterly abolish (Isa. 2:18).

Rather than have feelings of dismay at this point, you and I should have a certain feeling of appreciation, if not a certain kind of joy and satisfaction. Even in having the things we hold dear taken away, we can trust Almighty God. Oh, how you and I need to remember the Lord Jesus Christ; how we need to call to mind the tenderness of His concern for us and the thoughtfulness of His interest in us, the faithfulness of His purpose on our behalf. Even though the hand of God comes down heavy at times when He takes things away from us and blasts our expectations for the future so that we are hurt and dismayed, we can look up into the face of God and trust Him.

I cannot interpret or predict everything that is happening now or will happen so far as we are concerned, but all who read the Scriptures and reflect on history will feel moved to be sober and humble before God. So far as this world is concerned, we can be sure of absolutely nothing; any day we could have the hand of God upon us. Over and over again, He will do more for us than we can think or ask, but He will never let us get to the place where we will be completely satisfied with the things that are happening around us. We may be fortunate, yet there will be instances when there will be much sorrow and grief.

I recently had the privilege of meeting some people who were fortunate. They had family — all good people — around them. They were in a strong church and had a preacher who was faithful to the Bible. Their young people cared about spiritual things. One of them said he felt they had been very favored and that it was not like that in every place. What bothered me was that it would not be that way with him all of the time. We are not living in that kind of world. The boat you are riding in may be waterproof right now, but it can spring a leak any time. Such things can happen when least expected. However, I can point to One who is always true. You could put your trust in God. You can thank Him for every favor and rejoice in every good thing. Then if chastening comes, you can humble yourself under the mighty hand of God, and expect Him to exalt you in due time. He has his own way of doing things, He expects us to put our trust in Him.

After he has said in verse 18, "And the idols he shall utterly abolish," Isaiah tells us something about the idols of that day:

> And they shall go into the holes of the rocks, and into the caves of the earth, for fear of the Lord, and for the glory of his majesty, when he ariseth to shake terribly the earth. In that day a man shall cast his idols of silver, and his idols of gold, which they made each one for himself to worship, to the moles and to the bats (Isa. 2:19,20).

This can happen even in this present day. We have all known people who have labored to get rich, and suddenly something went wrong with the family or with their health. These people would have given everything they had if they could only have had something other than money at that particular time. There can be times when we give ourselves over to pleasure, and then, when all is said and done, we could just spew it out of our mouths. It turned out to be as nothing compared to something else, which was more important. That is what happened here. In the day that God rises up to manifest Himself and actually takes hold, a man shall cast his idols of silver and gold — the things he gave his heart to — to the moles and to the bats. He will throw these things away,

> to go into the clefts of the rocks, and into the tops of the ragged rocks, for fear of the Lord, and for the glory of his majesty, when he ariseth to shake terribly the earth (Isa. 2:21).

Then the prophet says:

> Cease ye from man, whose breath is in his nostrils: for wherein is he to be accounted of? (Isa. 2:22).

Isaiah is saying it is useless to trust in man, who is weak and mortal and of no account. Instead, we should trust in the Lord, who by His grace and mercy can and does restore man to worth and dignity.

Now we come to the third chapter. The first eight verses in chapter 3 are one passage. This is to be part of the judgment of God. Isaiah has just said God is going to bring man down and humble him and cause him to throw away his idols. Now he tells us something else that will happen. What is this judgment of God? In Israel and in Judah competent leadership would not be found. God will take away the leaders who have good sense (and that is a terrible thing to happen to any group) or He will, so far as we individually are concerned, so confuse us that when we act, we do not have good sense.

> For, behold, the Lord, the Lord of hosts, doth take away from Jerusalem and from Judah the stay and the staff, the whole stay of bread, and the whole stay of water, the mighty man, and the man of war, the judge, and the prophet, and the prudent, and the ancient, the captain of fifty, and the honourable man, and the counsellor, and the cunning artificer, and the eloquent orator (Isa. 3:1-3).

We have there a list of all capable public leaders. When any person is willing to accept leadership in public affairs, this means he will leave his own business and tend to everybody else's business for their sake. Every person who accepts a position of leadership, whether in government or the church, is going to have to leave home and family at times. This can be costly. Isaiah warns Judah that God will remove from willing leadership the good men in the group.

> And I will give children to be their princes, and babes shall rule over them (Isa. 3:4).

This does not necessarily mean children who are five or six years of age, but men who *act* as if they were five or six years old. When you put a man or woman who acts that age in charge, you will have trouble in your Sunday school. Anytime there is unseasoned, irresponsible leadership, it will not be good for the people. When the person in the place of leadership does not direct, this causes chaos and confusion, and people begin to hurt each other.

> And the people shall be oppressed, every one by another, and every one by his neighbour: the child shall behave himself proudly against the ancient, and the base against the honourable (Isa. 3:5).

There is no clear-cut leadership in such a situation. Why isn't there?

> When a man shall take hold of his brother of the house of his father, saying, Thou hast clothing, be thou our ruler, and let this ruin be under thy hand . . . (Isa. 3:6).

You and I may not realize it in this favored country, but there are certain people who could not take an office if elected to it because they cannot dress well enough for it. So they go to a man who has money and ask him to be their ruler. The only way I can interpret that is to think that at this moment Isaiah was almost an American! You know how he would have expressed it if he had said this in American English? "You be in charge of this mess." That is exactly what "this ruin" means.

> In that day shall he swear, saying, I will not be a healer; for in my house is neither bread nor clothing: make me not a ruler of the people (Isa. 3:7).

Have you ever seen anyone like that? The man who has money, faking and protesting that he has none. As for making him a ruler, he will protest loudly that he could never come to meetings because he has to work day and night in his business.

He will have always a sufficient alibi with a deep lament. Why? Because he does not want to do it. When God has withdrawn His favor, capable men will not want to be responsible.

> For Jerusalem is ruined, and Judah is fallen: because their tongue and their doings are against the Lord, to provoke the eyes of his glory (Isa. 3:8).

Isaiah is pointing out a very sober truth. It is something that you and I can carry everywhere we go. In the Lord's work, in the fellowship of the Lord's people, in a congregation or a denomination this principle will operate. It will be true of a Bible class; and it will be true so far as your own home is concerned. In fact, it will be true in your own soul. The best part of you will not be willing to serve the Lord, unless you have the blessing of God. If you have the blessing of God in your heart, the best things in you will want to serve Him; and the best persons in your family will want to serve Him; and the most competent people in the church will be willing to serve Him. When this is the situation, you are being honored and favored by God.

Chapter 8

THE LORD'S HOUSE WILL REIGN
IN TRIUMPH

We will now take a last look at the second aspect of God's way of dealing with His sinning people in the second chapter. You will remember that the general plan of God's dealing with His people when they have gone wrong is sketched for us in the last part of the first chapter of Isaiah and in the first part of the second chapter. In the last part of the first chapter is revealed how God uses chastisement to purge His people from their dross and to cleanse them from their sin. Then in the second chapter we see that victory will come by the inward rule of God through His Word in their hearts.

> The word that Isaiah the son of Amoz saw concerning Judah and Jerusalem. And it shall come to pass in the last days, that the mountain of the Lord's house shall be established in the top of the mountains, and shall be exalted above the hills; and all nations shall flow unto it (Isa. 2:1,2).

This is a poetic description to indicate that the government that is under God's control will dominate all other governments on the face of the earth. We read in Scripture that the kingdoms of this world will become the kingdoms of our Lord and His Christ. Here "the mountain of the Lord's house" is spoken of. The word *mountain* was associated with the function of government because in those days the one in authority would be stationed on a hilltop: the highest position in the community and the highest point in the whole landscape, from which control would go out over the entire community.

The Scriptures commonly speak of "the house of Saul" or "the house of David" or "the house of Aaron" when it refers to that person's family and everyone associated with him. I believe "the Lord's house" directly refers to the Son of God, implying what God and His Son will do. I think elsewhere in the Old Testament this is often brought out as it is also in Scripture as a whole.

The language used in Isaiah 2:2 is political, geographical, and earthly, because that is what Israel was. But the truth revealed is spiritual and it may be understood to have this significance for me as a believer. In my own personality there are certain interests that dominate me. When I am interested in pleasure, for which I would forego other pleasures, that particular pleasure dominates others. In business there could be some matters I am more interested in, and other matters I am less interested in: those in which I am most interested dominate in my thinking. Again and again in our plans, as we live day in and day out, there can be different things in which we may be interested, but because of a certain commitment on our part, one or two of these will dominate all others. Someone who has been interested in many activities may enroll in a school program; now that he is a student the things that have to do with his curriculum and his program are dominant over all others. These correspond in the language of Isaiah to a "mountain," because they are higher than other interests.

When I apply this second verse to my own heart and soul, I am saying that it will come to pass that when God has accomplished His final purpose in me, the control of the Lord Jesus Christ inside me will overrule all other interests I have, so that "the mountain of the Lord's house" in my own soul will be lifted up to the top of the mountain. All other interests I have — political, financial, social, amusement, personal — will take second place to this one thing: "Thou shalt love the Lord thy God with all thy heart, and with all thy soul, and with all thy mind." And when God completes His work of grace in any individual believer, the will of the Lord will be the first thing to which that person is committed. All units of interest he has will come under that control.

We shift our focus back to Israel, which at that time was a political nation. We understand the children of Israel were examples for believers today. God illustrated this in the way He did with the tabernacle. God illustrated in the tabernacle and the temple the truth that is inside the church, in the same way that He illustrated in the nation of Israel the truth that is in every personality committed to Him.

> And many people shall go and say, Come ye, and let us go up to the mountain of the Lord, to the house of the God of Jacob; and he will teach us of his ways, and we will walk in his paths: for out of Zion shall go forth the law, and the word of the Lord from Jerusalem (Isa. 2:3).

For the political nation of Israel this was the picture that was held before them: the time would come when God had completed His program, when His whole purpose would be finally achieved and many people would say, "Let us go up to the mountain of the Lord, to the house of the God of Jacob." The word *Zion* is another name for the city of Jerusalem, the place where God's presence and His control are centered. So Israel could expect many people to come to them for instruction in the truth.

The temple in the nation of Israel was the place where God met with His people. We know that God "dwelleth not in temples made with hands"; He dwells in His church and in His believers. But it was illustrated that way in the Old Testament. In the city of Jerusalem was the temple and in the temple was God, and from the throne of God would go His Word, His Law. It is significant to note that the Word of the Lord comes only from Almighty God with authority and power. The Word of God is not some good man's idea of what might be done in the world; the Word of God is a revelation of the will of Almighty God, who has power and who is able to save to the uttermost those who come to God through the Lord Jesus Christ. This Almighty God has given His Word, and that Word He will perform. That is why that Word has power. I will never understand the Scriptures unless I recognize God on the throne in my life. There must be on my part a willingness to recognize Him (John 7:17) before the truth will come into my soul. Believers actually go up to "Zion," which is the place where God's throne is, up to "Jerusalem," the place where His government is centered; and there they will listen and He will teach them.

In New Testament Scripture the Word of God incarnate was Jesus Christ Himself. And so, while we read the Scriptures, the Word of God literate, we are looking at the person of the

Lord Jesus Christ, who is the Word of God incarnate. Thus we can have communion with the Holy Spirit; and that will be the Word of God activated in us. Then the will of Almighty God is made clear to our hearts; and that is what the Word of God is: the Word of God revealing His will for us. God will speak to me, showing me what He would have me to do and telling me what He will do, so that I can follow Him obediently. The statement "And he shall judge among the nations" indicates that the presence of the Lord and of the Spirit of God in my heart will judge among the different ideas and interests that may be lodged there. Who are "the nations" on the face of the earth? These are groups of human beings with distinct and varying interests. So far as all mankind is concerned, there are many nations, each with its own individual interests; so far as my own human personality is concerned, in my consciousness, there are many interests, each of which has a little interest of its own.

When the presence of the Lord and the law of God, when the will of God and the thoughts of God are lodged in my soul, when all these different things are in me and put in their proper place, then what looks big to me is not so big and what looks insignificant to me is bigger than I thought it was. All of this comes out clearly when I am in the presence of God. In my own soul and consciousness there are many things there naturally that should not be allowed to have their own way; and the very presence of God and His Word rebuke in me many things, which in themselves are ordinarily natural.

Jesus of Nazareth taught, "I am the vine, ye are the branches. My Father is the husbandman." He is the gardener who prunes, taking away the things that are not fruitful, so that the rest can bear better fruit. This is what happens inside my own soul; and this is the end phase of God's program. God's great purpose in Christ Jesus is to save believers to the uttermost. When God has finally completed His purpose, what will we have? We will have Christ's will in us, doing the will of God through us. This will be the end: then we will have glory in God.

> . . . and shall rebuke many people: and they shall beat their swords into plowshares, and their spears into pruninghooks (Isa. 2:4).

What are their swords? These are weapons of offense, of conflict. They will be turned into productive tools. How many times it has happened with us when we have yielded ourselves to the indwelling presence of the Lord that we, having been filled with resentment against others, may even have wanted to do some kind thing to them instead. The New Testament says, "Let not the sun go down upon your wrath" (Eph. 4:26) and "If thine enemy hunger, feed him; if he thirst, give him drink" (Rom. 12:20). Here the Old Testament says they will "beat their swords into plowshares." This is not a command; it is a prediction of what will happen when the will of God is activated in the believer by the indwelling of the Holy Spirit in his life.

When the will of God is activated in our souls, our attention will be diverted from people who annoy and depress and distress us and directed to where we actually go to work to do something. The sword, which is for fighting, is to be exchanged for a plowshare, which is for producing. And the spear, which is for slaughtering people, is to be turned into a pruning hook, with which we will trim our trees to produce better fruit. God will enable us, when the impulse within us would have been to fight, to be directed to constructive attitudes. Then, instead of fussing, we will start producing, and the conclusion is this: "Neither shall they learn war any more." So we have completed again in this rather detailed fashion the grand outline of God's way of dealing with His wayward people.

God has a message to the world, which we will find in later chapters, but this was a message concerning Judah and Jerusalem, God's own people. Chapter 2 presents the next division. From 2:6 and through all of chapters 3, 4, and 5 there is a detailed interpretation of Israel's affairs. The benefit to us as we study this is that we will see what God's people can do when they get out of the will of God. "Therefore thou hast forsaken thy people the house of Jacob," not because of what we read in 1:1 to 2:5 but because of what we read in 2:6 through 5:30. For these reasons God has forsaken His people, the house of Jacob.

Each of the instances to be mentioned is significant because "they will be replenished from the east." In those days this meant Babylon, Chaldea, and Persia, which were the source of pagan thinking. In the days of Israel, about all that were known to the west were Palestine, Tyre, Sidon, and Phoenicia. Strange as it may seem, the people of Greece were relatively undeveloped, and Rome was a wilderness. Spain, France, and Germany were peopled by undeveloped, uneducated, nomadic tribes with no culture of any stature. The great areas of human understanding and wisdom were Egypt to the south; Arabia, Assyria, Chaldea, and the land of the Medes and Persians; and, farther east, what is now India, the land of the Hindus. All these people had great ideas. They were the philosophers of the day with a certain type of religion sometimes referred to as Zoroastrianism (Zoroaster lived about the time of Jeremiah).

At the time when the great prophets of Israel were preaching, the countries of the east — Babylon, Persia, India — were developing a considerable intellectual life. They had great philosophies featured by pagan thoughts. Today one need not go to Babylon, to the Medes and Persians, for such ideas. We can go to our own intellectual centers of learning, where ideas are derived from all human beings. The people to whom we refer as Babylonians, Medes, and Persians were human beings; the Greeks and the Romans were human beings. Today many of our thinkers offer insight into life without admitting that Jesus Christ is the way, the truth, and the life. Most of our philosophers consider Christianity to be a sect. Israel was listening to the Babylonians and to the Persians to get their ideas. The counterpart of that today would be a congregation or an individual believer who listens to pagan philosophers for ideas, who knows more about Plato and Aristotle than he knows about Paul and John, and who can talk more fluently about some contemporary thinker than he can about Moses. God would take note of me, for example, if I were more affected by the human authors I read than by the Word of God. God would say that I am being replenished by the mind of man and He would hold that against me.

Chapter 9

TRAITS OF SINFUL PEOPLE

As we think about this book of the prophet Isaiah, we should keep in mind this is a message that was sent to believing people. Of all the people on the face of the earth, those who believe in God, and especially those who follow His Word and His promises, live in a special relationship with Him. They are to do what He says, and then He will bless them. They are to believe in Him, and from Him they will receive the benefits that He gives in His grace and mercy. This relationship with God is to be permanent. Just as God is everlasting and His Word is everlasting, so the person who believes in God and puts His trust in Him is to walk with the Lord forever. That is God's plan and it is the outlook of the person who is turning to God. However, the best resolutions men have tend to weaken, humans being what they are, and something that seems now to be the kind of thing men would want to do forever may in coming days and months and years grow weaker. Other ideas may arise and the believer's purpose and faithfulness in following the Lord may vary and falter from time to time.

God has that in mind and He gives grace to the willing to enable them to be faithful in following Him. He also deals with His people in providence, and by His providence day by day He makes His people aware of their dependence on Him. But the human heart is such that believers can fall into habits that lead them to wander away from the Lord. Because of this, God deals with them in drastic ways to correct their thinking. He sends them messengers as prophets.

All through the history of God's people some persons have been teachers. They have been the leaders, the judges, of God's people. They have also been kings, priests, and prophets for God's people. In all these functions God provides that the people of God may be drawn nearer to Him. This enables us to understand the work of the prophet Isaiah. The major function of the prophet was to reveal the will of God to the people. Israel had missed it, and because they had grown careless, the prophet would oftentimes appear in the role of a preacher. He would take the truth of God, hold it before the people, and press it to their consciousness by various techniques and methods. In such a passage as the second chapter, Isaiah is revealing to God's people what God thinks of them. This passage has specific reference to their times, but we study it in order that we may learn what God has to say also to us.

> Therefore thou hast forsaken thy people the house of Jacob, because they be replenished from the east, and are soothsayers like the Philistines, and they please themselves in the children of strangers (Isa. 2:6).

In the preceding chapter we took note of the statement "they be replenished from the east" and drew your attention to the fact that this meant they had adopted the point of view and the philosophy of the pagan people, who had developed a religion of their own. The next statement "and are soothsayers like the Philistines" refers to persons we would name "fortune tellers" who seek to divine the future by certain techniques. Today some read tea leaves, while others tell fortunes with cards. Some read the palm of the hand and some tell fortunes by going into a kind of spiritual seance. Among pagan people such practices were not uncommon and among the Philistines there were those who claimed to have such psychic powers. The word *sooth* is etymologically related to *truth*. "Forsooth" in some old English literature means "for the truth of the matter." These soothsayers were people who tried to tell the truth about anything by employing a kind of clairvoyant insight and vision. Such practices were linked with the religious beliefs of these people and the children of Israel were following along with that philosophy. They were trying to get at truth by listening to human beings "and they please[d] themselves in the children of strangers." The people were preferring other ideas than those their fathers had taught them.

There was at that time in Israel a tendency to think that the old-fashioned way of doing things was no longer good enough.

Everybody knew what Abraham, Isaac, and Jacob had said, and everybody knew about Moses and Aaron, but here was something brand new, something from the outside. We can almost feel the contemporary character of this line of thought: the tendency is strong today to follow someone who comes forward with something that has been uncovered recently and that seems both contemporary and strange to the Scriptures. God takes note of that. Human beings are inclined that way. Men are always looking for something different: that is the tendency of the wayward human heart. But this does not make for integrity or inward strength in the individual.

The person who is inwardly committed to that which is sure is one thing, but the person who is not committed, who has heard what parents have said and what is taught in Sunday school and preached in the pulpit, and then has an ear for something else, something new and different and contrary to God's Word, that person will be called progressive. Many look with favor upon such, but Almighty God, looking down upon His people and seeing this tendency to shift from that which has been revealed to something new, judges this and He intends to forsake them.

As we read on, we find something of a different nature, but which belongs in the same setting.

> Their land also is full of silver and gold, neither is there any end of their treasures; their land is also full of horses, neither is there any end of their chariots (Isa. 2:7).

The people had become rich and powerful. The prophet used military language, the kind that describes their military strength. In the days when most fighting was done by men on foot, as Gideon, Samson, and David fought, the armies that were equipped with horses had a tremendous advantage. The horse gave greater mobility and striking power, so the armies could move faster and win victories. Many armies used chariots with their horses when they went to battle. One can imagine what a tremendous advantage that man would have in battle who could charge down upon the enemy in a horse-drawn chariot. These chariots were built with long sicklelike swords protruding from the wheels in such a way that they could cut down the soldiers, tearing through them.

> Their land also is full of idols; they worship the work of their own
> hands, that which their own fingers have made: and the mean
> man boweth down, and the great man humbleth himself: there-
> fore forgive them not (Isa. 2:8,9).

Now the real meaning of an idol is apparent when we compare it with the idea of God. Ask yourself the question "What should God be to a human being?" He should not only be the Creator, Keeper, and Judge, but He should be the Center of that human being's confidence. Man should put his trust in God and desire above everything else that he be right with God. Man should seek the face of God. When one's heart is given over to anyone or anything other than God, we call that thing an "idol." An idol could be money, power, pleasure, or some form of self-indulgence. Another idol could be a form of ambition. Men tend to worship what they think is really the most powerful element in their lives.

The Scriptures reveal that the first and great commandment is "Thou shalt love the Lord thy God with all thy heart, and with all thy soul, and with all thy mind. . . . Thou shalt love thy neighbor as thyself" (Matt. 22:37,39). One must put God first in his heart. In Israel at the time of Isaiah the land was full of idols and all kinds of things that people preferred to God. Paul speaks of people who were "lovers of pleasure rather than lovers of God" (2 Tim. 3:4). Such persons make an idol out of their amusement, so that comes first. "Their land also is full of idols; they worship the work of their own hands, that which their own fingers have made." It is natural for one to have special affection for something he has made or accomplished, and to these people these had become idols.

The prophet said that it did not make any difference where one looked, they were all the same. The great and the small, the rich and the poor were all the same in that their hearts had been given over to things in their possession, which they preferred above everything else. The prophet agreed with the judgment of God, and he asked in prayer to God, "Forgive them not." Why would this prophet pray that they should not be forgiven? Because he cared about the name and glory of God. So far as a person's conduct toward me is concerned, I could forgive him if I wished; but that man's conduct with reference to God I could not overlook. That man would have to deal with God about that.

A man may take advantage of me in that he may ignore me, cheat me, or do me harm, and I can forgive him. But when a man casts aspersion on the name of the Lord Jesus Christ, when he turns his back on Almighty God, when he does violence to the Word and the work of God, to the house and the name of God, then it is not my privilege to forgive him. That is God's privilege. Yet there is no forgiveness apart from repentance, and refusal to respond to the work of the Holy Spirit is to blaspheme the Holy Spirit. What is the work of the Holy Spirit? To show us the things of Christ. It is not for us to judge or to condemn; it is God's business to do that. That is revealed not only here in Isaiah but also in the Psalms.

Some Psalms are imprecatory; that is, the psalmist prays to Almighty God to destroy His enemies. That may seem harsh, but the truth is that the enemies of God are to be destroyed. When a person enters into the truth of God, he will find in his heart the same feeling that the Lord Jesus Christ had; His feeling was like that so far as those are concerned who reject His Father. However, when it is written here "forgive them not," it does not necessarily mean that He is to destroy them utterly, but rather that He is to chasten them.

In Isaiah 2:10-22 there is the description of what God will do for people whom He has forsaken and what God will do in judgment upon people who have disobeyed Him.

> Enter into the rock, and hide thee in the dust, for fear of the Lord, and for the glory of his majesty. The lofty looks of man shall be humbled, and the haughtiness of men shall be bowed down, and the Lord alone shall be exalted in that day (Isa. 2:10,11).

This is to say that Almighty God is coming in judgment and if you are here as a bystander, get into a safe place, because this is going to be bad. A terrible judgment is coming. The lofty looks of man, his pride, shall be humbled and his arrogant self-confidence shall be bowed down.

This brings to mind the basic truth that when man gets big, God gets small. But when God gets big, man gets small. If our hearts are filled with thoughts of the greatness of God, we are, at the same time, conscious of the humbleness of mankind and the smallness and weakness of man. If our attention is focused on man in such a way that we magnify man and begin to think that man is wonderful, God gets to be small, for just as surely as we exalt man we abase God, but when we exalt God we humble man. The wholesome and healthy thing to do is to exalt God. That is what the prophet was setting forth for the people to do, and God was going to see that this was done when the time would come for Him to establish His great plan and purpose.

Chapter 10

THE DIRE COLLAPSE OF SOCIETY

In Isaiah 3:12-15 it is revealed that when the leaders of God's people have not done what they should have done, they tend to lead them into error.

> O my people, they which lead thee cause thee to err, and destroy the way of thy paths (Isa. 3:12).

How can a leader destroy the way of the paths of the people? It is not difficult to understand if you will think for a moment. How do paths come to be? People walk on them. What is a path, then? A characteristic way of doing things. What was the path from your house to the well when you lived out in the country? That was the route you took to get water. In the city that is not so important but in the country it is very important because that is the way the little children know where to go; they are carefully taught by their parents to stay on the path. As long as children, young people, and, for that matter, grown people have pathways, they can find their way through a forest; but if someone comes along and destroys the pathway, takes down the landmarks, and cuts new roads, until they cannot recognize where they are going, they can get lost.

Sometimes there are people in places of leadership who seem to be perhaps unconsciously, perhaps consciously, beset with the idea that they have to change whatever is being done. A family, we will say, has always gone to church; so now they are not going to church. They are going to be different. Or a family has always returned thanks at meals and a young person out of that home, who starts a new family in which he is the leader, decides he will not do that. He is going to do something else. He may decide to worship God while they read the Bible, or when they are at church, whatever the case may be. You may be sure that if the leading person in the house does not care about returning thanks at the table, it will not be long until the children will not know whether to return thanks or not. The same is true in other ways: if ordinarily a person takes off his hat when he comes into the house, since that is the custom, and if then someone of importance, who does not take off his hat, comes to live there, it will not be long until all the young people leave their hats on. What we are discussing is far more important than taking off a hat, but I have used that by way of illustration. Leaders destroy the way of our paths, not by doing things differently, but by forsaking good ways and replacing them with ways that are not good.

It is surprising that, when you talk about Christian experience, many people do not want to speak about being "saved." They will talk about being integrated, or being reconstructed, perhaps, and you may wonder what in the world they mean by these words. What they actually mean is something that was once meant when people talked about being "saved." However, actually the word *saved* meant more than anything they would say, because it meant everything that the Lord Jesus Christ did. "Saved" is a biblical word. Some persons do not like the phrase "the blood of Christ." They do not like the word "blood" at all, so they just leave it out. Before you realize it, they have left out what the blood stood for. You may not have been conscious of it, but after you have listened to the preaching of such leaders for a while, you may have altogether gone past the point where you are aware that your sins are forgiven because Christ Jesus died for you. That is why they are forgiven, and that would have stayed in your mind if the word "blood" had been used, but "they which lead thee cause thee to err. They destroy the way of thy paths."

There was a time when in any ordinary Protestant church there were prayer meetings, but some leader may have come along who was more "contemporary," and prayer meetings were discontinued. Such leaders would not say you should not pray, but they just do not make arrangements for praying. God always overrules, and many times when a church has stopped having prayer meetings, praying has been started in individual homes. Often when churches have discontinued their Sunday evening services, members will go elsewhere to an evening service, because the hungry heart is going to find a way of getting the truth of God. What I particularly want to emphasize here is that when God's blessing is not on a situation, you may have a leadership that destroys the way of the paths of the people, causing them to wander and to err.

All that I have discussed has taken place in a church. Now let us bring it back to ourselves, deep down in our own hearts. If I as an individual Christian have wandered away from the Lord, my dominant thoughts will not lead me in the old spiritual ways of seeking the face of God. They will go contrary to the habits I once had of reading the Bible, of praying, and of turning to God in times of trouble. I will not have the faith I once had, and I will not be doing the things I once did. My thoughts that now lead me are causing me to err and the things I now prefer are destroying the old pathways that my soul once followed. Such would be an application of this truth revealed here in Isaiah.

In Isaiah 3:16–4:1 a serious condition is described; this is what happens to a nation such as Israel when the favor of God is not with them. Two things are brought out here: vanity will increase and social disorder will spread. Vanity will cause frivolous ways of doing things; and social disorder will move through war into moral disorganization.

> Moreover the Lord saith, Because the daughters of Zion are haughty, and walk with stretched forth necks and wanton eyes, walking and mincing as they go, and making a tinkling with their feet . . . (Isa. 3:16).

Zion is another name for Jerusalem, the city of God. The term "the daughters of Zion" refers to the people of God in general, whose sinful activities can take place in your own soul, be you man or woman. It is almost as though Isaiah saw the future. Though he actually saw only the people of his day, times really do not change so much. This description is intended to depict the frivolous attitude of the women, which was strongly significant.

> Therefore the Lord will smite with a scab the crown of the head of the daughters of Zion, and the Lord will discover their secret parts. In that day the Lord will take away the bravery of their tinkling ornaments about their feet, and their cauls, and their round tires like the moon, the chains, and the bracelets, and the

> mufflers, the bonnets, and the ornaments of the legs, and the
> headbands, and the tablets, and the earrings, the rings, and
> nose jewels, the changeable suits of apparel, and the mantles,
> and the wimples, and the crisping pins, the glasses, and the fine
> linen, and the hoods, and the veils (Isa. 3:17-23).

Why do you suppose all that was recorded in the Bible?
Because all those things taken together indicate something that
words alone cannot convey. When a person's mind is taken up
with all that, it shows what has attracted attention. It should be
remembered that when the women become frivolous, it is
because the men want them that way.

But God says:

> And it shall come to pass, that instead of sweet smell there shall
> be stink; and instead of a girdle a rent; and instead of well set hair
> baldness; and instead of a stomacher a girding of sackcloth; and
> burning instead of beauty (Isa. 3:24).

This is a rather drastic way of saying that all the attempts to
appear attractive will be turned into real disaster.

> Thy men shall fall by the sword, and thy mighty in the war. And
> her gates shall lament and mourn; and she being desolate shall
> sit upon the ground (Isa. 3:25,26).

Here is something that is as true as human society and I can't
tell you which comes first: periods of war are coincident with a
breakdown in morals, and a breakdown in morals is coincident
with the outbreak of war. You can study the history of the world
from the beginning and find this to be so. In this country we
have lived through several wars in the lifetime of most of us,
and each time we have seen social standards deteriorate. Those
of us who have served in the army or in any military force know
the terrific pressure there is to make one careless in his thinking and in his way of doing things. One's life is in danger, he
cannot do as he pleases, and for that reason he does not care
what he does. Everyone in the service is brought under that
pressure; however, in that situation, some young men have
had the most profound spiritual experiences they ever had in
their lives.

Many people, in reading the revealing story of Samson's
personal life, will be inclined to shudder in distaste and to
wonder how God could use a man like that, since his social
standards seemed to be so loose. Yet Samson is mentioned in

Hebrews 11 as one of the heroes of faith. He was affected by the culture in which he lived, and before we condemn the man we should remember something about the days in which he lived.

The frivolity of women on one hand and the loose conduct of men on the other is self-condemned. These two conditions always go together and they are a mark of a lack of the blessing of God. When God blesses men and women, they become self-controlled and characterized by virtue. A person blessed of God can readily understand other people, and if they do things that hurt him, he does not seek revenge. If they step on his feet, the next time he does not put his feet in that place; he tries to walk around. He seeks peace and pursues it. When that kind of man looks at a woman, he looks at her heart. Many women are inspired to seek the better things of life because of their association with men who appreciate the better things of life. We do not find these aspirations better expressed anywhere at any time than by the apostle Paul: "This one thing I do, forgetting those things which are behind, and reaching forth unto those things which are before, I press toward the mark for the prize of the high calling of God in Christ Jesus" (Phil. 3:13,14). Let us remember that women were the last at the cross and the first at the grave; there is no greater faithfulness than that which we read about women in the Bible as a whole.

Now when God has withdrawn His favor because of sin, and people have wandered away from Him, the tendency of a woman to be interested in her appearance runs to frivolous things and the aggressive tendency in man runs to violence. This always happens in the same society at the same time. Moral degeneration and frivolity always go together. Famine, pestilence, and disease always accompany a breakdown of morals. Calamity is ruinous to the human spirit. You can get so hungry you no longer care about conduct, and stealing is as nothing. You can be sick and diseased so that you do not care anymore. All these things are a terrific burden to the human spirit, but believing people know that they — God's people — are lifted above wars and destruction and vanity by the power and grace of God.

The last part of this sad story comes in Isaiah 4:1. We have already noted in Isaiah 3:25,26: "Thy men shall fall by the sword, and thy mighty in the war. And her gates shall lament and mourn; and she being desolate shall sit upon the ground." Now we read:

> And in that day seven women shall take hold of one man, saying, We will eat our own bread, and wear our own apparel: only let us be called by thy name, to take away our reproach (Isa. 4:1).

In our day we would call that polygamy. Why would women ever do such a thing? When war is severe enough, it kills off the men. There have been wars that caused women to outnumber men three to one. In this case it was seven to one. The consequent deterioration of the home and of marriage relationships is far more profound than we would ordinarily think. It is very hard to maintain your balance, and as a human being you cannot do it, when the situation is completely tilted to one side. The only possible way this imbalance can be overcome is by the grace of God.

> In that day shall the branch of the Lord be beautiful and glorious, and the fruit of the earth shall be excellent and comely for them that are escaped of Israel. And it shall come to pass, that he that is left in Zion, and he that remaineth in Jerusalem, shall be called holy, even every one that is written among the living in Jerusalem: when the Lord shall have washed away the filth of the daughters of Zion, and shall have purged the blood of Jerusalem from the midst thereof by the spirit of judgment, and by the spirit of burning. And the Lord will create upon every dwelling place of mount Zion, and upon her assemblies, a cloud and smoke by day, and the shining of a flaming fire by night: for upon all the glory shall be a defence. And there shall be a tabernacle for a shadow in the daytime from the heat, and for a place of refuge, and for a covert from storm and from rain (Isa. 4:2-6).

In the darkest hour God will send salvation.

Chapter 11

SALVATION WILL COME

In Isaiah 4:2-5 there is something of a repetition of the first three chapters. Some of the same things are expressed differently: we may wonder about that in the Bible. Often in reading the Psalms, especially, we find an idea expressed one way and in the next half of the verse the same idea is stated differently. We might ask ourselves why some anthems and hymns have the same words sung over and over. It is so that by repetition certain ideas become fixed in the mind. Isaiah was not writing an essay or an editorial. He was a preacher and because of that, he sometimes repeated a single thought and idea over and over. Any time we find any one idea repeated over and over in the Bible we can be sure it is an important one that we need to understand.

So as we go into this part of Isaiah we will find thoughts similar to some we read before, yet slightly different. The principle theme all the way through the first three chapters is the fact that Israel had sinned by turning away from God. They are the people who had said they would put their trust in God, claiming before the world that they were getting their help from God. God's name belonged, as it were, to these people, but this prophecy presents the rather sobering truth that God's own people can go wrong; they can fail to achieve their possibilities.

The next thing that is revealed is that God does not leave them there. He brings pressure to bear on them and He has ways of chastening them, of dealing with them as a father deals with his child. If a child does wrong, the father does not disown the child; he corrects him because he loves him. Our heavenly Father loves His people and when once He has committed Himself to them and they have committed themselves to Him,

He watches over them. If they wander away, He calls them back to Himself and warns them what will happen if they continue to stray. He does not arbitrarily force them to do His will, but He sets the consequences before them. If they continue doing wrong, God uses other measures. One of the measures God uses is to send prophets who come to His people to explain why they are having trouble and to warn them of further trouble they will have unless they change their ways. The prophets emphasize the fact that a person can start out walking with God and can move away from the will of God. Although He belongs to God in a sense, he can do the things that God does not want him to do.

We have learned in the early chapters of this book what God will do, and it was grievous to think about. We got an uncomfortable feeling because we realized that many people are doing just as these people did, and just as surely they will incur the disfavor of God. In the third chapter much was said about God judging His people in a chastening way; He led them through severe suffering experiences to bring them to Himself. The prophet now points out the dawning of new and brighter things, as set forth in Isaiah 4:2-6. All through this section the day of the Lord seems to be the time when God will move to bring His will to pass: "In that day shall the branch of the Lord be beautiful and glorious." We are inclined to believe this phrase refers to the Messiah, the One who is to come and to serve God. All the way through the Old Testament Scripture this coming is spoken of, and Isaiah will say much about it before this book is finished. What we need to think of here is that something is going to be good — after three chapters of one bad thing after another.

> In that day shall the branch of the Lord be beautiful and glorious, and the fruit of the earth shall be excellent and comely for them that are escaped of Israel (Isa. 4:2).

It appears that some will escape. Judgment will come upon Israel and that will be grievous. It will be grievous in wars and in many other ways. There will be character deterioration and spiritual suffering of various kinds, but some will escape.

> And it shall come to pass, that he that is left in Zion, and he that remaineth in Jerusalem, shall be called holy, even every one that is written among the living in Jerusalem (Isa. 4:3).

After God is through dealing with them and has allowed many to be killed off and degenerated, there will be some left — the faithful ones.

"The branch of the Lord," which I take to be the Messiah of the Old Testament, Christ of the New Testament, will be beautiful and glorious in spite of the darkness of human history. God will do a wonderful thing in Christ, His Servant. Some will be saved. Sodom and Gomorrah were destroyed, but Lot and his family were delivered. Again and again in the Bible there was widespread judgment, such as the judgment over the whole land of Egypt, but those who put the blood on the doorposts escaped and the Lord passed over them. Always this truth is evident: some will escape. Which ones? Those who put their trust in Him. We are then told:

> When the Lord shall have washed away the filth of the daughters of Zion, and shall have purged the blood of Jerusalem from the midst thereof by the spirit of judgment, and by the spirit of burning (Isa. 4:4).

Many times we read the first part of that statement and rejoice in it. We think how wonderful it is that some are going to be all cleaned up, but many times we fail to understand exactly what is mentioned following that. How will this be done? "By the spirit of judgment, and by the spirit of burning." Generally speaking, the figure used for cleansing is washing by water but here is it cleansing by fire, such as sterilizing dirty utensils, for instance. This seems a strange thing. I have the impression this is about the way it will happen: the sinner who does not know the Lord, who in ignorance wanders away and does things that are wrong, will have the experience of being washed by the water, like bathing. But for the believers, the ones who know the Lord, there will be periods of chastening that will be like fire. In other words, the faith of a Christian is like gold that is refined by fire. And that is truly suggestive. I am inclined to think that, so far as the unbeliever is concerned, trouble will not come with the idea of turning him to God; I rather think the words that will be spoken to him will be the gentle words of forgiveness and peace: "Come unto me, all ye that labor and are heavy laden, and I will give you rest." But when a person who already knows the Lord is wayward, I should expect that in some sense there will be scourging. This is suggested to me in this passage because here the washing and the purging take place by the spirit of judgment and the spirit of burning.

> And the Lord will create upon every dwelling place of mount Zion, and upon her assemblies, a cloud and smoke by day, and the shining of a flaming fire by night: for upon all the glory shall be a defence (Isa. 4:5).

When we read this, we immediately think about Israel traveling through the desert, guided by the cloud by day and the fire by night, because the Lord God was leading them, surrounding them, and keeping them all that time. This is what He says will happen to those who escape from Jerusalem. "Every dwelling place" may mean each individual heart and "her assemblies" may mean every group. You and I can expect the guidance of God individually and as a group, when the cloud by day and the pillar of fire by night will guide us, because "upon all the glory shall be a defence."

The believer is to learn that as he makes up his mind and does his thinking, as he goes along from day to day, the course of his action and the course of his life do not depend primarily on his own ideas. As surely as he belongs to the Lord, it will not depend a great deal on his own decision, because Almighty God will overrule if the heart is given over to Him. God will make all things work together for good. I would say that when the believer is praying about what he should do, he should be concerned that he feel God's hand on his, and he should then leave the rest to Him. "Sufficient unto the day is the evil thereof." No man knows what the day will bring forth, but we know Him. The next time, and any time, that the believer wonders where he is going and what he is going to do, he should make sure he is walking in the presence of the Lord. If I were giving practical advice, I would suggest that the believer look to see where the good road is and walk in it. The chances are that is where God wanted him to go. Just as surely as the believer is walking with God, He will overrule to bring him where He wants the believer to be.

> And there shall be a tabernacle for a shadow in the daytime from the heat, and for a place of refuge, and for a covert from storm and from rain (Isa. 4:6).

As we live along in this world, there will be days when it will be stormy, when things go wrong. Now God does not stop the storm on our account; He is not going to sweep all the clouds out of the sky on our account, but He will give us shelter. If we are in a good shelter, let it rain, the rain on the roof does not sound so bad, does it? There will be shade in the daytime in the heat and a place of refuge from rain; there will be safety.

In the fifth chapter there is a recapitulation: a repetition of the same things previously written. Isaiah 5:1-7 sets forth something that will resemble the opening verses of the book, when the prophet said that they had "forsaken the Lord [and] gone away backward" In chapter 1 Isaiah recorded God's lament: "The ox knoweth his owner, and the ass his master's crib: but Israel doth not know, my people doth not consider" (v. 3). Here the prophet uses the illustration of domesticated animals: they at least know whether they are fed, and they come back to the hand that feeds them; but so far as Israel was concerned, they did not come back to God, although He had taken care of them before this time. In Isaiah 5:1-7 Isaiah uses a parable, a graphic one, and as it unfolds, the meaning becomes obvious:

> Now will I sing to my well-beloved a song of my beloved touching his vineyard. My well-beloved hath a vineyard in a very fruitful hill: and he fenced it, and gathered out the stones thereof, and planted it with the choicest vine, and built a tower in the midst of it, and also made a winepress therein: and he looked that it should bring forth grapes, and it brought forth wild grapes (Isa. 5:1,2).

This is the parable, a story told to illustrate a point.

> And now, O inhabitants of Jerusalem, and men of Judah, judge, I pray you, betwixt me and my vineyard. What could have been done more to my vineyard, that I have not done in it? wherefore, when I looked that it should bring forth grapes, brought it forth wild grapes? And now go to; I will tell you what I will do to my vineyard: I will take away the hedge thereof, and it shall be eaten up; and break down the wall thereof, and it shall be trodden down: and I will lay it waste: it shall not be pruned, nor digged; but there shall come up briers and thorns: I will also command the clouds that they rain no rain upon it. For the vineyard of the Lord of hosts is the house of Israel, and the men of Judah his pleasant plant: and he looked for judgment, but behold oppression; for righteousness, but behold a cry (Isa. 5:3-7).

That is the poetic way the prophet has of bringing an illustration before these people and telling them that God will deal with them in judgment. What will the judgment be? God is going to take away His protection. He will let them suffer the consequences. More than that, He will put on even more distress. He will not send rain. And inwardly they will have no more grace in their hearts than they used to have. Throughout this fifth chapter Isaiah continues to tell what God will do, and as we study that, we will see the full extent of the chastening treatment God will give His own people because He loves them. If He did not love them, He would not treat them this way. But because He loves them, He will not let them continue doing wrong and not know that it is wrong.

Chapter 12

IMPENDING DOOM BECAUSE OF SIN

Isaiah 5:8-30 presents a sketch, as it were, of the judgment of God. I suspect many people are like me when they think about the judgment of God. I could understand it as lightning that would strike a man dead, or perhaps a flood that would swallow him up, or an earthquake or some other violent force to sweep him from the earth. It might also be considered His judgment if a fire destroyed your place of business, or a hailstorm destroyed your crop, or war came in which a great many people were killed.

Perhaps we are not altogether prepared to realize that the judgment of God can show itself in such things as the heart's becoming wayward, the weakening of faith, the development of a perverseness, and a turning away from Him. In other words, the judgment of God does not always have to do with violence in physical things; it can actually appear in spiritual ways as well. Many times we may have the idea that turning away from God is simply a matter of faith. We would say here is one man who believes and here is another man who does not believe, and the man who does not believe has turned away from God. But it is not quite as simple as that. The man who turns away from God and does not lay hold on God's strength but lives in himself, trying to do the best he can in himself, will find his own efforts inadequate and he will personally deteriorate.

I sometimes describe this in various ways as we find it here in Isaiah 5:8-30, suggesting that this is like describing the appearance of a man who has smallpox, by just drawing attention to one pock after another on his face. Verses 24 and 25 seem to be the key verses in this chapter:

70

> Therefore as the fire devoureth the stubble, and the flame
> consumeth the chaff, so their root shall be as rottenness, and
> their blossom shall go up as dust; because they have cast away
> the law of the Lord of hosts, and despised the word of the Holy
> One of Israel (Isa. 5:24).

Verses 8 to 23 describe what that judgment is like, but the real crux of the matter is the reason why judgment is coming: "They have cast away the law of the Lord of hosts, and despised the word of the Holy One of Israel." Had God's people kept His Word, they would not have wandered away.

> Therefore is the anger of the Lord kindled against his people,
> and he hath stretched forth his hand against them, and hath
> smitten them: and the hills did tremble, and their carcases were
> torn in the midst of the streets. For all this his anger is not
> turned away, but his hand is stretched out still (Isa. 5:25).

These various sins are the result of having neglected to follow the Word of God:

> Woe unto them that join house to house, that lay field to field,
> till there be no place that they may be placed alone in the midst
> of the earth! (Isa. 5:8).

This is a description of people with a covetous, acquisitive attitude. These are persons who want to get hold of everything for themselves. Of course, they take away from everyone else just so they can get a lot for themselves.

> In mine ears said the Lord of hosts, Of a truth many houses shall
> be desolate, even great and fair, without inhabitant. Yea, ten
> acres of vineyard shall yield one bath, and the seed of a homer
> shall yield an ephah (Isa. 5:9,10).

This seems to reveal that God will not prosper them in their plans; He will see to it that no blessing comes to them. The Bible tells us over and over that if a man is covetous and selfish, he will lose what he gained.

> Woe unto them that rise up early in the morning, that they may
> follow strong drink; that continue until night, till wine inflame
> them! And the harp, and the viol, the tabret, and pipe, and
> wine, are in their feasts: but they regard not the work of the
> Lord, neither consider the operation of his hands (Isa. 5:11,12).

This poetic language pictures indulgent, riotous people who are having a glorious time, so to speak, but do not consider the work of the Lord, neither consider the operation of His hands. When the prophet says, "Woe unto them," he is saying in effect that that is the kind of thing God will judge.

> Therefore my people are gone into captivity, because they have no knowledge: and their honourable men are famished, and their multitude dried up with thirst. Therefore hell hath enlarged herself, and opened her mouth without measure: and their glory, and their multitude, and their pomp, and he that rejoiceth, shall descend into it. And the mean man shall be brought down, and the mighty man shall be humbled, and the eyes of the lofty shall be humbled: but the Lord of hosts shall be exalted in judgment, and God that is holy shall be sanctified in righteousness. Then shall the lambs feed after their manner, and the waste places of the fat ones shall strangers eat. Woe unto them that draw iniquity with cords of vanity, and sin as it were with a cart rope: that say, Let him make speed, and hasten his work, that we may see it: and let the counsel of the Holy One of Israel draw nigh and come, that we may know it! (Isa. 5:13-19).

The language here is rather awkward for us but what it amounts to is this: these people are ignorant; they are impudent and are going in the wrong direction. They pursue their wicked ways hilariously and make a big to-do about it. This is a description of people who have no real knowledge, they are wicked in what they do, and they will be destroyed.

> Woe unto them that call evil good, and good evil; that put darkness for light, and light for darkness; that put bitter for sweet, and sweet for bitter! (Isa. 5:20).

There are people like that. If they hear someone say that this is the right thing to do, they ask what makes it right. If someone says this is a good thing to do, they ask why it is good. These people are perverse. There are people who not only talk that way but also think that way. They go after things that are not good and turn their back on things that are good. This is a condition of people bringing forth wild grapes instead of good grapes. Although God has done good things for them, they do not respond. This shows what happens in a sinful heart.

> Woe unto them that are wise in their own eyes, and prudent in their own sight! (Isa. 5:21).

Do you know that the tendency to be conceited and vain and proud of oneself belongs to the human heart? Every now and again some of us would have the feeling there are some people who certainly should not be proud of themselves, but I wonder if we are always conscious of the fact that we usually have it figured out that we have something about ourselves that is really worthwhile. May I say that will shrivel up, and when you come into the presence of the Lord, you will not be moved to pride.

> Woe unto them that are mighty to drink wine, and men of strength to mingle strong drink (Isa. 5:22).

What we read before had to do with self-indulgence. Here the reference is to those who have given themselves over to intoxicating liquors.

> Which justify the wicked for reward, and take away the righteousness of the righteous from him! (Isa. 5:23).

This sketch has shown one thing after another that was wrong. Unjust people were exercising injustice, taking the place of those who were in a position of judgment. We can be that way in our hearts. When we justify the wicked for reward, the reward may not always be money. Sometimes we favor our friends just because they are friends, to the extent that we will actually excuse them no matter what they do. We want to make it seem that what they do is all right. All of these people are to be consumed as stubble before the fire.

> Therefore as the fire devoureth the stubble, and the flame consumeth the chaff, so their root shall be as rottenness, and their blossom shall go up as dust: because they have cast away the law of the Lord of hosts, and despised the word of the Holy One of Israel (Isa. 5:24).

This will help us to understand that Isaiah is speaking about people who know the Lord. Only the people who have the law can cast it away, just as one cannot despise something he has not heard. Those who have the Bible and believe it to be the Word of God, yet pay no attention to it, are far more responsible than the people who do not have the Bible at all and who cannot throw it away because they do not have it.

In the latter part of this chapter we are told what the judgment and the anger of the Lord will be. It is sobering to listen to.

> Therefore is the anger of the Lord kindled against his people, and he hath stretched forth his hand against them, and hath smitten them: and the hills did tremble, and their carcases were torn in the midst of the streets. For all this his anger is not turned away, but his hand is stretched out still (Isa. 5:25).

It is still further described in more detail:

> And he will lift up an ensign to the nations from far, and will hiss unto them from the end of the earth: and, behold, they shall come with speed swiftly: none shall be weary nor stumble among them; none shall slumber nor sleep; neither shall the girdle of their loins be loosed, nor the latchet of their shoes be broken: whose arrows are sharp, and all their bows bent, their horses' hoofs shall be counted like flint, and their wheels like a whirlwind: their roaring shall be like a lion, they shall roar like young lions: yea, they shall roar, and lay hold of the prey, and shall carry it away safe, and none shall deliver it. And in that day they shall roar against them like the roaring of the sea: and if one look unto the land, behold darkness and sorrow, and the light is darkened in the heavens thereof (Isa. 5:26-30).

Isaiah is describing an enemy so powerful and mighty as to be dreadful. God will bring in from the outside this enemy who will destroy His people. The immediate thought many may have is that this implies there would be political war, and so it was for Israel. What actually happened to Israel was that first Syria, then Assyria, and then Babylon, came in and destroyed the country. This was God's way of judging His people. It would be easy to feel that this is the way it could be with us today: that if a certain nation did not obey the laws of God, He would let some other political entity come with military might and destroy it. Although that is the pattern shown here, I suggest that the deeper and true meaning of this passage does not point to contemporary political situations. I do not know of any country in the world today whose people could claim to be the people of God. Practically all nations today exist for political purposes, for economic and social reasons. Modern nations are largely made up as they are because they live together in the same location and have common interests.

In recent years, more than a dozen new nations were formed in the continent of Africa. Not one was formed because the people believed in God. So far as the nations in the United Nations are concerned, I do not know what people would claim that theirs is a nation because they believe in God. I think that since we are living in the New Testament days, in the days of the Spirit, this Scripture is best understood as intimating that God will bring judgment on His people spiritually. A denomination that fails to obey God, that does not follow the Scriptures, and, instead of praying to discover the mind of the Lord, works by various other means through committees to bring to pass the things they think should be done, is a group that should expect the judgment of God.

A congregation could lose the truth if they ignore the importance of prayer and neglect the work of the Holy Spirit. An enemy could come in from the outside and do harm to this group — some spiritual enemy. The results would show up in the way it happened in Judah: the young men would lose their lives, that is to say, young people in the congregation would not come to faith. Such a congregation could lose the things it treasured. And this would, in my estimation, be the fulfillment of a contemporary application of this passage in Isaiah.

Chapter 13

THE CALL OF ISAIAH

Chapter 6 deals particularly with the call of Isaiah. Some of the great things revealed about God in this chapter are these: He is on the throne; He is sovereign; and He is holy — so holy that the seraphim dare not look at Him. His glory fills the temple. The account of Isaiah's experience shows his sense of personal unfitness, his feeling of inward sin:

> Woe is me! for I am undone; because I am a man of unclean lips, and I dwell in the midst of a people of unclean lips: for mine eyes have seen the King, the Lord of hosts (Isa. 6:5).

Isaiah felt that he was ruined.

The account moves swiftly on to record a great act of grace. Coming from the presence of God, one of the seraphim with tongs lifted a live coal off the altar and touched the lips of Isaiah, saying, "Thine iniquity is taken away, and thy sin purged." Here we see God acting to remove sin. We should pause here for a moment to rejoice in that. It is everlastingly wonderful that all through the Scriptures this truth is set forth: God takes away our sins. It is difficult for the human heart to understand it, but it is gloriously true. It is God who cleanses and delivers. The live coal, taken from the altar, the very place of worship, was used to cleanse. Those of us who have the New Testament in mind will think of how the Lord Jesus Christ spent His life doing the work of God and laid Himself on the altar as a sacrifice to do God's will. He was put to death with cruel hands and His blood was shed; but it is His blood that cleanses me from my sin. And it is God who does it.

Then Isaiah "heard the voice of the Lord, saying, Whom shall I send, and who will go for us? Then said I, Here am I; send me" (Isa. 6:8). Almighty God had a work to be done. He needed a service to be rendered, and He issued the call: Who will go? Isaiah's ready response is classic. This is the kind of response one makes whose heart and mind have been touched by the Lord. The person who serves God freely and gladly is the person who is forgiven. When Jesus of Nazareth was in the house of Simon the Pharisee, the woman who had been cleansed came and washed His feet with her tears, dried them with her hair, and anointed them with ointment. Later in the house of Lazarus, a similar situation arose when Mary came with a box of precious ointment and anointed the feet of the Lord Jesus Christ. Both of these women were people who served Him out of a full heart gladly because they had been forgiven by Him. Isaiah, too, was willing to serve in this wholehearted way.

Now in verse 9 we learn that he was to go and tell his people. After this there are several statements difficult to interpret in our English translation, but similar quotations elsewhere indicate their meaning.

> And he said, Go, and tell this people, Hear ye indeed, but understand not; and see ye indeed, but perceive not. Make the heart of this people fat, and make their ears heavy, and shut their eyes; lest they see with their eyes, and hear with their ears, and understand with their heart, and convert, and be healed (Isa. 6:9,10).

Elsewhere in the Old Testament we read that is what the people did: they closed their ears and shut their eyes so they would not hear and see what the prophets said. Because they did this, their hearts became hard, and the preaching did not reach them.

This same truth was brought out in the New Testament when Jesus of Nazareth was teaching. His disciples asked why He taught in parables, why He was always using illustrations when He talked. And He answered:

> For this people's heart is waxed gross, and their ears are dull of hearing, and their eyes they have closed (Matt. 13:15).

All that Isaiah was given to understand at this point is that he was to go and preach and the people would not listen; they would shut their ears and their eyes, lest in listening they would have to change their ways.

Then said I, Lord, how long? And he answered, Until the cities be wasted without inhabitant, and the houses without man, and the land be utterly desolate, and the Lord have removed men far away, and there be a great forsaking in the midst of the land (Isa. 6:11,12).

Isaiah was to keep on preaching until everything dried up. Like many other prophets he was called on to preach when the tide was running out, and there was nothing he could do in his preaching to stop that tide from ebbing. In a sense, his mission was to preach as if he were a doctor who was called in when the patient was dying; the doctor is just there to ease the patient's dying. I suspect many doctors get real satisfaction when they are called in under circumstances when their service actually helps a person get well, rather than just to be called to be there when the patient dies. Perhaps even more satisfying is to help in the prevention of illness. My doctor once said to me, "Ordinarily I am called a doctor of medicine. I wish that I could be known as a doctor of health. Usually I am called to minister to people who are already sick, but I wish I were called on to help people stay well."

In the natural world "it is appointed unto men once to die" (Heb. 9:27). Regardless of who the doctor is, dying will take place. But in the spiritual world it is not necessary to die. Isaiah was called on, however, to come to these people and preach when their spiritual condition was getting worse and worse, and he was told to preach until the whole thing was completely ruined. I am of the opinion that a human being can be just like Israel. Perhaps in your family there may be individuals who have rebelled against God. They have turned away from Him, and now no voice, however strong and kind, can turn them from their way; they will go on ruining themselves and everything they touch. Many times a man has to get down to the very bottom before he is willing to turn. Human nature is like that. Sometimes we are called on to be friendly to people who are determined to disobey God. When that happens with someone in your own family, you can have some idea of what Isaiah felt. You may sometimes wonder whether or not God will let those persons live long enough to turn and come back.

Isaiah was a good man, a great preacher, called into a situation to preach when all the preaching he could do could not

turn them from the road to ruin. In spite of Isaiah — and for
that matter in spite of Amos, Micah, Hosea, and Jeremiah —
these people went wrong. And Isaiah said, "Lord, how long?"
With reference to our own ministry today, we sometimes
wonder how long we must warn. Yet after Isaiah had been
shown all this it is written:

> But yet in it shall be a tenth, and it shall return, and shall be
> eaten: as a teil tree, and as an oak, whose substance is in them,
> when they cast their leaves: so the holy seed shall be the
> substance thereof (Isa. 6:13).

The Lord said to Isaiah in effect that he should preach until
the leaves would turn color and die and fall off the trees, until
winter would come into the soul of the nation. Though he
would tell the truth, they would not pay any attention to him.
The leaves would all drop off and the trees look dead, but
they would not be dead. Inside would be the sap, the life-
giving fluid that makes a tree grow. That would be the remnant in Israel. God will never lose sight of those who belong to Him. They will be there, ready to grow when spring
comes.

How many times will this be true for people from a spiritual
point of view? This can happen among believing people. We
see believing people become wayward in spirit. They stop
praying; they stop reading the Bible. They believe in God and
they believe in the Lord Jesus Christ. They are properly called
believers, but they are not obedient. Their life is miserable.
While we should not call them unbelievers, they are not at one
with God; they are estranged from Him. Yet even with such
people there will be in them something that God will never let
go. The part in them that God puts there will never be forsaken. In such times of waywardness that we may experience,
as long as there is in our hearts any inward confidence in God,
despite the way we feel and despite the way we act, we will yet
know that God is true and that He is kind; we will know that
Christ Jesus died for us.

Paul says that if we suffer with Him, we shall reign with Him.
If we serve Him, we shall be blessed with Him, and if we deny
Him, yet He remains faithful. He cannot deny Himself. That is
the point at which God does more than we can ask or think. He
will be faithful even if we are not.

This, then, was Isaiah's call: to minister to a nation that belonged to God but was wayward and had become worldly. Many times when a man stands before others and declares the Word of God, the heart of the listener has a tendency to deviate from the truth and turn away from God. This was Isaiah's experience, but he was to preach anyway. This whole message does not have to do with unbelieving sinners; Isaiah was dealing with believing people.

The next section of the book of Isaiah, chapters 7 to 12, have to do with the situation that arose at the time of the Syrian crisis. The land of Judah was in danger of being attacked by two other countries. The land of Judah was around the city of Jerusalem. Just north of Judah was the northern kingdom called "Israel," whose capital city was Samaria. Judah and Israel were two nations, both of whom were supposed to believe in God. Although the temple was in Jerusalem in the south, the people of the north claimed they belonged to God through the covenant with Abraham and the law of Moses. There was often war between these two kingdoms. In general, the people of Judah were the people who wanted to walk closer with God. All but one of the kings of Judah were good men, whereas all of the kings of Israel were wicked. In the Christian church today there is in a general way a division between two classes of believers: those who work at Christian living and those who do not work at it. The latter just go along for the ride. They are professing believers who do not read their Bibles, do not pray, and have no particular interest in missions. They feel they are doing all that can be expected of them if they bring their children to Sunday school and if they themselves come to church perhaps two or three times a month. They are respectable people who have their names on the church rolls and contribute something to the church. Those I have described here may properly be called "worldly Christians."

I would like to speak of the one group as the worldly Christians and the other group as the spiritual Christians. Any church has these two groups. It is not exactly black and white or completely all day and all night. There are twilight zones. There are some people who are somewhat gray. They have a good feel of interest in spiritual matters and a lot of interest in the world as well. They live in between. And so, when you are thinking in the study of Isaiah about Israel and Judah, you can be thinking of two ordinary groups of Christian people: those who are worldly in spirit and those who are godly and spiritual in spirit. Between these there is often contention.

Chapter 14

THE SYRIAN CRISIS

We are now entering more definitely into that portion of the book that is based on the events in Judah's history when they were threatened by the danger of Israel and Syria conspiring against them. When the children of Israel had become established in the land of Canaan, the government they set up lasted several generations. Saul became the first king and he was a failure. David, who followed him, was probably the greatest king Israel ever had. Solomon, the most glorious king, followed him, and after him came Rehoboam, in whose time the nation was divided.

You will remember that Isaiah lived in the southern, small kingdom of Judah. Judah was situated in the mountains, whereas the large northern kingdom was in the plains. The military advantage of living in the mountains was such that although Judah was small, oftentimes in battle her armies were able to hold their own against, and even defeat, Israel. Another country near them was Syria. The capital of Syria was Damascus. Occasionally the three countries were referred to by their capital cities — Samaria in Israel, Jerusalem in Judah, and Damascus in Syria. One of the reasons for the conflict between Judah and Israel was that both claimed the land east of the Jordan, sometimes Judah took it and held it for a while, then Israel would take it. Since Syria was on the other side of Jordan, they became interested in it from time to time. And so it was a bone of contention among these three nations.

At the time this section of Isaiah was written, the political situation was something like this: Israel and Syria combined against Judah. The actual historic incident is very simple.

> And it came to pass in the days of Ahaz the son of Jotham, the son
> of Uzziah, king of Judah, that Rezin the king of Syria, and Pekah
> the son of Remaliah, king of Israel, went up toward Jerusalem to
> war against it, but could not prevail against it. And it was told the
> house of David, saying, Syria is confederate with Ephraim. And
> his heart was moved, and the heart of his people, as the trees of
> the wood are moved with the wind (Isa. 7:1,2).

The two larger nations combined against the smaller Judah,
and the people were scared to death.

> Then said the Lord unto Isaiah, Go forth now to meet Ahaz,
> thou, and Shearjashub thy son, at the end of the conduit of the
> upper pool in the highway of the fuller's field; and say unto him,
> Take heed, and be quiet; fear not, neither be fainthearted for the
> two tails of these smoking firebrands, for the fierce anger of
> Rezin with Syria, and of the son of Remaliah. Because Syria,
> Ephraim, and the son of Remaliah, have taken evil counsel
> against thee, saying, Let us go up against Judah, and vex it, and
> let us make a breach therein for us, and set a king in the midst of
> it, even the son of Tabeal: thus saith the Lord God, It shall not
> stand, neither shall it come to pass. For the head of Syria is
> Damascus, and the head of Damascus is Rezin; and within
> threescore and five years shall Ephraim be broken, that it be not
> a people (Isa. 7:3-8).

Isaiah was to go to Ahaz, king of Judah and say in effect, "Don't
let enemies frighten you. The Lord God has said it will not
come to pass."

Now that was the political picture at the time Isaiah brought
his message. When we interpret and understand that for ourselves, we can be very sure that this was recorded in Scripture
also for us, to give us the political situation in Judah. What do
we see here? We see Judah, the people who sincerely believed
in God, confronted and threatened by a combination of Israel
(the worldly believers) and Syria (whose people made no profession of God). The Syrians were unbelievers interested in
values that were cherished by God's people. What made this so
serious was that Judah's welfare was at stake. In the time of
Isaiah this was spelled out in material terms. It was a matter of
good crops and a bumper harvest. It was a matter of the
security of their treasure, that their gold and silver might be
saved. And it was a matter of having liberty to do as they saw fit
to do in their country, all spelled out in a human and political
fashion.

That is the way it was in those days, and when we think about ourselves today, we will miss the point in interpretation of Scripture if we try to bring that over and refer it to our *material* situation. Those things happened to them for examples, in which they dealt with external things, which God specially controlled in providence to teach us something. But the truth is this: the reality of God, the blessing of God, is not a matter of food and drink or gold or silver. It is not a matter of political or personal liberty in this world but it is spiritual. What, then, are some of the values we have as believers? It is human nature to spell out every value in terms of physical things: if God would bless us, we would get more money; if God would bless me, I would never be sick and I would not have any trouble. Far be it from me to decry the providence of God in natural things, because He shows forth His kindness many times; but that is not the real essence of the blessing we have in Christ Jesus. These are matters of an eternal nature.

What are some of these things? One of the greatest blessings we can have is our own faith in God. Now faith in God is not a simple thing. Even people who have it do not have as much as they want. You cannot just make up your mind to believe God; that would be make-believe. You have to have something to go on; you must have an inward conviction about some things, and God has a hand in that. When you are blessed of God, you have an inward faith in Him that will not be shaken by anything, and you thank God for your faith.

Another blessing is your confidence in His providence: "Though he slay me, yet will I trust him," said Job (Job 13:15). It is marvelous to have that kind of confidence in my heart, to know that no matter what happens, I am able in my heart to have the feeling that God meant it for good. Not everybody's faith stays at the same level. A person can believe more and more. The apostles prayed, "Lord increase our faith," because faith can grow. Furthermore, to have personal deliverance from my inward weaknesses, to be delivered from the domination of my desires, and to be able to look at something that I want and then to be able not to take it: all of these are blessings. It is not possible to have a strong faith without the help of God.

Telling a man to believe in the Lord is not going to help him believe in the Lord. You have to tell him what the Lord will do for him, and all the time you have to be praying to Almighty God to give that person the grace to believe. There are various ways in which faith comes. "Faith cometh by hearing and hearing by the word of God" (Rom. 10:17). A child brought up in a home where God is honored will find it easy to honor God. Apart from the Word of God there is no faith, and the Word of God can be taught, lived, and shown to others in many ways in the home. The same is true in a church. If the man in the pulpit believes the Bible, in God, in prayer, and in the reality of spiritual matters, it will be a natural thing for members of that congretation to also believe in God. That is a blessing of God.

Now let us consider this situation in Judah at the time of Isaiah. When we study this experience of Judah, we are going to find the truth, as it were, about certain conditions under which we can be blessed with faith and with hope and with love. These precious blessings we are speaking of — the blessings of the Spirit — are not of our own making. They are given to us in His Word. They are activated in us by His Spirit and they are realized by us in His presence.

Who are our enemies? Those who would weaken our faith and destroy our confidence, who would shake our quietness and peace by the way they deal with the things in which we are trusting.

> For we wrestle not against flesh and blood, but against principalities, against powers, against the rulers of the darkness of this world, against spiritual wickedness in high places (Eph. 6:12).

We do not fight after the flesh or use carnal weapons; we use spiritual weapons in this struggle in which we are.

Who then are the worldly believers referred to in Isaiah 7, such as Ephraim, the northern kingdom Israel, who are among us today? They are the ones who claim to be believers, but whose manner of life is not grounded in faith. They develop their personal lives according to their own desires or benefit, as the case may be. This was the Israel of Isaiah's time — those who said they believed in God but who did not worship God according to the way it is written. We have people among us today who pay lip homage to the Bible. They say the Bible is the Word of God, yet they never read it. Often their ministers preach what is in their own minds.

Today there are people who are sincerely interested in Bible study and in prayer and in evangelism, and right around them, sometimes in the same congregation, are people who say they are interested in these things, but who are not. Sometimes a feeling of difference develops in a church like that, and often the people who say they stand for the same things believers do actually hold out against the sincere people and oppose them in many ways. Israel was like that.

Syria may well represent unbelieving persons interested solely in what they have, who covet the blessings of the believers. There are unbelievers who have heard that believers have peace of heart and mind and they would like also to have these blessings.

There are people who do not believe in the Lord Jesus Christ personally, but they would like to have peace. They are interested in examining the peace believers have. They analyze that peace and examine it from a psychological point of view to try to find out how believers attain it. Then they try to have the same peace that believers enjoy who have the peace of God in their hearts and minds. That is Syria, who did not believe in God at all, but wanted the land that Judah owned.

The same is true with reference to virtue. Many people who do not have any particular interest in the gospel often admire honest, clean people. Such unbelievers like good homes and reliability in business. Sometimes there are people so interested in the welfare of the community that they admit they are terribly afraid we will have a business depression if we do not have a revival. In that case they say it would be better to have a revival, because they do not want to lose their money. Rather than lose their money, they yield to the churches to have a revival. Such persons are like Syria in this period of history.

Chapter 15

PROMISE OF GOD'S HELP

In chapters 7–12 we will consider just what the situation pictured means to us in our day. We recognize that the political crisis that developed in chapter 7 came about because the country of Judah was confronted by the threat of opposition from two other larger countries: Israel and Syria. Israel was called by the name of God and counted themselves as believers. Syria, on the other hand, was composed of a large number of people who did not claim any relation to God. Both were fighting against Judah for the reason all fighting takes place: Judah had something they both wanted — the land on the other side of Jordan.

Believing people are inclined to obey the laws of the land and to live orderly lives. There are people who prefer these things but who do not want to give the Lord any credit for them. Many philanthropic enterprises today are carried on openly — distinctly divorced from the church or from the name of the Lord, with the insinuation that a person can be charitable even if he does not believe in God and in the Lord Jesus Christ. Such persons want the blessings that originally come from the gospel and have been promoted only in countries where the gospel is preached. There are many who talk about peace but deny God. These are the people represented in this interpretation by the nation of Syria. Then there are worldly believers who want to be known as believers but who do not really intend to do anything about it. They would reduce all the spiritual interest of sincere believers to a form of sanctimoniousness. Such were the people of the northern kingdom of Israel.

It is not easy for a spiritually minded believer to stand up in sincere belief in God and in the Lord Jesus Christ when many others in the church do not believe in those things. That is what Judah faced in the nation of Israel. Syria represents those who want all the benefits of Christianity but do not want to give any glory to the name of the Lord Jesus Christ. They reject the spiritual basis if believers speak of peace and of love, of doing for the poor, of quietness of mind and heart because they believe in the Lord Jesus Christ. Believers make these claims because God has forgiven them for Christ's sake and Christ shed His blood for them. Unbelievers claim that our gospel is a cultural myth of some kind, that we use symbolic language whenever we refer to spiritual ideas. This disturbs many sincere Christians. After all, other people claim many of the same things we do, but they do not give any credit to the Lord Jesus Christ. What actually develops is a terrible conflict.

In Isaiah's time a war was involved. Judah, with two tribes, was standing alone against the great power of ten tribes and against Syria as well. In many ways the children of this world are smarter than the children of light and they "come at us" from all directions. It was no wonder then that when Judah heard about the combination against them, their hearts were moved as the trees are moved in the wind. They were frightened because this was a crisis. Judah rightly felt that her very life was at stake. What we may overlook is that we, too, are at war. When many people claim every blessing we have and give no credit to the Lord Jesus Christ, this can have a stifling effect on our own spirit, and this becomes a real spiritual struggle. This is what the apostle Paul had in mind when he said, "For we wrestle not against flesh and blood, but against principalities, against powers, against the rulers of the darkness of this world, against spiritual wickedness in high places" (Eph. 6:12).

> And it was told the house of David, saying, Syria is confederate with Ephraim. And his heart was moved, and the heart of his people, as the trees of the wood are moved with the wind (Isa. 7:2).

Fear and dread came upon Judah because of a desperate feeling of helplessness. How many times has it been true that an earnest Christian, confronted with certain situations, feels completely helpless?

Then said the Lord unto Isaiah, Go forth now to meet Ahaz,
thou, and Shearjashub thy son, at the end of the conduit of
the upper pool in the highway of the fuller's field; and say unto
him, Take heed, and be quiet; fear not, neither be fainthearted
for the two tails of these smoking firebrands, for the fierce
anger of Rezin with Syria, and of the son of Remaliah (Isa.
7:3,4).

Certainly the enemies are greater than the believer, and in the
ordinary course of human events the believer will not be able
to convince them of the truth of God's Word. They will
examine everything the believer says and will turn his own
words against him, making him look like a fool. But from the
Lord God comes this assurance: "It shall not stand, neither
shall it come to pass" (Isa. 7:7). God will keep His word and He
will keep His people. The course of such natural enemies to the
truth will soon run out, and what is clear here is that within
sixty-five years Ephraim would be destroyed. Their time is
limited and their days numbered.

I am much impressed by this: God will not give many of us
the opportunity to see any great victory outwardly in this
world. Believers are the kind of people who in this world will
be defeated and laughed at. The chances are that smart folks
are going to have it all over them in any conflict, but the Lord is
their God and their trust is in Him. Their confidence is not
based on superficial victory in some argument. The believer
can say:

I know whom I have believed, and am persuaded that he is able
to keep that which I have committed unto him against that day
(2 Tim. 1:12).

Isaiah spoke to Ahaz, telling him not to get excited or upset,
God would not let the enemies win. He would be with His
people. Then comes an amazing promise: He told Ahaz to ask
for a sign, and Ahaz said he would not ask for a sign; then Isaiah
said these famous words:

Therefore the Lord himself shall give you a sign; Behold, a
virgin shall conceive, and bear a son, and shall call his name
Immanuel (Isa. 7:14).

That verse was quoted in the New Testament (Matt. 1:23)
when the Lord Jesus was born. His birth was the fulfillment of
the word that was spoken by Isaiah. God told His people not to

worry or get panicky, for He would send His Son into this world incarnate.

Now you and I are standing 2,000 years this side of that event. God has sent His Son. This is God's answer to all of the contention about how to secure blessing from Him: the incarnation of the Son of God, the Lord Jesus Christ. In the last analysis, every argument for the gospel is solved in the face of the Lord Jesus Christ. We bring every argument of every sort right to Jesus Christ, the Son of God, our Savior and our Lord. When you and I stand by Him, we are safe. He is the Refuge, and to this day, right now, we can do no better in the face of any threat than to put our trust in Jesus Christ and Him crucified, as set forth in the Scriptures. Let us keep this in mind as Christian people: Whom are we trusting? Jesus Christ died for us and now we can test anyone, anywhere, any time in the face of Jesus Christ. And anyone, anywhere, who needs an explanation about how to receive blessing, we bring face to face with Jesus Christ.

Keep this in mind: when Jesus of Nazareth was born into this world and lived His thirty-plus years here, He was God in human form. The outstanding characteristic of Jesus of Nazareth was that He did all things that pleased His Father. That is now and forever will be the highest principle value on the face of this earth: that a man should do the will of his Creator. "Remember now thy creator in the days of thy youth" (Eccl. 12:1). This is the one word we say to all young people, any time, any place.

In the remainder of the chapter it is revealed that God will utterly destroy the very forces that threatened His people. But here is an amazing thing: He is going to destroy them by bringing in other forces against them. The fly from Egypt and the bee from Assyria will come in swarms to cover the land. In other words, Judah will not destroy them; God's people will stand still, trusting in God, and God will undo the opposition and bring them to nothing, while those who put their trust in Him shall never be moved.

That is what Isaiah was preaching and teaching in his time.

> In the same day shall the Lord shave with a razor that is hired, namely, by them beyond the river, by the king of Assyria, the head, and the hair of the feet: and it shall also consume the

> beard. And it shall come to pass in that day, that a man shall
> nourish a young cow, and two sheep; and it shall come to pass,
> for the abundance of milk that they shall give, he shall eat butter:
> for butter and honey shall every one eat that is left in the land.
> And it shall come to pass in that day, that every place shall be,
> where there were a thousand vines at a thousand silverlings, it
> shall even be for briers and thorns. With arrows and with bows
> shall men come thither; because all the land shall become briers
> and thorns. And on all hills that shall be digged with the mat-
> tock, there shall not come thither the fear of briers and thorns:
> but it shall be for the sending forth of oxen, and for the treading
> of lesser cattle (Isa. 7:20-25).

There will be terrible consequences over the whole country
when God moves to undo those who have resisted His people.
Judah is to see it happen but is not to lift a hand to help it.

Let me remind you, it will never be given to God's people to
have the privilege of pointing, as it were, to their superiority.
They will never be able to lead any great victory parades, so far
as this world is concerned. Believers are going to win in Christ
Jesus. God always causes them to triumph in Him, but many
believers will live through their lifetime and never see their
victory openly demonstrated and vindicated to their own satisfaction. Many parents have dealt with a child, disciplined him,
and tried to show him the right way; and that child may have
become wayward and stayed away from them. Finally, years
later, some stranger may come along and say certain things to
that child (perhaps the very truth the mother had taught), and
he will be given all the credit when that child believes and
changes. God knows these things. Situations often develop in
which all we can do is just stand for what we know to be right.
There will be no great victory; we just stand for what we think is
right even though we are outvoted nine to one, as the case may
be. The apostle Paul wrote to the Corinthians:

> Therefore, my beloved brethren, be ye steadfast, unmovable,
> always abounding in the work of the Lord, forasmuch as ye know
> that your labour is not in vain in the Lord (1 Cor. 15:58).

So far as Judah was concerned, they were going to be pro-
tected. But it was not to be given to them in any human way to
flaunt themselves as being great. They had been frightened by
the opposition, for they had no strength to face it. But God was
on their side and He had said, "Take heed and be quiet.

Neither be fainthearted because of these threats." Almighty God has taken note of the whole situation and what they said they would do would not come to pass. God will utterly destroy them. He will send forth His own Son into this world and you are going to put your trust in Him.

This is the marvelous teaching of Isaiah 7. We will find more of the same as we look at chapters 8 and 9.

Chapter 16

GOD'S PROMISE OF THE MESSIAH

In the eighth chapter of Isaiah the situation continues to be described in certain political circumstances. We will remember that our attention is focused on the people of Judah because Isaiah ministered to them. These people represent those on earth who have committed themselves to walk in the ways of God. They are a type of spiritually minded believers who have conviction about the reality of God and who want the blessing of God in their lives. How are they different from other people? They have the temple of God among them, and God is dwelling in their midst. They trust in God for protection and for health and they have committed themselves to walk in the ways of God.

But they are still human beings living in this world and it is characteristic of them that their faith does not always remain strong; it can grow weaker. Their sense of spiritual things may grow more dim while their sense of material things becomes stronger. God is invisible — we cannot hear, see, or touch Him — yet He is real, but the human heart tends not to remember that. This world is so much a part of us, and so day in and day out we need to do many things to live in it, with the result that the spiritual or invisible things, the things that have to do with eternity and God, become dim in our consciousness. When that happens, we tend to act according to the material things; and when we act according to the material elements, the things of this world, we are not acting in the will of God, because the will of God and setting our hearts on the things of this world do not go together.

On one occasion the Lord Jesus said, "For that which is highly esteemed among men is abomination in the sight of

93

God" (Luke 16:15). Many believers have found that they want to do certain things in the flesh, whereas in the spirit, in obedience to God, it seems they should be doing other things. This causes tension and distress in the average believer's life. In this passage of Scripture Judah represents that group of believing people who want the blessing of God. We call them spiritually minded believers. Another group in the political situation was Israel, the ten northern tribes at that time. They obviously represent people who say they belong to God, but in their actual history they do not seek His face. They represent what we call worldly believers, carnal persons. Sometimes the tensions between these two groups broke into open conflict, and they went to war with each other. At other times they attempted to collaborate with each other, but always danger was there. Invariably, when Judah associated with Israel, there would be dissatisfaction and trouble. Where did Syria come in? They coveted territory that belonged to Judah. Who would the Syrians represent in our day and time? I suggest they represent people who, seeing the benefits of living the believing life, want those benefits, but they do not want the religion that is involved in it. They will try to produce the integrity, joy, and peace of mind the believer enjoys, but not through faith.

And so this situation developed in the history of that time: Judah was confronted by a coalition made up of Israel (the worldly believers) and Syria (the people outside the company of faith, who coveted some of the things they had). Isaiah told Judah they did not need to be distressed or panicky because Israel and Syria had joined together against them; God would fight for them and they would have the victory through Him. They were told that God would raise up another nation, Assyria, who would move in to destroy first Syria, then Israel, after which they would besiege Jerusalem.

> The Lord spake also unto me again, saying, Forasmuch as this people refuseth the waters of Shiloah that go softly, and rejoice in Rezin and Remaliah's son; now therefore, behold, the Lord bringeth up upon them the waters of the river, strong and many, even the king of Assyria, and all his glory: and he shall come up over all his channels, and go over all his banks (Isa. 8:5-7).

The expression "the waters of Shiloah" apparently refers to the blessing that comes from the place of God, since Shiloah is a place where God was being worshiped. The waters of Shiloah were the rivers that flowed by the city of God. That refers to the source of blessings that come from God, but the people of Israel and Syria did not rejoice in those. They refused those waters of Shiloah that go softly and they rejoiced in Rezin, the king of Syria, and Remaliah's son, Peka, the king of Israel.

> And he shall pass through Judah; he shall overflow and go over, he shall reach even to the neck; and the stretching out of his wings shall fill the breadth of thy land, O Immanuel (Isa. 8:8).

This is a poetic way of saying that Assyria will come in like a flood and overflow Syria and Israel, down to the very gates of Jerusalem itself. The water will reach even "to the neck," which means the flood will get so high it will almost drown them; even Judah would almost be destroyed.

As it turned out, Judah was not destroyed, but was very seriously threatened. So Isaiah said that because Syria and Israel did not put their trust in God, He would bring out of the pagan world another power that would destroy them. The prophet said to Israel and Syria:

> Associate yourselves, O ye people, and ye shall be broken in pieces; and give ear, all ye of far countries: gird yourselves, and ye shall be broken in pieces; gird yourselves, and ye shall be broken in pieces. Take counsel together, and it shall come to nought; speak the word, and it shall not stand: for God is with us (Isa. 8:9,10).

All their planning would amount to nothing. The one thing that would give Judah their strength in all this conflict and strife was that God was with them.

> For the Lord spake thus to me with a strong hand, and instructed me that I should not walk in the way of this people, saying, Say ye not, A confederacy, to all them to whom this people shall say, A confederacy; neither fear ye their fear, nor be afraid (Isa. 8:11,12).

Isaiah was saying God had spoken to him and told him not to join in with the people who were promoting a confederacy, nor to be affected by their fears. It is characteristic of the people of the world that they imagine that by getting together they will be able to get things done. This happens over and over again. We remember the tower of Babel when the people said "Go to, let us make brick . . . let us build us a city and a tower, whose top may reach unto heaven; and let us make us a name, lest we be scattered abroad upon the face of the whole earth" (Gen. 11:3,4). Almighty God looked down upon them and said in effect, "See what they do. If they would succeed in this there would not be anything in their vanity and pride they would not get done" and He arranged that they would never be able to get along together. He touched them in such a way they did not understand each other's speech, and so their grand plans for union were shattered.

God even now has things fixed so that when men get together and try to figure things out, it will not work. Why? It is just as if He made them part of a jigsaw puzzle and He is the third part; two won't make a picture. That is how it would be with reference to anything when man leaves God out of his plans. Now God has it fixed that way so far as the whole world is concerned; and it was like that with reference to Israel and Syria. Judah was alone against them. Now God told Isaiah, who interpreted the mind of God to Judah, not to form a confederacy with Israel and Syria.

> Sanctify the Lord of hosts himself; and let him be your fear, and let him be your dread (Isa. 8:13).

Isaiah was urging Judah not to be afraid of people; they should be afraid of God. The word *afraid* should be taken in a broad sense, meaning they should not give heed primarily to those nations, but consider God primarily.

> And he shall be for a sanctuary; but for a stone of stumbling and for a rock of offence to both the houses of Israel, for a gin and for a snare to the inhabitants of Jerusalem. And many among them shall stumble, and fall, and be broken, and be snared, and be taken (Isa. 8:14,15).

This same God will become a sanctuary to those who trust Him and will become a stone of stumbling and a rock of offense to people who do not trust Him.

> Bind up the testimony, seal the law among my disciples. And I will wait upon the Lord, that hideth his face from the house of Jacob, and I will look for him (Isa. 8:16,17).

Isn't that an interesting expression? In my experience in Bible teaching I have become convinced that we cannot make the Bible completely clear to everybody; only the willing heart will understand the Word of God. In coming to understand Scripture, it is important for us to seek to know the mind of God. Unless there is a hunger and a thirst for the knowledge of God, we will miss it.

> Behold, I and the children whom the Lord hath given me are for signs and for wonders in Israel from the Lord of hosts, which dwelleth in mount Zion (Isa. 8:18).

I think Isaiah is just admitting that he personally is an illustration of the truth to everybody. Every man who preaches will feel like the apostle Paul, who said that this happened to him that he might be an example to those who would afterward believe on Christ to life everlasting (2 Tim. 1:16).

> And when they shall say unto you, Seek unto them that have familiar spirits, and unto wizards that peep, and that mutter: should not a people seek unto their God? for the living to the dead? (Isa. 8:19).

There were people even in those days who claimed they could get in touch with God through the spiritual world. We have people today who want to get in touch with God, but they do not come by the way of the cross of Calvary. Claiming they can worship God in other ways, they do not come by the way of the Lord Jesus Christ. But the Lord Jesus said, "I am the door: by me if any man enter in, he shall be saved" (John 10:9). He also said if any man "climbeth up some other way, the same is a thief and a robber" (John 10:1). In another place He said, "I am the way, the truth, and the life: no man cometh unto the Father, but by me" (John 14:6).

Some people want to get in touch with the Creator of the universe, but they do not come by the way of the cross; they do not make forgiveness of sin the basis of their relationship with God. They do not deal with sins at all. Rather, they come before God perhaps saying they are weak and they want Him to give them strength, or they look for comfort or blessing. When anyone comes with some new way of interpreting spiritual experience and says that you can have the blessing of God without being a believer in Christ, arguing that there are pagan people who likely will be able to get the blessing of God because they worship God, you have this very situation. Isaiah says, "If they speak not according to this word, it is because there is no light in them" (Isa. 8:20).

I am willing to think that some people may be led better than they know and they may say some of the very things that are true, but these things will be true because they are according to the Word of God. When it is true, it will not be contrary to what we find in Scripture. However, if it is contrary to what we find in Scripture, contrary to the law and to the testimony, it will be because the ideas are wholly or partly false. This is what the prophet Isaiah is saying:

> And they shall pass through it, hardly bestead and hungry: and it shall come to pass, that when they shall be hungry, they shall fret themselves, and curse their king and their God, and look upward. And they shall look unto the earth; and behold trouble and darkness, dimness of anguish; and they shall be driven to darkness (Isa. 8:21,22).

Such people would never be satisfied. There will be people who will claim they have always done the right thing, yet they do not seem to get anywhere, and their hearts are filled with bitterness, even against God Himself. Actually, such never did trust in the Lord Jesus Christ and they did not come to God by Him. "They shall look unto the earth; and behold trouble and darkness." This, then, is the message we have in Isaiah 8, in which Isaiah is revealing to the people of his day what God will do so far as their experiences are concerned.

Chapter 17

GOD'S JUDGMENT ON ASSYRIA

In the course of our study thus far, Isaiah has been teaching Judah not to be afraid of the confederation of Israel and Syria, but to depend on God, for God would take care of them. That has been set forth in various ways. In chapters 9 to 11 we will see how God will work things out. Isaiah's message begins at 9:8.

> The Lord sent a word into Jacob, and it hath lighted upon Israel. And all the people shall know, even Ephraim and the inhabitant of Samaria, that say in the pride and stoutness of heart, The bricks are fallen down, but we will build with hewn stones: the sycamores are cut down, but we will change them into cedars (Isa. 9:8-10).

Do you recognize that language? They are saying, "We have had it bad, we have had trouble, but we will come out of it all right." So they speak up to encourage each other in self-confidence.

> Therefore the Lord shall set up the adversaries of Rezin against him, and join his enemies together; the Syrians before, and the Philistines behind; and they shall devour Israel with open mouth. For all this his anger is not turned away, but his hand is stretched out still (Isa. 9:11,12).

God reveals that Israel will be desolated: enemies will gang up on them from behind and in front and will destroy Israel.

> For the people turneth not unto him that smiteth them, neither do they seek the Lord of hosts (Isa. 9:13).

That is the condition they were in. That is what was at fault with Israel.

Almighty God in faithfulness chastises those who put their trust in Him. He is too faithful to let a wayward child wander

99

away from Him. A person who believes in God will interpret every calamity, every sorrow, every grief as from the Lord. Sometimes people are inclined to think that if people have suffering to endure, it will make them good. That does not follow. Suffering makes a good person better but it makes a bad person worse. Suffering does not make everybody gentle; it makes some people harsh. Suffering does not make everybody sweet; it makes some people bitter. When the hand that falls upon you is heavy, the course of events in providence as it comes to affect your life actually brings a burden upon you. How are you going to interpret this? If you interpret it as from the Lord, as I verily believe it is, and He lets this thing happen to you, what will your attitude be? Strange as it may seem, some people will, in a sense, rebel against God even when the hand is heavy upon them. Even when they are being chastened, they will fight back, and when they are suffering, they will curse God because of this suffering.

That is the mark of an unrepentant heart and a sure sign that a person does not belong to God. I will never forget the first time I seriously chastised our oldest child. I spanked the baby because she was impudent to her mother. Why did I do it? I did it because in faithfulness to her I had to do it. I will never forget that when I was through punishing her, she ran to me and, throwing her arms around my neck, cried, "Daddy, Daddy, Daddy!" I was astonished beyond words. I did not know about children; I did not even know about human nature. I not only did not know about human love, I did not know about the love of God. That is the way it happens when they love you. Now I can understand how it happens with God: when real Christians suffer, they turn to God as never before. Above everything else, they do not want God to let them go. They can endure anything but separation from God. When people in the ordinary course of life experience suffering and do not turn to Him, it is obvious their heart is not right. And that is what Isaiah says about these people:

> For the people turneth not unto him that smiteth them, neither do they seek the Lord of hosts (Isa. 9:13).

They were not repentant.

> Therefore the Lord will cut off from Israel head and tail, branch and rush, in one day (Isa. 9:14).

That is the way of saying He will clean them out — lock, stock, and barrel.

> For the leaders of this people cause them to err; and they that are led of them are destroyed (Isa. 9:16).

The leadership of Israel was wrong. That the followers — the younger, weaker, and more recent adherents — could falter can be understood, but when the leaders faltered, the situation was hopeless. That was the way it was with these people.

> Therefore the Lord shall have no joy in their young men, neither shall have mercy on their fatherless and widows: for every one is an hypocrite and an evildoer, and every mouth speaketh folly. For all this his anger is not turned away, but his hand is stretched out still. For wickedness burneth as the fire: it shall devour the briers and thorns, and shall kindle in the thickets of the forest, and they shall mount up like the lifting up of smoke. Through the wrath of the Lord of hosts is the land darkened, and the people shall be as the fuel of the fire: no man shall spare his brother (Isa. 9:17-19).

This is a further description of their distress due to disobedience to God.

In chapter 10 we find how the will of God will be done. There is a refrain all through this passage.

> For all this his anger is not turned away, but his hand is stretched out still (Isa. 10:4).

In other words, from Isaiah 9:8 through 10:4 the fate of Israel is described. The finger was pointed at this one thing: they would not repent, they followed false leaders and their destruction was sure. God would really destroy them. That is what the message of God is concerning worldly minded believers, people who claim to know God but will not submit themselves under the providence of God or to His chastening hand. They follow false leaders who cause them to err. Such people will suffer total loss.

Now in Isaiah 10:5-19 attention is focused on Assyria. As the story unfolds, it is Assyria that destroys Syria; and Assyria is again a type of religious unbelievers. The interesting thing is that God undoes one set of unbelievers with·another set of unbelievers. Syria had joined with Israel against Judah. Then Syria was destroyed when Assyria came through Syria and Israel and attacked Judah. They became an enemy of God's people, though they were the very ones who were to help them. But now this is what is said about them: Assyria will be destroyed; God will undo them. Here is a very interesting fact: God will use Assyria to destroy Syria and Israel. He will use these pagan people to destroy other heathen people, even though He does not approve of Assyrian motives or Assyrian principles and procedures, and will one day utterly destroy Assyria. We learn from this that so far as the world as a whole is concerned, some great leader may rise up, perhaps such a leader as Hitler or Mussolini were in their times. Then over against him another nation may be raised up — one that will help to crush the Hitler or the Mussolini.

According to the course of history as it is seen in Scripture, God may even now be raising up the people who will undo the present great power in turn. These things happen over and over again. There are waves of human power. One person rises up and controls for a length of time, and just about the time he seems to be established the next one comes along. This happens like the waves of the sea, one following another, again and again. So Assyria is used to destroy Syria, but Assyria will also be destroyed, as Isaiah wrote:

> O Assyrian, the rod of mine anger [God says], and the staff in their hand is mine indignation. [When the Assyrian armies devastate Syria, that is what God wants to do to Syria.] I will send him against a hypocritical nation [He will send the Assyrians down against Israel itself], and against the people of my wrath will I give him a charge, to take the spoil, and to take the prey, and to tread them down like the mire of the streets. Howbeit he meaneth not so [the Assyrian king did not do this for God's sake], neither doth his heart think so [he is not thinking of doing the will of God. He is doing the will of God but he doesn't know it], but it is in his heart to destroy and cut off nations not a few. For he saith, Are not my princes altogether kings?" (Isa. 10:5-8).

God is shown in His sovereignty.

> Wherefore it shall come to pass, that when the Lord hath performed his whole work upon mount Zion and on Jerusalem, I will punish the fruit of the stout heart of the king of Assyria, and the glory of his high looks (Isa. 10:12).

God will use this Assyrian power to accomplish His purpose, and then He will cut the ground out from under it. He is able to make the wrath of man to praise Him.

Some people have felt that a similar thing occurred to Judas. They say that since the Lord Jesus Christ needed to die, did not Judas, in betraying Him, actually do the will of God? But we answer that he did not intend to do this for God's sake. What Judas was actually after was thirty pieces of silver, but God in His great almighty wisdom and sovereignty let this traitor sell his Lord that the Lord Jesus might be taken by wicked hands, be crucified, and become our Savior. When the Roman soldiers put Him to death, they did not intend to offer Him up as an offering to God, they put Him to death as a common malefactor. God was able to make Judas' selling Him for thirty pieces of silver and the Roman soldiers' treating Him the way they did be the very things that gave us our Lord and Savior Jesus Christ. Judas went out and hanged himself. He was responsible for what he had done. And I believe a similar principle is true here with reference to Assyria. We are told how the Assyrian boasts:

> For he saith, By the strength of my hand I have done it, and by my wisdom; for I am prudent: and I have removed the bounds of the people, and have robbed their treasures, and I have put down the inhabitants like a valiant man (Isa. 10:13).

The Assyrian was successful because it pleased God to allow it, but the moment it did not suit God there was no more success. At this point it would be perfectly proper for us to remind ourselves of one thing when we think of the affairs in the world: no matter how mighty any hostile enemy or power may be in this world, there is a God in heaven who has marked the bounds of the sea. The sea is not going to roll one bit farther than Almighty God will let it roll. No king, no dictator, no leader of any kind will be able to go one step farther than Almighty God in heaven will let him go. God will have His own way and He will bring them to their fate in His own time.

It is your privilege and mine to keep our trust in Almighty God at all times.

Chapter 18

THERE WILL BE A REMNANT

By way of understanding this part of the book of Isaiah, let us bear in mind certain groups of people in Isaiah's world for whom he had a special message. We will remind ourselves that when the nation of Israel was divided into two parts, the two tribes in the south around the city of Jerusalem took the name of Judah and the ten tribes in the north around the city of Samaria took the name of Israel. In the course of time, Judah had the true worship as it was ministered by the priests, who were, generally speaking, closer to God — a group who could be counted on as those who seriously wanted the blessing of God. Israel, on the other hand, though they also named the name of God, did not come to Jerusalem to worship and did not follow the Levitical ceremonies of worship. Generally speaking, in the course of their history they practiced more evil and less righteousness than the people in the south.

I am inclined to believe that Israel and Judah represent two common groups of people among those who call themselves the Lord's people. Normally in any company of people who call themselves believers in God there are few who seriously seek the face of God. There are more who take the name of God and claim to belong to Him, and who are in favor of the things of God, though they do not actually mean to live that way. When Isaiah is speaking to Judah, he is speaking to the spiritually minded believers. There are some people, even in the church, about whom it could be said that they are not spiritually minded people. I do not wish to be harsh with them; I would say they are the kind who never read the Bible to get to know the will of God. They never pray to seek the will of God. When they try to figure out what to do, they are thinking in terms of what would be pleasing to themselves. If someone should suggest to them that God wants them to do this or that, they would be irritated. They live their lives very much as they see fit. They believe in God and if they have children, they want to have them baptized. They are inclined to make a big social affair of the baptizing and would pay far more attention to the dress the child is wearing than to the promises they are making. When they get married, they would not think of being married without a preacher; they might even have a church wedding. They might even have the Lord's Prayer sung at the service, if the organist is good and the soloist gifted. You cannot call such persons pagans. You could say they are believers, but you and I know right well that deep down inside nothing is going on, so they are not really believers in the full sense of the word.

Who are those people? I would say they are like the northern nation, Israel. We would call them worldly. I am willing to call them believers because the Bible, I think, might count them as such.

When I think of people who are like Syria, I think of people who do not belong to any church. Such people might claim that their nation is a Christian nation. They are against other nations in the world that are not Christian. They appreciate the fact that the gospel makes a person strong in character, honest in business, and faithful in service; and they appreciate such a person's high ideals in ethics.

Then there are people in the world today who make no pretense at all and who do not want anything we have. They would prefer we were not in the world. If they had their way, they would kill all believers.

God is over all people just as He was in Isaiah's time. All human beings on the face of the earth are creatures whom God has made, and He deals with each one. Every human being is going to stand before God and give an account for deeds done in the body; every knee will bow and every tongue confess that Jesus is Lord to the glory of God the Father. These people who do not profess to know Him will be dealt with also. We can notice in Isaiah's book that he has certain things to say to Assyria, the distant people who do not know God at all, but over whom God rules as sovereign and with whom He deals as He sees fit. He has some things to say to Syria, the nation that knows God's people and wants what God's people have but does not want to give God the glory. Then God has a word for the northern kingdom, Israel, whose people profess to know God but their hearts are far from Him. And He has something to say to His own people, to Judah, who are trusting in and believing in Him but are having trouble. They believe that Almighty God is the Ruler, but they perceive other people to be stronger than they themselves and they are face to face with the ruination of their hopes and ambitions.

In this portion of Scripture many of the things said are repetitions of what has been said before, but we learn by going over and over the same things. All of us should have in mind that God knows how things are! He knows that some people want to be near Him and that others would like to have His favor but do not want to do His will. He knows there are people in this world who are ignorant of Him and are going their own way. We have noticed in Isaiah 9:8–10:4 that Israel, the worldly people, would be desolated. Then in Isaiah 10:5-19 the general idea is brought out that Assyria, the distant nation that does not even know God, will be destroyed. God will deal in judgment with those people. One reason why God can judge all people on the face of earth is that His law applies to all people: "Whatsoever a man soweth, that shall he also reap" (Gal. 6:7). That is true for all, whether they know God or not.

Now in Isaiah 10:20-23 something is said to those among worldly minded people who really hunger for the things of God:

> And it shall come to pass in that day, that the remnant of Israel, and such as are escaped of the house of Jacob, shall no more again stay upon him that smote them; but shall stay upon the Lord, the Holy One of Israel, in truth. The remnant shall return, even the remnant of Jacob, unto the mighty God. For though thy people Israel be as the sand of the sea, yet a remnant of them shall return: the consumption decreed shall overflow with righteousness (Isa. 10:20-22).

Even among the worldly minded group of people some will come to God. Every person who has ever heard the gospel at all is touched in some way, and so there may be something in that person who as yet does not have anything to do with God. It is an amazing thing that a human being need not have a perfect score to have blessings from God; if any person has faith as a grain of mustard seed, it will be sufficient to bring him a great blessing. And so it can be said that even if one's heart is worldly and turned away from spiritual things, yet there may be in that person some yearning after God that He recognizes and honors. God said that the remnant would be saved, because no matter how wayward they had been, they would really believe in God and turn to Him.

In Isaiah 10:24–12:6 is revealed the great truth that Judah will be comforted. The people who put their trust in God will be comforted. In this world they may be beset by many troubles, and if they really believe in God, those troubles can be very hard. But the promise is that those troubles will be destroyed.

> Therefore thus saith the Lord God of hosts, O my people that dwellest in Zion, be not afraid of the Assyrian; he shall smite thee with a rod, and shall lift up his staff against thee, after the manner of Egypt. For yet a very little while, and the indignation shall cease, and mine anger in their destruction. And the Lord of hosts shall stir up a scourge for him according to the slaughter of Midian at the rock of Oreb: and as his rod was upon the sea, so shall he lift it up after the manner of Egypt. And it shall come to pass in that day, that his burden shall be taken away from off thy shoulder, and his yoke from off thy neck, and the yoke shall be destroyed because of the anointing (Isa. 10:24-27).

The forces of evil can hurt the people of God, but their time is limited.

Habakkuk cried "O Lord, how long shall I cry, and thou wilt not hear!" (Hab. 1:2). Many believers in God have wondered how long God will wait before He moves to bring relief. But the promise is there. And the believer is a person who is able to look ahead into the future and when he sees the dark clouds of trouble, the powerful forces over which he has no control, and is aware that he is in the pathway of destructive forces that could completely destroy him, he knows that God can overrule! God speaks to His people to reassure them. He has all things in hand and in His own good time God will destroy those forces that threaten to destroy His people. That is what He is saying here to the remnant.

In chapter 11 the remarkable promise is plainly revealed:

the Messiah will come. That is God's hidden weapon: His secret weapon. God will send His Son. God will not only manipulate the processes of nature, He will not only judge justly so far as those processes of nature are concerned, but He will do more than that: He will send into this world a Savior. That is of special significance to those who believe. And in chapter 12 an amazing truth is revealed about this Messiah, the anointed One whom God will send to deliver and bring into glory those who put their trust in Him.

And so, at this point when we are studying the Book of Isaiah, we can call these things to mind. We can think of what the Lord has to say to His own people that is different from what He has to say to the outside world. So far as Assyria is concerned, that pagan element of the world that does not even know God, the one great thing revealed is that God has His time measured. In due time He will destroy, not because He is evil or unjust, but in all fairness and justice God will destroy that which is evil on the face of the earth. So far as the worldly people are concerned, they will suffer loss, but any one among them who will turn to God will be saved. So far as God's own people are concerned, those who really seek His face, there is this remarkable promise we have just been discussing. God will destroy their enemies and He will send them a Savior.

Chapter 19

THE DAY OF THE LORD UPON PAGANS

As we begin chapter 13 of Isaiah, we find an interesting portion of this book where we get a clear picture of what the message of the Bible should be to the outside world. The gospel is the message about what God will do for anyone through Jesus Christ. The people who believe the gospel and receive the Lord Jesus Christ as Savior are people the Bible calls Christians. There is a message to believers and what the outside world may not always know is that a pastor's first responsibility is to believers, to feed them so that their faith may become strong. Perhaps some days a believer has more confidence than on other days. Perhaps there are times he feels surer than he does at other times. The time may come when a person may begin to doubt a friend; the same can be true with reference to his faith in God. Faith in God is faith in Someone who has never been seen, but Someone whose Word has been received in the Scriptures by those who have been moved inwardly to believe. The inward persuasion that this Scripture is true is something like strength in the body: it is a strength that must be exerted to believe.

There is always a reason why a person believes more or believes less. "Faith cometh by hearing, and hearing by the word of God" (Rom. 10:17). Generally, the more a person knows about the Bible, the more he will believe in God; and the less a person knows about the Bible, the less he will believe in God.

The church is made up of people who say they believe the gospel. When a pastor is called, his business is to shepherd the flock; he is to minister to believers. People who are outside in the world may wonder why believers need to be ministered to.

It is simple: they need to be fed. Peter writes, "As newborn babes, desire the sincere milk of the word, that ye may grow thereby" (1 Peter 2:2). Fortunately God has resources in addition to preaching whereby He ministers to the hearts of people; but they can never become strong nor can they become effective in spiritual experience, unless their faith is kept strong.

When anyone in a congregation is in trouble, the pastor will go to him, because he has human sympathy. But more importantly, he has some insight into God's providence that he can share with that person, and he can encourage him to believe that God really does care for him. While ordinarily most of the preaching is to believers, this should not be misunderstood. It is unfortunate that a preacher often seems to assume that all in the congregation are believers, because this is a false assumption. All people need to be told, "He that hath the Son hath life; and he that hath not the Son of God hath not life" (1 John 5:12). But does the minister have anything to say to the world outside? Is there a message from God's man in the community to the people outside the church? There may be those who are not necessarily opposed to Christ but who are not yet organized in the church. In the Epistles there are few references to the people on the outside of the group of believers. Believers are told in the Epistles to walk circumspectly so that the people outside will understand, and they are told to maintain good works. They are also told to conduct their public worship services so simply that when the unlearned and ignorant (ignorant of the gospel) come in, they will understand enough to know that God is present there.

But does God have a message to people outside of Christ? Is He interested in worldly people? He created all men. All people are His. Almighty God is the Keeper of every human being on earth and nobody has the power to raise a hand unless God gives it to him. No carpenter ever drove a nail, no engineer ever planned a building, no construction man ever put up a building without God's giving that person the strength physically and mentally to be able to plan such things and accomplish them. Yes, God is interested in all people and He has a way of dealing with them. Human beings are sinful, and, as Paul would say, they all seek their own — not each other's, but their own. Everybody is interested in what he can get for himself. The Bible tells us that God sees the whole world lying in the lap of the evil one. "There is none righteous, no, not one" (Rom. 3:10).

The world may not like to hear this, and that is one reason why, in the body of society as a whole, there is a deep-rooted resentment against the gospel. The average person wants nothing to do with what the church stands for. Why are the people of the world alienated from God? Because they are guilty and they will be judged. I remember in my agnostic days that if anyone had told me these things, I would have been filled with resentment. What I did not know in the days of my agnosticism, and what the world outside does not realize, is that God cares for the world. He does not approve and He does not condone the world's sinful walk; but He is so concerned about the people in the world, that He gave His own Son to die for them so that "whosoever believeth in him should not perish but have everlasting life" (John 3:16).

There is an amazing prophecy of what God has to say about all human activity in Isaiah 13 to 23 — in a series of messages directed to people who are not Israel. God made them, but they do not know Him. These are messages to ten different nations — among them are Babylon, Moab, Ethiopia, and Egypt. In chapter 20 there is a most interesting short message that tells how Isaiah preached. There is a message to the desert of the sea — probably the desert around the Dead Sea — and also to the city of Tyre. In other words, here is a message to folks on the outside, who do not belong to God's people.

Howl ye; for the day of the Lord is at hand (Isa. 13:6).

This is the time when God will take action. That day will come as a destruction from the Almighty. The reason that preaching to the world outside is not easy is that the only message of truth must be one that tells of their death sentence. Believers know they will be saved; but many of the people on the outside wish that somehow what they dread is going to happen, just will not happen.

Behold, the day of the Lord cometh, cruel both with wrath and fierce anger, to lay the land desolate: and he shall destroy the sinners thereof out of it. . . . And I will punish the world for their evil, and the wicked for their iniquity; and I will cause the

> arrogancy of the proud to cease, and will lay low the haughtiness
> of the terrible. . . . Behold, I will stir up the Medes against them
> (Isa. 13:9,11,17).

The Medes and the Persians moved in on Babylon and destroyed that city. What God is pointing out here is that these people do not even know God, that He is their Judge.

God sees the weaknesses and wrongdoings of the pagans, even as they think they are better than other people and take advantage of them. God will move others to destroy them. When people in this world prey upon others, no one should think that Almighty God is unaware.

> Their bows also shall dash the young men to pieces; and they
> shall have no pity on the fruit of the womb; their eye shall not
> spare children (Isa. 13:18).

Wartime atrocities are not new in human history. When men get into a killing mood as in war, they kill anything and everything. In the natural world the attitude of natural human beings toward each other is cruel and vicious.

> And Babylon, the glory of kingdoms, the beauty of the Chal-
> deans' excellency, shall be as when God overthrew Sodom and
> Gomorrah. It shall never be inhabited. . . . For the Lord will
> have mercy on Jacob, and will yet choose Israel, and set them in
> their own land (Isa. 13:19,20; 14:1).

The message to the world outside tells the pagans they will reap the harvest of their sins, as over against this message of the gospel. God will have mercy on Jacob; that is, on all those who believe in Him. And God "will yet choose Israel." God will choose those who believe in the Lord Jesus Christ. He will do for them in grace and mercy what they could never do for themselves. "And the strangers shall be joined with them." People who never knew God, the Gentiles, people who are unbelievers will be joined with them "and they shall cleave to the house of Jacob."

> And the people shall take them, and bring them to their place:
> and the house of Israel shall possess them in the land of the Lord
> for servants and handmaids: and they shall take them captives,
> whose captives they were; and they shall rule over their oppres-
> sors. And it shall come to pass in the day that the Lord shall give
> thee rest from thy sorrow, and from thy fear, and from the hard
> bondage wherein thou wast made to serve (Isa. 14:2,3).

And so to the world outside the preacher takes this message: Human nature in itself is unable to serve God. Selfishness, indulgence, pride, and vanity render people unacceptable in the sight of God, but Almighty God will save to the uttermost those who come to Him through the Lord Jesus Christ. The whole world lies in the lap of the evil one, and God's judgment is on all the earth; but those who believe in the Lord Jesus Christ will be saved, and they will be given rest from their sorrow and fear and from the hard bondage in which they were made to serve. That is the kind of message a preacher can preach in the world today.

Chapter 20

GOD WILL DESTROY THE UNREPENTANT

Isaiah 14:4-23 is a message addressed to the king of Babylon. Some scholars think this has a hidden reference to Satan.

> That thou shalt take up this proverb against the king of Babylon, and say, How hath the oppressor ceased! the golden city ceased! (Isa. 14:4).

> How art thou fallen from heaven, O Lucifer, son of the morning! how art thou cut down to the ground, which didst weaken the nations! (Isa. 14:12).

It seems these verses could refer to the king of Babylon in historical fashion, but the king of Babylon very likely was a person who showed in himself the very nature and character of Satan.

In the New Testament the prince of the power of the air is spoken of as Satan. There it is written:

> For we wrestle not against flesh and blood, but against principalities, against powers, against the rulers of the darkness of this world, against spiritual wickedness in high places (Eph. 6:12).

There seem to be various passages of New Testament Scriptures that indicate that the kings of this earth are being motivated by Satan — far more than we realize. Satan, who is himself a spirit, is the great opponent of God. Satan as a spirit is maliciously intent upon destroying the work of God — especially man. But such is the providence of God that Satan cannot touch a person whom God does not allow him to touch. In fact, apparently Satan is not able to touch any person who does not yield in some fashion to Satan's suggestions.

Satan is very cunning. The way he approaches us is to appeal to our own interests and disposition in those things wherein we are liable to become selfish and self-indulgent. That probably covers everything that happens in the world.

According to 2 Thessalonians, Antichrist in the New Testament is he who sets himself up in the temple as equal to God (2 Thess. 2:3,4). That is very sobering language for those of us in the Christian life, because our bodies are the temple of the Holy Ghost. And so in the temple of my own body, insofar as I have the disposition, I could be setting myself up in the place of God. That is to say, I could be intending to do what I want to do, rather than what God wants me to do. In such an event I would be motivated by the spirit of Antichrist; and that, I think, is the spirit of Lucifer here. Notice what this is as we look into it here:

> How art thou fallen from heaven, O Lucifer, son of the morning! how art thou cut down to the ground, which didst weaken the nations! For thou hast said in thine heart, I will ascend into heaven, I will exalt my throne above the stars of God: I will sit also upon the mount of the congregation, in the sides of the north: I will ascend above the heights of the clouds; I will be like the most High (Isa. 14:12-14).

That disposition to elevate oneself, to make oneself the most important, and to have the final word so far as events are concerned is the very disposition that the prophet said will be cut down.

> Yet thou shalt be brought down to hell, to the sides of the pit. They that see thee shall narrowly look upon thee, and consider thee, saying, Is this the man that made the earth to tremble, that did shake kingdoms; that made the world as a wilderness, and destroyed the cities thereof; that opened not the house of his prisoners? (Isa. 14:15-17).

Is this the person who selfishly pursued his own way regardless of other people? This is the message for him: God will bring him down. And this message is here tied up with Babylon — this worldly unit. As we summarize all that is in this first message to Babylon (chapters 13 and 14) we can think of Babylon as a typical human activity. Babylon was human beings gathered together in one city to make of themselves the best they could according to their own plans, motivated by a disposition to make themselves great. Their efforts were offensive to God and He would destroy them. He will put the power of His judgment against this spirit anywhere, any time.

And now there is written a remarkable statement:

> The Lord of hosts hath sworn, saying, Surely as I have thought, so shall it come to pass; and as I have purposed, so shall it stand: that I will break the Assyrian in my land, and upon my mountains tread him under foot: then shall his yoke depart from off them, and his burden depart from off their shoulders (Isa. 14:24,25).

God is saying He will break this human control.

> This is the purpose that is purposed upon the whole earth: and this is the hand that is stretched out upon all the nations. For the Lord of hosts hath purposed, and who shall disannul it? and his hand is stretched out, and who shall turn it back? (Isa. 14:26,27).

This purpose of God will bring judgment to bear upon the activities of man and bring the haughtiness and pride of man to ruin; God will smash what man is trying to do, but He will save Jacob. He will save Israel, i.e., those who put their trust in Him. The sovereignty of Almighty God will establish it and who is to stop Him from doing this, the prophet says.

> What shall one then answer the messengers of the nation? That the Lord hath founded Zion, and the poor of his people shall trust in it (Isa. 14:32).

The final word is that Almighty God intends to save those who put their trust in Him.

Is there evidence in the world at large that would enable us to believe it will be like that? Do you doubt there is much misery? Do you have any doubt that in the world there is heartache, sorrow, pain, frustrated hope, and shattered plans? Yet God is over all. What actually happens in this world is death: "The grass withereth and the flower fadeth." The grave is the end of everything that we see on the face of the earth. If we are to understand this earth in which we live, we must understand that man will die. There is but one avenue of escape from destruction: it is through the Lord Jesus Christ. Into this world the gospel has come and light has been shown to the ends of the earth. God is able to save to the uttermost those who put their trust in Him. The joy of the believer is that of believing in the Lord Jesus Christ. Joy will not be found in the things of this world.

What was written by Isaiah plainly points out that Babylon

was like the city of New York today. Isaiah was like a country preacher who would refer to New York or to any other big city where there is wealth and a display of human power and ingenuity and wisdom, and say all these great things will come to nothing; all will be destroyed. We are reminded of Jesus of Nazareth as He walked through the buildings of the temple that was forty years in building — the temple of Herod. He said not one stone of that building would be left upon another (Matt. 24:2). This world is doomed. The few times we have in our lifetime to enjoy health and strength, catching a fish, reading a book, or winning a baseball game are small compared with the widespread suffering, misery, and distress to be found on every side. But in the midst of this sobering pronouncement of coming doom shines this great truth: "I will have mercy on Jacob, and will yet choose Israel."

It may indeed be sobering to note that there was not one hint that Babylon could improve itself to escape judgment. There was no hint that Babylon and Judah would come together or that somehow Babylon and Israel could get together. The gospel does not associate the church with the world outside. If you put the church and the world together, you lose the church. Believers in the Lord Jesus Christ differ from those outside the Lord Jesus Christ. There is no word here that implies Babylon will escape its fate, just as there is no word in Scripture that holds out the prospect that the world can be saved from destruction. There is no way known to keep a human being living forever. "It is appointed unto men once to die" (Heb. 9:27). God has let this be seen to show all the more clearly the wonder of His promise in the gospel. "Whosoever will" can be saved through the work of the Lord Jesus Christ.

The message to Moab begins in much the same way:

> Because in the night Ar of Moab is laid waste, and brought to silence; because in the night Kir of Moab is laid waste, and brought to silence; he is gone up to Bajith, and to Dibon, the high places, to weep: Moab shall howl over Nebo, and over Medeba: on all their heads shall be baldness, and every beard cut off. In their streets they shall gird themselves with sackcloth: on the tops of their houses, and in their streets, every one shall howl, weeping abundantly (Isa. 15:1-3).

The prophet had no pleasure in this, for he says, "My heart

shall cry out for Moab." Anyone who ministers the gospel can
have no satisfaction declaring the destruction of the world. The
only joy we have in this is to know that God can save people
from destruction.

Isaiah offered a clue about this whole matter, as to why it was
as it was.

> We have heard of the pride of Moab; he is very proud: even of
> his haughtiness, and his pride, and his wrath: but his lies shall
> not be so. Therefore shall Moab howl for Moab, every one shall
> howl: for the foundations of Kirhareseth shall ye mourn; surely
> they are stricken. . . . Therefore I will bewail with the weeping
> of Jazer the vine of Sibmah: I will water thee with my tears, O
> Heshbon, and Elealeh: for the shouting for thy summer fruits
> and for thy harvest is fallen. And gladness is taken away, and joy
> out of the plentiful field; and in the vineyards there shall be no
> singing, neither shall there be shouting: the treaders shall tread
> out no wine in their presses; I have made their vintage shouting
> to cease. Wherefore my bowels shall sound like a harp for Moab,
> and mine inward parts for Kirharesh. And it shall come to pass,
> when it is seen that Moab is weary on the high place, that he
> shall come to his sanctuary to pray; but he shall not prevail (Isa.
> 16:6,7,9-12).

Whenever I read this portion of Scripture, for many years
there was a deep sadness in my heart. When Moab has worn
himself out and then wants to turn to God, he shall not prevail.
Isn't that an awful plight? It is terrible to think a person could
come to the place where he wants to pray and cannot. There
will be a sad awakening for some people because they will find
that it is too late for them. There are those who may think it will
never be too late, and I would say it is never too late for a
sincere soul, but there are some people who are not sincere in
turning to God. What they bring to God is a very tattered and
bedraggled remnant of what is left after they have spent themselves doing as they pleased.

Let us as believing people remind ourselves of this: God is
more faithful than we are. If we reach the point where we
cannot do a thing, if we have the Lord Jesus Christ as our
Savior, He will carry us when we cannot even walk. If I could
not have turned to God when I was worn out, when every effort
of my own had failed, and then found that God could do more
than I could ask or think, I would have been ruined long ago.
Sometimes when I did not anticipate my spiritual needs and

did not devote myself to God first, seeking His will, then I have come to God without any joy, because I had no sense of strength at that time. Taking Moab as an example, we know there are people in the world who do not know Christ, but who think about prayer when in trouble, and this touches the heart. They would turn to God if they knew how. I want to share this word: Such people as in pride exhaust themselves, being "weary on the high places," doing the things they want to do, shall not prevail when they come to God's sanctuary. There is also a message to Damascus: "Behold, Damascus is taken away from being a city, and it shall be a ruinous heap" (Isa. 17:1). So far as this world is concerned, those who do not obey God will be ruined. But all the way through this portion of Scripture is the message that the Lord will redeem those who put their trust in Him. Even in Damascus there will be a remnant, and we can thank the Lord for that.

Chapter 21

UNGODLY NATIONS ARE DOOMED

In this study we are not primarily concerned about what the message meant for Judah in those days. We do not think the Book of Isaiah was written as a history of Israel and Judah or a biography of Isaiah. We think the book was written as part of the revelation of God, who sets forth His whole truth in Jesus of Nazareth, our Lord and Savior, Jesus Christ. So far as you and I are concerned, we come to the study of the Bible with faith in Jesus Christ. I trust each one of my readers is looking to the Lord Jesus Christ for the salvation of his soul. We understand that He died for our sins and, believing in Him, we trust that Almighty God will forgive us, make us His own, regenerate us, fill us with the Holy Spirit, live in us, and walk with us all the days of our life upon earth. In time, He will bring us before Himself, and we will stand before Him and see our Redeemer face to face. We will be forever with the Lord.

We need to understand the ways of God so that we may intelligently walk with Him. The ways of God are expressed in the person of the Lord Jesus Christ and they were actually revealed in dealing with His people in Old Testament times. We ask ourselves if it is not Israel, Judah, or Isaiah we are interested in, then who *are* we interested in? We are interested in the truth of God's dealing with people, as seen in those days. Who then were Judah and Israel? They were the people who believed in God, just as today there are some people who believe in God. The way in which God dealt with Israel is the way He still deals with His people. What was Isaiah's relation to God's people? He was a prophet who explained the will of God, the Word of God. He told the people what God wanted them to know about His will for them. There are some things

God will do in His grace, which He will do only when people trust in Him.

There are some things God does apart from human faith. The sun shines and the rain falls without regard to whether one believes these things will happen or not. All the processes of nature go on whether one believes they will or not. But when it comes to the matter of a person being forgiven his sins, of getting right with God who is his Judge, for that there must be faith. It is necessary to know that God has promised it and that the individual human being must trust in God. What does that involve? Believing in God means the believer yields himself into the will of God and trusts God to supply him with what he needs. That involves many things that must be learned. A person must know the will of God and the mind of God before he can believe, but not every human being can equally understand these. Many persons are beginners. So God gives to certain persons special insight: the gift of understanding the will of God; and so there are pastors, apostles, evangelists, and teachers who communicate to others what the gospel of God is. In the Old Testament days there were prophets who interpreted to the people what the will of God was for them. Such a man was Isaiah, who interpreted to them the will of God, just as the preacher does today.

At this point we may again raise the question: Does the person who is preaching the gospel of Jesus Christ and ministering to the believers of the Lord Jesus Christ have a message to unbelievers? In Isaiah 17 there is a general statement for these people: The only message that can be given to Damascus is that it will come to ruin.

> The fortress also shall cease from Ephraim, and the kingdom from Damascus, and the remnant of Syria: they shall be as the glory of the children of Israel, saith the Lord of hosts (Isa. 17:3).

Buried in that third verse is this fact: Though the political governments of these nations will collapse, there will be a remnant. There will be some people even in Syria who will believe, and when they come to believe, they will be just like the children of Israel. Verses 6 to 8 tell us more clearly that there will be a remnant: "Yet gleaning grapes shall be left in it." In the days of Israel when a farmer harvested his grapes, and the few late ones were not harvested because they were too green (they would ripen later), it was written in the law of Moses that a farmer should not go back and pick his grapes a second time. The poor would come and pick those. The same was true with their grain. A Jewish farmer was not to pick up the ears of grain that fell on the ground; those were for the poor who would come later and glean.

Here Isaiah is saying that just as gleaning grapes should be left for the poor when harvest was done, so it would be with the remnant of those who would believe. God would bring His judgment upon the nation as a whole, but there would be a few left, a gleaning:

> Yet gleaning grapes shall be left in it, as the shaking of an olive tree, two or three berries in the top of the uppermost bough, four or five in the outmost fruitful branches thereof, saith the Lord God of Israel (Isa. 17:6).

These would be the remnant. Here is something that should make us very sober. Jesus of Nazareth said, "Many are called, but few are chosen" (Matt. 22:14). Each of us is responsible in himself toward God, and each must turn to God in himself or herself. One cannot wait until everybody else comes, because not everybody is coming. Few will come; but there will be some who will turn to God, even in Syria among unbelieving people, even among people who have not been brought up to know the gospel.

> At that day shall a man look to his Maker, and his eyes shall have respect to the Holy One of Israel (Isa. 17:7).

There will be people who will turn from worldliness to God, even in the most worldly circumstances.

> And he shall not look to the altars, the work of his hands, neither shall respect that which his fingers have made, either the groves, or the images (Isa. 17:8).

This remnant will turn their attention to God.

One more word as to what will happen to Syria is written in verses 9 to 11, telling how ruin will come upon them:

> In that day shall his strong cities be as a forsaken bough, and an uppermost branch, which they left because of the children of Israel: and there shall be desolation. Because thou hast forgotten the God of thy salvation, and hast not been mindful of the rock of thy strength, therefore shalt thou plant pleasant plants,

> and shalt set it with strange slips: in the day shalt thou make thy
> plant to grow, and in the morning shalt thou make thy seed to
> flourish: but the harvest shall be a heap in the day of grief and of
> desperate sorrow (Isa. 17:9-11).

Things will not work out for those people. How many brave
projects are begun today, whose common result is that they
come to nothing. It was characteristic of these people in Syria
that their projects did not come to pass.

> Woe to the land shadowing with wings, which is beyond the
> rivers of Ethiopia (Isa. 18:1).

The words "woe to the land" mean ruin is for them, too.

> In that time shall the present be brought unto the Lord of hosts
> of a people scattered and peeled, and from a people terrible
> from their beginning hitherto (Isa. 18:7).

The message to Egypt comes next. The specific description
of the fate of each of these ten countries is a little different.
Although there is a different way of saying it, yet always there is
ruin, ruin.

> The grass withereth, the flower fadeth: but the word of our God
> shall stand for ever (Isa. 40:8).

> And I will set the Egyptians against the Egyptians: and they
> shall fight every one against his brother (Isa. 19:2).

There is here a description of what we would call civil war —
brother against brother. I think that what has been said in
succession about Babylon, Moab, Damascus, Ethiopia, and
now Egypt with its civil war, is characteristic of human nature.
These are some of the blemishes that fall upon human nature:
quarreling, fighting, discord.

> And the Egyptians will I give over into the hand of a cruel lord;
> and a fierce king shall rule over them (Isa. 19:4).

A common historical experience is to be found over and over
in the history of mankind: when folks start falling out with each
other, somebody else comes in and controls both of them. The
same is true with us individually. If deep down in my own
personality there is conflict, so that I can never be united in
myself, someone starts telling me what to do. There is even
more in this description of the fate of Egypt.

> The Lord hath mingled a perverse spirit in the midst thereof:

> and they have caused Egypt to err in every work thereof, as a
> drunken man staggereth in his vomit. Neither shall there be any
> work for Egypt, which the head or tail, branch or rush, may do.
> In that day shall Egypt be like unto women: and it shall be afraid
> and fear because of the shaking of the hand of the Lord of hosts,
> which he shaketh over it (Isa. 19:14-16).

God will fill Egypt with a great sense of confusion and frustra-
tion, and the people will never be able to get anything
straightened out.

> In that day shall five cities in the land of Egypt speak the
> language of Canaan, and swear to the Lord of hosts; one shall be
> called, The city of destruction. In that day shall there be an altar
> to the Lord in the midst of the land of Egypt, and a pillar at the
> border thereof to the Lord. And it shall be for a sign and for a
> witness unto the Lord of hosts in the land of Egypt: for they shall
> cry unto the Lord because of the oppressors, and he shall send
> them a saviour, and a great one, and he shall deliver them (Isa.
> 19:18-20).

I am not sure whether this means that at some time in the
future something was to happen to Egypt historically that we
can place either in past history or in future history. I prefer to
take this passage in its spiritual meaning for what it says to me,
that even among the people in the world who are not brought
up in the Word of God, some can turn to God and His great
grace can call them.

> And the Lord shall be known to Egypt, and the Egyptians shall
> know the Lord in that day (Isa. 19:21).

There are missionaries in Egypt today and in other Middle
East countries, and there are many Egyptians who believe.
There are Ethiopians, Syrians, and Armenians who believe. I
think further that this message is not meant in Scripture to
apply only to the physical descendants of the Egyptians; I think
this message could apply also to Chinese, Indians, Hindus,
and Germans. I see in this a pre-Christian missionary view;
here the prophet Isaiah sees Gentile people coming to the
Lord.

At the time the gospel was being revealed and Jesus of
Nazareth was walking in the streets of Jerusalem, my
forefathers in northern Europe were worshiping trees, the
sun, moon, and stars. They were worshiping the spirits in

trees: they believed the oak was a sacred thing. They had never heard of Abraham, Isaac, and Jacob. They knew nothing about the promises of the Old Testament or the expectations of the Messiah. Not for hundreds of years after Jesus Christ lived did my forefathers know any of those things. It was hundreds of years later when the gospel came to them and they learned about the Lord Jesus Christ. They were not even described in this prophecy of Isaiah. I am one of them, and so are some of you, who have since come to believe.

I think this is actually a prophetic pre-Christian missionary view that Isaiah had when he saw pagan people, Gentile people, coming to God by the grace of God. It sounds strange to read:

> In that day shall there be a highway out of Egypt to Assyria, and the Assyrian shall come into Egypt, and the Egyptian into Assyria, and the Egyptians shall serve with the Assyrians. In that day shall Israel be the third with Egypt and with Assyria, even a blessing in the midst of the land: whom the Lord of hosts shall bless, saying, Blessed be Egypt my people, and Assyria the work of my hands, and Israel mine inheritance (Isa. 19:23-25).

I believe that is happening today. Here in Isaiah God is saying He will bring His blessing upon all the people all over the world who believe in the Lord Jesus Christ, people of all classes and all races who believe in Him.

Chapter 22

GOD WILL CHASTEN, THEN BLESS, HIS PEOPLE

Our study in Isaiah brings us now to chapter 20, a very interesting interlude in the story. If you have noticed the organization of the book, you will have found that in chapters 13 to 23 are messages to the nations, while chapters 24 to 35 have to do with messages to God's own people. Chapter 20 is just six verses long. It is a description of Isaiah's homiletic technique. Isaiah was a preacher, and every preacher in the course of time tends to develop some personal peculiarity in his presentation. In some congregations anything demonstrative is frowned upon, but in certain circumstances, in order for a man to get his point across, he has to do considerable preaching, and with that goes all forms of sensational procedures. A number of people would perhaps feel that the shouting and the clapping, the pounding of the pulpit or the stomping around on the rostrum, would be the kind of thing they would want.

You will be interested to know that some of the Old Testament prophets were told by the Lord just what they should do. I could refer to Ezekiel, whose book is usually considered very difficult. Ezekiel was told the people would consider him a fluent speaker and a beautiful orator, but they would not do anything he admonished them to do. So God told Ezekiel to stamp with his feet and smite with his hands, and to preach sensationally; because the people he was preaching to were apathetic and dull. They had no life in them. It was explained differently to Ezekiel. He was told their foreheads were hard. That was using a figure that anybody who has been around sheep would understand, because when sheep start fighting with each other they have no teeth with which to bite and they do not have the kind of hooves with which to hurt each other; so the way they hurt each other is by butting their heads together. The one with the hardest head wins. When the Lord told Ezekiel his listeners have hard heads, He meant to say they would belligerently oppose him by butting against him when he was preaching. The Lord promised Ezekiel to make his forehead harder, so that he could count on winning. Ezekiel was involved in conflict: when those people butted against him, he butted back against them. Another thing God said to Ezekiel is interesting to us: God told Ezekiel he would not be sent to a foreign nation that could not speak his language. He was to preach to his fellow countrymen.

Isaiah is called the princely prophet. One reason for that, it is assumed, was that it appears he was a nephew of the king. By virtue of being a member of the royal household, he would be considered a very sophisticated person; probably very dignified in his procedure. Yet it is astonishing to read:

> And the Lord said, Like as my servant Isaiah hath walked naked and barefoot three years for a sign and wonder upon Egypt and upon Ethiopia; so shall the king of Assyria lead away the Egyptians prisoners, and the Ethiopians captives, young and old, naked and barefoot, even with their buttocks uncovered, to the shame of Egypt. And they shall be afraid and ashamed of Ethiopia their expectation, and of Egypt their glory (Isa. 20:3-5).

Have you recognized all the way through God would do this only with Egypt and Ethiopia? He would not do it with Israel and Judah, but with the worldly minded people. I am sure the pagans looked upon Isaiah with horror and astonishment, and I suspect he was the scandal of the whole community; but they knew what he was saying. His actions said "Just take a look at me; that is the way it will be with you." The next time you are inclined to criticize a man because he bangs the pulpit too much, look around; chances are he is doing this because he feels he should. The thing you and I need to worry about is this: Did he get his message across?

Chapter 21 refers to three different localities. "The desert of the sea" is what we commonly call the Arabian Desert beyond the Dead Sea. The inhabitants there are to be in misery and finally destroyed. In verse 11 the "burden of Dumah" conveys practically the same idea, as does "the burden upon Arabia" in verse 13. God is letting these people know He is thinking about them and making a claim on them. He is revealing through Isaiah what will happen to them in His will. It will be nothing good because they have not been obedient.

There is some question among Bible interpreters about the meaning of "the valley of vision" in chapter 22. I am inclined to think Isaiah is referring to the country that his own people occupy — the country of God's own people. If one should wonder why they would be mentioned here, it could be because even among God's own people there is worldliness. We would be unwise if we assume that all of the members of our church are spiritually minded. It is possible that some are not really believers, and so are not saved.

When I was a young man preparing for the ministry, I had an idea that we should get rid of those people in the congregation who were not real believers. Then my father-in-law would say to me, "What are you in the world for?" And I remembered I was going to try to seek and save the lost, and of course right in the church is where many of these can be found. He drew my attention to the three stories of the lost in Luke 15. The shepherd went out after the lost sheep and brought it home. Then there was the lost coin, and the woman swept until she found it. And there was the "lost" son, the prodigal, who went away. Nobody went after him, because he knew the way home. The sheep knew it was lost but did not know the way home, so someone was needed to help him; but the coin did not know it was lost right in the house. He drew my attention to what I have since learned that other interpreters of Scripture have pointed out. There may well be such people who are brought up in the church, but who have never accepted the Lord Jesus Christ. We can rejoice to realize God has as much joy in heaven over the coin that is found right in the house as He has over the sheep that went far away, or as the father had in the son who came home afterwards.

> Therefore said I, Look away from me; I will weep bitterly, labour not to comfort me, because of the spoiling of the daughter of my people (Isa. 22:4).

That word *spoil* can be translated "despoil," and that is something we fear when there are people in the church who do not really enter into the fullness of Christ. They do not realize they have lost everything they had at the beginning. They can lose their confidence in the Bible and even their faith in God and so finally be worse off than the pagan people who never heard the gospel at all. That is what the prophet is lamenting about.

> For it is a day of trouble, and of treading down, and of perplexity by the Lord God of hosts in the valley of vision, breaking down the walls, and of crying to the mountains (Isa. 22:5).

The prophet then talks about that and goes on to show how this has to do with his own people:

> And he discovered the covering of Judah, and thou didst look in that day to the armor of the house of the forest. Ye have seen also the breaches of the city of David, that they are many: and ye gathered together the waters of the lower pool (Isa. 22:8,9).

A breach means a breakdown in the walls, something neglected. Isaiah saw in the city of the people of God many neglected areas where things were allowed to go to pieces.

> Ye made also a ditch between the two walls for the water of the old pool: but ye have not looked unto the maker thereof, neither had respect unto him that fashioned it long ago (Isa. 22:11).

They did things in their own strength and did not look to God; this was their failure. They did not do what God wanted them to do, so the prophet called them to weep, to mourn, and to dedicate themselves in seeking the face of God in prayer and in girding with sackcloth.

The girding with sackcloth meant they would take off their comfortable clothing and put on rough, uncomfortable clothing that would keep them awake so they could pray and turn their mind to God. It is an old custom among God's people that if they really want to draw near to God, they set themselves to follow a regimen that is not pleasant to the flesh. That is the reason some people fast. When they are hungry, their hearts and their spirits draw nearer to God. There are any number of people who do not run to the full excess of riot as others do, because they want to save themselves for a certain relationship with God.

> And in that day did the Lord God of hosts call to weeping, and to mourning, and to baldness, and to girding with sackcloth: and behold joy and gladness, slaying oxen, and killing sheep, eating flesh, and drinking wine: let us eat and drink; for tomorrow we shall die (Isa. 22:12,13).

Instead of seeking the face of the Lord, they banqueted and caroused. That attitude probably originated with the Greeks; we hear about it in Paul's letter to the Corinthians. I had that idea myself in Canada before I was a Christian. I had the idea that if you have to live through this world, you might as well have a good time. Fortunately, I had a conscience, and when I began reading the Bible, my thinking about these things underwent a profound change.

At this point in the discussion Isaiah emphasizes something new. God will change the leadership.

> Thus saith the Lord God of hosts, Go, get thee unto this treasurer, even unto Shebna, which is over the house, and say, What hast thou here? and whom hast thou here, that thou hast hewed thee out a sepulchre here, as he that heweth him out a sepulchre on high, and that graveth a habitation for himself in a rock? (Isa. 22:15,16).

Isaiah found that the man who was in the position of leadership made himself a nice spot so that he could enjoy himself.

> Behold, the Lord will carry thee away with a mighty captivity, and will surely cover thee. He will surely violently turn and toss thee like a ball into a large country: there shalt thou die, and there the chariots of thy glory shall be the shame of thy Lord's house. And I will drive thee from thy station, and from thy state shall he pull thee down (Isa. 22:17-19).

Who? The man who was in the place of leadership at a time when the people indulged themselves instead of praying.

> And it shall come to pass in that day, that I will call my servant Eliakim the son of Hilkiah: and I will clothe him with thy robe, and strengthen him with thy girdle, and I will commit thy government into his hand: and he shall be a father to the inhabitants of Jerusalem, and to the house of Judah. And the key of the house of David will I lay upon his shoulder; so he shall open, and none shall shut; and he shall shut, and none shall open (Isa. 22:20-22).

This implies a change from human leadership to that of Christ. Here I can see this truth: If, in my own spiritual experience, I adopt the idea that I can live a worldly life and still be counted all right, if I am associating with those who talk about turning to God and never spend time in prayer, seeking to know His will for them, then I should not lay blame on the leaders. I never should have been following those human beings in the first place: I should have been following none other than the Lord Jesus Christ. No preacher died for me. The Lord Jesus died for me. He is my Savior, my Intercessor at the right hand of God; and He is my King. I am responsible to Him. His Holy Spirit comes into my heart and leads me. When I open my heart to see what the Lord is doing, I shall be on the road to blessing.

Chapter 23

GOD WILL DESTROY THE NATURAL
BUT SAVE THE SPIRITUAL

Isaiah 23–35 presents a description of how God will deal with the nations of the world and with those who are named by His name. Paul wrote:

> Now all these things happened unto them for examples: and they are written for our admonition, upon whom the ends of the world are come (1 Cor. 10:11).

So we read with the aim of noting what seems to have revelation for us.

"The burden of Tyre" is set forth in Isaiah 23. The prophet foresees total ruin. The dire prospect is amazing because Tyre was known as a "joyous city," "a crowning city," much esteemed in the world.

> The Lord of Hosts hath purposed it, to stain the pride of all glory, and to bring into contempt all the honourable of the earth (Isa. 23:9).

Tyre is typical of any natural situation where there is no relation with God in the consciousness.

> The whole world lieth in wickedness (1 John 5:19).

> God is angry with the wicked every day (Ps. 7:11).

There is no relief anywhere in sight for those who have rejected God. Any natural situation or person faces death and destruction.

Isaiah 24–35 is a lengthy portion that reveals over and over again what is going to happen in Canaan among people who are called by the name of God. The basic fact is that among those who profess to believe in God there are two quite different groups. In the course of history the larger number were persons who claimed the name of God but did not obey His law or seek His guidance. In our time such are commonly spoken of as "worldly Christians." Isaiah described their manner of life and worship in the opening chapter of prophecy:

> They have forsaken the Lord, they have provoked the Holy One of Israel unto anger, they are gone away backward (Isa. 1:4).

> Wherefore the Lord said, Forasmuch as this people draw near me with their mouth, and with their lips do honour me, but have removed their heart far from me, and their fear toward me is taught by the precept of men . . . (Isa. 29:13).

These are the people who "say, and do not."

There is a smaller group who may also be wayward in conduct but they are distinguished by a sincere belief in God. They listen to hear His word, believe His promises, confess their sin in repentant humility, and seek His forgiveness. These are called "the remnant" by the prophets. They are to be found when judgment has been executed: they cling to the promises of God and look for His mercy.

Paul later speaks of them as the "true Israel." They are among the descendants of Abraham and they qualify as being his seed because they share the faith he had. Perhaps one reason so much space is devoted to this situation is that it is both so strange and so important. Though the leaders and the great majority of the people are doomed because of their unbelief, yet among them will be found such as humbly confess their sin, repentantly turn to God, and look up to Him with expectancy, that they might be saved.

> Wide is the gate, and broad is the way, that leadeth to destruction, and many there be which go in thereat: because strait is the gate, and narrow is the way, which leadeth unto life, and few there be that find it (Matt. 7:13,14).

> Behold, the Lord maketh the earth empty, and maketh it waste, and turneth it upside down, and scattereth abroad the inhabitants thereof. . . . The land shall be utterly emptied, and utterly spoiled: for the Lord hath spoken this word (Isa. 24:1,3).

The terms *the earth* and *the land* in this portion refer to the promised land, Canaan, which Israel now occupied by the providence of God. This is the natural home of Israel as a natural people. Its fate is to be "utterly emptied" and "utterly spoiled" (despoiled). Because "the inhabitants" (Israel) have "transgressed the law," the result was that "the curse devoureth the earth." Total devastation would occur, but there shall be a remnant.

> When thus it shall be in the midst of the land among the people, there shall be as the shaking of an olive tree, and as the gleaning grapes when the vintage is done. They shall lift up their voice, they shall sing for the majesty of the Lord, they shall cry aloud from the sea (Isa. 24:13,14).

Isaiah 25 is poetical praise to God for His salvation that He will work out for the remnant.

> He will swallow up death in victory; and the Lord God will wipe away tears from off all faces; and the rebuke of his people shall he take away from off all the earth: for the Lord hath spoken it. And it shall be said in that day, Lo, this is our God; we have waited for him, and he will save us: this is the Lord; we have waited for him, we will be glad and rejoice in his salvation (Isa. 25:8,9).

This is indeed the song of the redeemed:

> Thou wilt keep him in perfect peace, whose mind is stayed on thee (Isa. 26:3).

Throughout this section of Isaiah (chapters 23 to 35) two lines of thought are intertwined in the course of events: there will be final judgment on the unrepentant, resulting in their destruction, and there will be salvation for the remnant who believe in God and seek His favor. Isaiah 27 emphasizes that when God has destroyed His opponents, He will deliver His own.

> Ye shall be gathered one by one, O ye children of Israel (Isa. 27:12).

Isaiah 28:1-15 portrays the judgment of God.

> The crown of pride, the drunkards of Ephraim, shall be trodden under feet (Isa. 28:3).

But this is followed by the assurance that after judgment God will bring His eternal purpose to pass.

> This also cometh forth from the Lord of hosts, which is wonderful in counsel, and excellent in working (Isa. 28:29).

In Isaiah 29:1-13 the prophet becomes more specific in predicting in so many words that Ariel (Jerusalem) will be destroyed; but then he reaffirms that God will work out His promise to Abraham by saving the remnant.

In Isaiah 30 and 31 the prophet refers to the fact that in distress Israel turned to Egypt for help rather than to God. God had given them His precious promise:

> In returning and rest shall ye be saved; in quietness and in confidence shall be your strength: and ye would not (Isa. 30:15).

Israel had persisted in turning to Egypt for help.

This brings to mind the fact that there are professing believers today who, in facing serious threats to personal peace, do not turn to God in prayer to seek guidance in His Word, but turn to science or some artfully contrived procedure in counseling to find what they need. For all that, His promise has never changed:

> As birds flying, so will the Lord of hosts defend Jerusalem; defending also he will deliver it; and passing over he will preserve it (Isa. 31:5).

The prophet then proceeds in Isaiah 32 to present a picture of God's final plan for the blessing of His people.

> Behold, a king shall reign in righteousness, and princes shall rule in judgment. And a man shall be as a hiding place from the wind, and a covert from the tempest; as rivers of water in a dry place, as the shadow of a great rock in a weary land. And the eyes of them that see shall not be dim, and the ears of them that hear shall hearken. The heart also of the rash shall understand knowledge, and the tongue of the stammerers shall be ready to speak plainly. . . . And the work of righteousness shall be peace; and the effect of righteousness quietness and assurance for ever (Isa. 32:1-4,17).

Chapters 33 and 34 of Isaiah are a recapitulation of what has been recorded thus far. The judgment of God has brought devastation on the natural land of Canaan.

> The Lord is exalted; for he dwelleth on high: he hath filled Zion with judgment and righteousness (Isa. 33:5).

But in line with His promises, God will deliver some by His grace.

> Thine eyes shall see the king in his beauty: they shall behold the land that is very far off (Isa. 33:17).

Isaiah 34 portrays the severity of "the day of the Lord's vengeance." The devastation of the natural land will be thorough and final. But even in this chapter the prophet inserts the assurance that the promises of God will not be forgotten (Isa. 34:16,17).

Isaiah 35 is a glorious description of the blessedness of the salvation of God.

> The wilderness and the solitary place shall be glad for them; and the desert shall rejoice, and blossom as the rose. . . . And the ransomed of the Lord shall return, and come to Zion with songs and everlasting joy upon their heads: they shall obtain joy and gladness, and sorrow and sighing shall flee away (Isa. 35:1,10).

Chapter 24

THE ASSYRIAN CRISIS

The portion of the Book of Isaiah that we will be looking at now is historical. There are several such passages. This one begins with chapter 36. I call it the Assyrian crisis because Assyria is the country involved. Let me refresh your memory about the countries surrounding Judah in the time of the prophets. North of Judah was the other part of the nation of Israel that was sometimes called Israel, sometimes Samaria, and, again, sometimes Ephraim. There were some ten tribes in that country. North of Israel was the country of Syria, whose capital city was Damascus; and northeast of Syria was the country of Assyria, whose capital city was Nineveh. Southeast of Judah was the country of Chaldea, whose capital city was Babylon, and still further east was the country of Persia, where Nehemiah was cupbearer to the king in the palace of Shushan.

Just now we will remember that in the early part of Isaiah's ministry the international trouble was with Syria, while in this part of the book the trouble is with Assyria. The actual trouble itself developed very simply. This big country of Assyria, with its superior armed forces, moved down and imposed its will on the smaller weaker nations, until its forces came to Jerusalem. At the opening of chapter 36 they reached Jerusalem. This is of interest to us because we see in this a movement from the people of the world against the people of God. The movement was big and strong, and the people of God were small and weak.

The king of Assyria, Sennacherib, had in mind that he would take over the whole country of what we now call Palestine. He had taken over Israel and then moved down and took over Judah.

> Now it came to pass in the fourteenth year of king Hezekiah, that
> Sennacherib king of Assyria came up against all the defenced
> cities of Judah, and took them (Isa. 36:1).

There seemed to be nothing that could stop him in his advance until he came to Jerusalem itself. The king of Assyria then sent Rabshakeh, a lesser general, to King Hezekiah with a great army to confer with the Jews about the surrender of Jerusalem.

> Then came forth unto him Eliakim, Hilkiah's son, which was
> over the house, and Shebna the scribe, and Joah, Asaph's son,
> the recorder (Isa. 36:3).

Eliakim was the representative of Hezekiah; if there had been an army, he would have been the head of it. These men came as a commission to negotiate with the Assyrians. We will find before the story is over that Isaiah was called upon for help in the matter of giving advice. It is of interest to us to notice the way Rabshakeh talked to the Jews, because when worldly people talk to the people of God, they belittle them.

From the fourth verse on we will notice some of the things that Rabshakeh said.

> And Rabshakeh said unto them, Say ye now to Hezekiah, Thus
> saith the great king, the king of Assyria, What confidence is this
> wherein thou trustest? I say, sayest thou, (but they are but vain
> words) I have counsel and strength for war: now on whom dost
> thou trust, that thou rebellest against me? Lo, thou trustest in
> the staff of this broken reed, on Egypt; whereon if a man lean, it
> will go into his hand, and pierce it: so is Pharaoh king of Egypt to
> all that trust in him (Isa. 36:4-6).

In other words, if you put your trust in Egypt, it will be as if a man had a cane that he was trying to lean on, but it was broken so that when he leaned on it, the sharp end of the cane would go into his hand.

> But if thou say to me, We trust in the Lord our God: is it not he,
> whose high places and whose altars Hezekiah hath taken away,
> and said to Judah and to Jerusalem, Ye shall worship before this
> altar? (Isa. 36:7).

This shows how the pagans misunderstood. Hezekiah had destroyed the pagan altars: but those people thought he was actually taking God away. That is interesting because it is so similar to some of the criticism that was leveled against the Christians in their early career. When the early church was founded, the Christians were living in a country that was dominated by Rome. When the people of Rome worshiped, they worshiped idols of stone, wood, gold, or silver. When the Christian people worshiped, they had no images, and so they were accused of being atheists.

> Now therefore give pledges, I pray thee, to my master the king of Assyria, and I will give thee two thousand horses, if thou be able on thy part to set riders upon them (Isa. 36:8).

That would be like two countries today preparing to fight and one saying to the other: "I'll give you a thousand fighting planes" when the other could not supply the pilots to handle them.

> How then wilt thou turn away the face of one captain of the least of my master's servants, and put thy trust on Egypt for chariots and for horsemen (Isa. 36:9)?

The whole tone is one of belittling the people who trust in God. Many, having given testimony of faith in the Lord Jesus Christ today, have found that even among their friends there is a tendency to belittle them.

> And am I now come up without the Lord against this land to destroy it? the Lord said unto me, Go up against this land, and destroy it (Isa. 36:10).

This is one of the unhappy results that follow when we get into an argument about the Bible. The other person can use the Bible too, whether he is right or wrong. The Scriptures can be turned around, and that is what any man can do. A careful reading of verses 11 to 22 will give you an idea of the unscrupulous tactics employed by this man, Rabshakeh, in his efforts to mislead Hezekiah's people. He accused Hezekiah of trying to deceive the people into thinking he could deliver them. Rabshakeh also made elaborate promises if they would come over.

> Eat ye every one of his vine, and every one of his fig tree, and drink ye every one the waters of his own cistern (Isa. 36:16).

These comments by Rabshakeh sound like typical political promises: vote for me and you will get everything you need.

> Until I come and take you away to a land like your own land, a land of corn and wine, a land of bread and vineyards (Isa. 36:17).

Those are the kinds of promises that appeal to people. Many

are led to think if they try to live as the Lord wants them to live, they may lose out: they won't have friends. This often leads them to think if they go along with others, they will get along fine. In this case the children of Israel followed a safe procedure:

> But they held their peace, and answered him not a word: for the king's commandment was, saying, Answer him not (Isa. 36:21).

When Hezekiah was told the words of Rabshakeh, he was deeply disturbed.

> And it came to pass, when king Hezekiah heard it, that he rent his clothes, and covered himself with sackcloth, and went into the house of the Lord (Isa. 37:1).

In the midst of his trouble, when he had nothing to say in self-defense and every accusation of his weakness could only be accepted as being true, this man went into the house of the Lord to pray. He called on the prophet for advice through his servants.

> And they said unto him, Thus saith Hezekiah, This day is a day of trouble, and of rebuke, and of blasphemy: for the children are come to the birth, and there is not strength to bring forth (Isa. 37:3).

This was an acknowledgment that the time was at hand to act, but they had no strength.

Hezekiah identified himself with God and claimed God for his people. In Isaiah 37:4-7 we read that Isaiah sent the servants back with the message that they should not fear, for Almighty God had matters in hand and when He would be ready to act, He would destroy this enemy. Then in Isaiah 37:8-13 the account is given that Rabshakeh returned and found Sennacherib warring against Libnah. Rabshakeh knew these enemies were forcing him to make a decision quickly because he now could not promote a prolonged campaign against Jerusalem. He sent word to Hezekiah saying:

> Let not thy God, in whom thou trusteth, deceive thee, saying, Jerusalem shall not be given into the hand of the king of Assyria. Behold, thou hast heard what the kings of Assyria have done to all lands by destroying them utterly; and shalt thou be delivered? (Isa. 37:10,11).

This message had a profound effect:

> And Hezekiah received the letter from the hand of the messen-

gers, and read it: and Hezekiah went up unto the house of the
Lord, and spread it before the Lord. And Hezekiah prayed unto
the Lord . . . (Isa. 37:14,15).

In his prayer, Hezekiah lifted up his voice to Almighty God,
recognized who He is and that He is over all; and he reminded
God that these people talked as if He were not anything
important. He asked God to show Himself in such a way that
everybody will know He is a living God. That is always a sound
basis for prayer.

> Then Isaiah the son of Amoz sent unto Hezekiah, saying, Thus
> saith the Lord God of Israel, Whereas thou hast prayed to me
> against Sennacherib king of Assyria: this is the word which the
> Lord hath spoken concerning him [and in poetic language we
> read when Sennacherib spoke against God he took on too much,
> reminding him it was God who won the victories he was boasting
> of. A sign is given that Assyria will be destroyed.] . . . for I will
> defend this city to save it for mine own sake, and for my servant
> David's sake (Isa. 37:21-35).

In this portion there is revealed a threat of a movement out of
the natural world that is stronger than the people of God are,
and far more imposing. This natural opposition moves against
believers with an insinuation that they have no strength and
taunts them about their weaknesses. Believers know they are
weak and they can actually be almost overcome by their discouragement because of the enemy's strength and their weakness: but Hezekiah shows them at this point what to do: turn to
God. Hezekiah is sure that if God takes a hand, He will stop
this enemy.

> Then the angel of the Lord went forth, and smote in the camp of
> the Assyrians a hundred and fourscore and five thousand: and
> when they arose early in the morning, behold, they were all
> dead corpses. So Sennacherib king of Assyria departed, and
> went and returned, and dwelt at Nineveh. And it came to pass,
> as he was worshiping in the house of Nisroch his god, that
> Adrammelech and Sharezer his sons smote him with the sword:
> and they escaped into the land of Armenia: and Esarhaddon his
> son reigned in his stead (Isa. 37:36-38).

Thus ended the career of Sennacherib.

Even today, every now and again, we hear that if the church
does not do thus and so, it will be wiped out; or if the church
does not succeed in this or that, the gospel will come to naught.

There are those who will say we had better change and join in with some other people, that we might derive some benefit from all the religions in the world, and so maybe we can make a new religion that will work. Yet at the time when those ideas are strong, there are always some people who put their trust in God; and they pray. Time and again the apparently invincible natural movements fall of their own weight. Often those who were considered important thirty or forty years ago are now almost forgotten, but the name of the Lord Jesus Christ is just as great and strong today as it ever was. Believers are called to put their trust in Him.

Sennacherib raised himself up as a great one; he came against the people of God and was undone and destroyed, all in one generation. May the Lord give us grace to trust in Him.

Chapter 25

HEZEKIAH'S PRAYER AND PRIDE

Isaiah 38 and 39 present Hezekiah as the chief character again, but the story is different. In our last study we saw Hezekiah as a man of God, trusting in Him in a day of great danger. We saw how the Lord stood by him and brought him through. Now we shall see another interesting thing that is human and very important in the history of this man.

> In those days was Hezekiah sick unto death. And Isaiah the prophet the son of Amoz came unto him, and said unto him, Thus saith the Lord, Set thine house in order: for thou shalt die, and not live (Isa. 38:1).

No doubt everyone would consider it a favor if he were told a few days in advance that he was going to die. There is a message in a prayer book that says, "From sudden death, Good Lord, deliver us." It may be that some have the feeling that sudden death is a blessing, because then one does not suffer. In any event, it behooves a person to be ready. Hezekiah had a favor granted to him. But what happened when he was told he would die?

> Then Hezekiah turned his face toward the wall, and prayed unto the Lord, and said, Remember now, O Lord, I beseech thee, how I have walked before thee in truth and with a perfect heart, and have done that which is good in thy sight. And Hezekiah wept sore (Isa. 38:2,3).

Here is a man who could say before God: "I have walked before thee in truth and with a perfect heart, and have done that which is good in thy sight." Then what did the Lord do? He sent Isaiah to tell Hezekiah:

> Behold, I will add unto thy days fifteen years (Isa. 38:5).

143

This is astonishing. It was God's plan that Hezekiah should die. This will cause us to be somewhat careful when we talk about God having arbitrarily fixed the future. God has settled the outcome, we know, but the Scriptures do not imply that God has filled in every detail between here and there. The Scriptures give the impression that when God needs more time, He can make time; and if there is something He intends to do, He can do it ten years from now, or fifteen years from now. He can extend time in any situation as He may need.

Jonah went to Nineveh and preached that in forty days Nineveh would be destroyed, but in forty days Nineveh was not destroyed. Jonah is not the only theologian who has had a headache over that. The Scripture records that Jonah was very angry and upset. Anger and being upset often go together; psychologically there is not much difference between them. Some people fill in the account by saying Jonah hated those people and wanted to see them destroyed. That seems slanderous to the name of Jonah. I do not feel we have to think that at all. There are those, also, who say he did not want to preach to Nineveh because he was afraid they would be saved, but that is filling in with contemporary ideas. We do not need to hunt for an astute reason why people do not want to do the will of God. Generally speaking, they have something else to do. There are some things we do know. All the time Jonah believed in God, he just did not understand Him. When Nineveh was not destroyed in forty days, Jonah was completely nonplussed. I think the account in Jonah reveals something about God: we should not try to bind Him to a time schedule. When it comes to His purposes, God binds Himself about that. But when it comes to time, we should remember, "It is not for you to know the times or the seasons" (Acts 1:7). They are in God's own hands. When He needs more time, He can make it. Actually, the message Jonah took to Nineveh was eventually fulfilled. Nineveh in due time was totally destroyed, and for the very reason that Jonah preached to them. But there was a period of respite Jonah did not know about. In the case of Hezekiah, the implication was plain: it was God's will that the king should die. Hezekiah did not want to die and so he "wept sore." Then God told Isaiah He had seen the king's tears and would add fifteen years to his days.

> And I will deliver thee and this city out of the hand of the king of
> Assyria: and I will defend this city. And this shall be a sign unto
> thee from the Lord, that the Lord will do this thing that he hath
> spoken; behold, I will bring again the shadow of the degrees,
> which is gone down in the sun dial of Ahaz, ten degrees back-
> ward. So the sun returned ten degrees, by which degrees it was
> gone down (Isa. 38:6-8).

This was a great miracle. If scientists say such action would
destroy the world, they are overlooking the fact that God is
above natural law. When the greatness of God is remembered,
miracles are not impossible.

Isaiah 38:9-20 records Hezekiah's song of praise. This is a
wonderful tribute of thanksgiving to God. We should note:

> For Isaiah had said, Let them take a lump of figs, and lay it for a
> plaster upon the boil, and he shall recover (Isa. 38:21).

This should keep us from being too superficial in our under-
standing of the ways of God. I think every miracle is in the
Bible for a reason, but I also believe certain incidents in the
Bible reveal that the ways of God are just natural processes.
God is the God of the natural processes, too; just as He is the
God of the miracles. I am inclined to think as I go through
Scripture as a whole that God does work wonders and miracles
on occasion to attract attention; but I am impressed by the fact
that with His own people He seldom does. Rather, He more
often uses the normal, natural processes. I believe it is easier
on us because of our psychological make-up to have things
come in a natural way. Because things happen according to
"whatsoever a man soweth that shall he also reap" and there is
an element of law and order in the procedures, one has more
quietness and confidence.

God can overrule all things and in this particular case He
did. I am sure He blessed what was done. Jesus of Nazareth
mixed clay and water and put it on a man's eyes, then told him
to wash and promised he would see. In obeying Christ, the
man saw. Paul was a man who often had answers to prayer, yet
in writing to Timothy he said, "Use a little wine for thy
stomach's sake and thine often infirmities" (1 Tim. 5:23).
Purely medicinal, doubtless, but still he tells Timothy to do it.
Some may say that all one needs to do is just to ask the Lord and
one will get over all his troubles. If the Lord should say, "Make

a poultice and put it on the boil," as He did with Isaiah and Hezekiah, don't be too proud to do it.

> Hezekiah also had said, What is the sign that I shall go up to the house of the Lord (Isa. 38:22)?

Here we have a marvelous answer to prayer. This shows that a believer may have the opportunity to ask the Lord for something that is not in the Lord's will, and the Lord may do it. Not only that, but He could confirm it with a great sign.

> At that time Merodach-baladan, the son of Baladan, king of Babylon, sent letters and a present to Hezekiah: for he had heard that he had been sick, and was recovered (Isa. 39:1).

Hezekiah was glad to see them and he took them on a tour. He showed them all the beautiful things he possessed in an exhibition of pride. What happened to Hezekiah shows that it is dangerous to let one's mind dwell on a series of successes with the Lord. Believers are human beings and they can be easily tricked because of their vanity. Isaiah took note of what had happened and asked, "What have they seen in thine house?" And when Hezekiah informed him they had seen everything, Isaiah replied:

> Behold, the days come, that all that is in thine house, and that which thy fathers have laid up in store until this day, shall be carried to Babylon: nothing shall be left, saith the Lord. And of thy sons that shall issue from thee, which thou shall beget, shall they take away; and they shall be eunuchs in the palace of the king of Babylon (Isa. 39:6,7).

This prophecy was fulfilled when Nebuchadnezzar conquered Jerusalem.

It is revealing to get the full picture by picking up other parts of the story. In that fifteen-year interval Hezekiah fathered Manasseh, the most wicked king Judah ever had. Had Hezekiah died when the Lord had planned, he never would have been responsible for the birth of Manasseh. We are told in the Bible that for the sins of Manasseh Judah was destroyed. If good king Hezekiah had just had the humility to accept God's will when God had announced he would die, he would have been better off. In all ways Hezekiah walked in the ways of God, save in the matter of the sundial when his heart was lifted up. He became proud.

The matter of prayer also is something for believers to think about. Believers may sometimes get what they insist on, even when it is not the best thing for them, even if they belong to the Lord. God will on occasion permit this. Do you remember when the children of Israel were in the desert? They did not want only manna, so they complained. They cried for meat, and finally the Lord told Moses He would give them meat until it would stick between their teeth. And He did, but they were in distress because of this.

The truth seems to be that in the matter of prayer, believers are better off to yield into the hand of God day by day. It is better to accept His way. The Lord's way will never be too hard. Remember Gethsemane. If a believer should deep down in his heart wish it otherwise, he could talk to the Lord about it, and he could say, "Father, if it be possible, let this cup pass from me so that I won't have to drink it." There is no sin in the believer's pleading, for God is able; but the final prayer should be "Nevertheless, not my will but thine be done." The believer should call upon all that is within him to yield himself under the mighty hand of God that He may exalt him in due time (1 Peter 5:6).

God understands everything that will ever happen to the believer, and His way is the best way. The believer should live through whatever he is called to face and if it seems too hard, he should look up into the face of the Lord and ask Him for help. Why not let God have His way in your life, and let Him do His holy will? It will be good. The Lord loves you.

Chapter 26

GOD'S CALL TO THE REMNANT

People who study the Book of Isaiah have become interested at one time or another in the authorship of the book. I have previously stated my observation that the New Testament quotes from the book at various times, always referring to what "Isaiah the prophet" said; e.g., " . . . as the Lord spake by Isaiah the prophet." Those who do think the book was prepared by different authors note that there seems to be a difference between the first thirty-nine chapters and the last twenty-seven chapters; i.e., beginning at chapter 40 the tone is different. That does not indicate necessarily that different people wrote the two sections, because all messengers deliver one type of message at one time and another type of message at another time. Nevertheless, the difference is apparent and we will consider it at this point.

In connection with this, there is something that is somewhat strange, yet true. There seems to be a division in the book, with thirty-nine chapters in the first section and twenty-seven chapters in the second, a major difference in ideas and in presentation at chapter forty, the beginning of the last twenty-seven chapters. There are thirty-nine books in the Old Testament and twenty-seven books in the New Testament. Chapter 40 seems to correspond to the Gospels in the New Testament. Chapter 40 begins with the very words that point to John the Baptist. This may be significant. I am not sure it has inspirational significance, since the selection of the canon of Scripture deciding on the sixty-six books that were in the Bible was apparently done by godly men in the history of the church, and I do not know whether anyone claims that the selection of those sixty-six books was an inspired act. There seems to be no doubt that God's providence was involved. I can accept these sixty-six books as being what God wants us to have as His Word, but they were chosen by human beings. God may have had a very definite hand in making the selection of the sixty-six books, but I am quite certain that when Isaiah wrote his prophecy, he did not write it in sixty-six chapters.

There were no chapters and there were no verses in the original manuscripts: they were brought into the Bible by scholars. Paul did not write his Epistles in the New Testament in verses; he wrote them straight through in manuscript form, in paragraphs. There are special markings that show where some paragraphs were indicated. Students of the Scripture and godly men selected the sixty-six books we have in the canon, and godly men divided the text into chapters and verses. Whether or not they realized what they were doing when they divided Isaiah into sixty-six chapters, putting the first thirty-nine in the first section and the next twenty-seven in the other, I do not know. But the division came right where John the Baptist appears in the New Testament, and that is interesting and it may be significant.

I personally understand these last twenty-seven chapters to consist of material actually aimed at those people who, in the Book of Isaiah, are called "the remnant." In the nation of Israel there were some people who sincerely wanted to be right with God; they humbly sought His face. These are spoken of as "the remnant." When Isaiah and other prophets pronounced the doom of Israel and Judah, they always recognized there would be some who would repent and turn to God and be saved. These were "the remnant."

I have the impression that the doom as it actually occurred for Israel and Judah was political and natural; it had to do with this world's affairs, and it destroyed Israel as a nation. The blessing that came to the remnant was a spiritual one; they could be involved in the destruction of the nation but they would never be lost so far as God was concerned. He preserves His people who put their trust in Him. They were the people who anticipated the real truth of the gospel of God, which is shown much more clearly in the New Testament.

I think that when the book of Isaiah was written, the first thirty-nine chapters were written first, and then the author turned the page, so to speak, and started writing the last twenty-seven chapters. I think that after Isaiah wrote on such subjects as we have studied, both historical references and national messages specially aimed at the national groups (all of which is found in the first thirty-nine chapters), he then gathered the material of the messages he had preached to the believers (and this formed the last twenty-seven chapters). I think his manuscript was divided up topically in this fashion. Something like this is in the Psalms also.

There are 150 Psalms and not one would claim that the first Psalm was written first and the 150th Psalm was written last. The Hebrew Bible actually divides the Psalms into five groups and names them according to the first five books of the Bible — the Pentateuch. So the five divisions of the Psalms are identified and named by what we would call Genesis, Exodus, Leviticus, Numbers, and Deuteronomy. In studying the Psalms, one can feel that something related to the message in Genesis is in the first portion, to Exodus in the second, and so on. The material in the Psalms is inspired, but the order in which the psalms are listed may vary according to human judgment.

As we look at Isaiah 40:1-8, we can see how similar this is to the message of John the Baptist. This is the message God sent to the true believers in a time when the nation as a whole was turning away from Him. It was a time when many people were disobedient and sin was rampant over the whole country. Danger threatened the nation. But these twenty-seven chapters are eternal rather than temporal. They are pertinent always, rather than just at some specific time in the history of Israel. In the first thirty-nine chapters there were local messages, specific in time, for that particular day and time in which they were preached. They had eternal principles in them, but I think the local application was the focus of that portion. However, in these last chapters I think we have eternal principles that are always true in speaking to the people who trust in God at any time.

> Comfort ye, comfort ye my people, saith your God. Speak ye comfortably to Jerusalem, and cry unto her, that her warfare is accomplished, that her iniquity is pardoned: for she hath received of the Lord's hand double for all her sins (Isa. 40:1,2).

This is the word that reveals God's everlasting word of comfort to people who have been chastened.

> For whom the Lord loveth he chasteneth, and scourgeth every son whom he receiveth (Heb. 12:6).

Every person who walks with the Lord is sometimes led through experiences of affliction because of the hand of God upon him. God leads believers through chastening experiences to refine and purify them, and to prepare them for a closer walk with Himself.

Speaking of that, the apostle Paul would say that if believers would judge themselves, they should not be judged, but if they do not judge themselves, then they will be chastened (1 Cor. 11:31,32). Things will happen to them because God will not let them go on in their foolishness or waywardness but will bring them back to Himself. He is quick to speak a word of comfort. There is a difference when the hand of God is upon a person whether that person interprets his sorrow and suffering as punishment or as chastening. If he interprets what has befallen him as punishment, the suffering he endures has no real inspiration or blessing to him. It will be a matter of his enduring and doggedly living through, wondering whether God will continue to hate him and wondering what will happen next. I think this is a great misunderstanding, if not a real slander against God. God will punish the wicked in His own time, but you and I are not living in the day of judgment. God is not now getting even with wicked people. There is a day of judgment coming, and in that day God will require that men will answer for every deed done in the body.

This is a day of grace in which God is working all things together for good to them that love Him. So while we shall not endeavor to pass judgment on what is happening to others, we will say for those who believe in God, that when trouble comes, they can look up to the Father in heaven and trust Him, knowing that the distresses they have all work together for good to them that love God. That is chastening and under those circumstances Paul would say we "glory in tribulation." When he says we "glory in tribulation," he does not mean that in any morbid fashion we are glad when we hurt. He means we are so confident in God that we are sure when He is hurting us that

He is working out His will. Sometimes when we have trouble, the result is that we actually come nearer to God than we ever were before.

Now to these people, the remnant, the people who out of their distress call upon God, Isaiah has a word of comfort and this is what we read in chapter 40. A preacher standing in the pulpit of the gospel can say to these people: trust God. And it is our privilege to speak words of comfort. In the days when I was beginning in the ministry this was an aspect I needed to learn. I would come back to Isaiah again and again and ask myself if I were preaching "comfortably" to the people. Sometimes I would be helped by what some of my parishioners had to say. Once one good woman spoke to my wife following a funeral service in which I had preached what was deep in my heart to people who had just lost a loved one. The woman said that, sitting there listening to me preach, she could wish she were going to heaven that very day to be with God. Then she added: "Why doesn't he preach like that on Sunday?" I did not get over that for years. I found out the truth was that I had not entered deeply enough into the gospel of the Lord Jesus Christ. When our Lord stood up in the synagogue and preached, those who heard Him marveled at all the gracious words He uttered. I realized that many people listening to me would be amazed at God's kindness and goodness, because I as the preacher was actually trying to "lay them out." But I was not preaching the whole truth! Persons need to know what their sins are, but no preacher needs to uncover sins if he cannot offer a cure. "The light that reveals is the light that heals," and the reason a preacher refers to sin is not that he is glad people sin, but he is glad to preach that sin can be taken away, that God can deliver from sin.

This is what God wanted His people to hear in Isaiah's time. These poor people had seen their nation collapse and had seen first the Syrians come in and then the Assyrians. Isaiah knew that the Babylonians would come next, and after that the Persians, until the country was run over again and again by hostile forces that would crush the nation. God told His prophet to "speak comfortably to my people."

> The voice of him that crieth in the wilderness, Prepare ye the way of the Lord, make straight in the desert a highway for our

> God. Every valley shall be exalted, and every mountain and hill
> shall be made low: and the crooked shall be made straight, and
> the rough places plain (Isa. 40:3,4).

God will build a highway that will be straight and smooth; all
obstructions will be taken away and low places will be filled in.
How can we straighten things out? In our own hearts are hills
and valleys; our own sin has made all kinds of obstructions in
us. The preaching we need to hear will be preaching that opens
the heart to the coming of the Lord Jesus Christ. What will
smooth out the valleys and bring down the hills? What can do
this but the kind of preaching that leads to repentance?

> And the glory of the Lord shall be revealed, and all flesh shall see
> it together: for the mouth of the Lord hath spoken it. The voice
> said, Cry. And he said, What shall I cry? All flesh is grass, and all
> the goodliness thereof is as the flower of the field: the grass
> withereth, the flower fadeth: because the spirit of the Lord
> bloweth upon it: surely the people is grass. The grass withereth,
> the flower fadeth: but the word of our God shall stand for ever
> (Isa. 40:5-8).

Thus we find that the message brought to these people at the
beginning of this section conveys the idea they are to be
comforted now by God.

Here is the basic thing for us to learn: we are to get ready for
the coming of the Lord into our hearts. The thing we are to
understand is that flesh is weak. All flesh is like grass. The best
thing the human being can do is not good enough. It will not
last for eternity. The word of our God will stand forever. The
arm of flesh will fail; we should put our trust in Almighty God.
He alone is able. The prophet will point out how great this God
is. All chastening is to make us aware of our weakness, so that
each one of us can look up to Almighty God and acknowledge,
"I am nothing." The promise is that although all flesh is like
grass, and the grass withereth, the Word of our God will stand
forever.

Chapter 27

"BEHOLD YOUR GOD!"

The Bible promises that God has in mind to do good and that He will carry out His purposes. God gives us reason to confidently expect He will do that.

> O Zion, that bringest good tidings, get thee up into the high mountain; O Jerusalem, that bringest good tidings, lift up thy voice with strength; lift it up, be not afraid; say unto the cities of Judah, Behold your God! (Isa. 40:9).

That reference to getting "up into the high mountains" suggests that they should get high enough so they will have the advantage of their voice being heard. What are they going to say? They will start by pointing to God; and here is the first word from Almighty God that would be a comfort to the heart: "Behold your God!" Actually, that is saying, "Don't look at your troubles first or last. Don't look at people first or last. Don't look at yourself first or last. Look at God first, then you can look at troubles and people and yourself, and God last. Start and finish with God, and you will be comforted, because God is greater than anything that is wrong with you." Greater is the One in whom they could put their trust than anything that could be against them.

"Behold your God!" That word *behold* means more than to just take a glimpse or a quick look. It has in it the idea of gazing, studying something. Let your eyes fasten upon God while you are considering Him.

> Behold, the Lord God will come with strong hand, and his arm shall rule for him: behold, his reward is with him, and his work before him (Isa. 40:10).

The idea in the word *reward* implies that He will judge. Almighty God will come, and He will come into this world to rule. But this should be noted: "He shall feed his flock like a shepherd" (Isa. 40:11). That is different. He will rule the world, but He will feed His flock. "He shall gather the lambs with his arm, and carry them in his bosom . . ." (Isa. 40:11). There is probably nothing so suggestive of tenderness and solicitation as a shepherd carrying a baby lamb. " . . . and shall gently lead those that are with young." He will gently lead those who are in any kind of situation where matters are beyond their strength; He will gently lead those who need Him in a special way.

But now Isaiah proposes another line of thought.

> Who hath measured the waters in the hollow of his hand, and meted out heaven with the span, and comprehended the dust of the earth in a measure, and weighed the mountains in scales, and the hills in a balance? (Isa. 40:12).

This implies something of God's creative power — Almighty God, in whom they are to put their trust.

> The heavens declare the glory of God; and the firmament showeth his handiwork. Day unto day uttereth speech, and night unto night showeth knowledge (Ps. 19:1,2).

The creation of God reveals the greatness of God.

> Behold, the nations are as a drop of a bucket, and are counted as the small dust of the balance: behold, he taketh up the isles as a very little thing (Isa. 40:15).

God is greater than all nations. The nations are like the drop of a bucket. When one pours water out of a bucket, there may be a few drops left. You know how insignificant they are. That is the way God feels so far as the nations of the world are concerned. What a comfort to know that as believers in Christ, we can keep this in mind: over all is One who is greater than all others; they are like a drop in the bottom of the bucket. "They are counted as the small dust of the balance." The balance refers to scales used in drugstores to weigh powders used in mixing medicines of various kinds. Such scales have little trays for the powders, and little weights for balance. If a person wanted to weigh gold dust, he would hold up that tray and blow on it to get rid of any common dust. That is what God thinks of the nations: they are like nothing at all compared to His greatness. Isaiah said this at a time when nations were thundering across the Arabian Peninsula into Palestine. These invading nations had military might that was similar to that of our greatest nations today. The power they had was terrifying, but Isaiah tells the people Almighty God is so much greater than these human beings that they are like the common dust that gathers in the scales. They can just be blown away. "Behold, he taketh up the isles as a very little thing." This may refer to the fact that some invading nations made islands in the Mediterranean into bases for military campaigns.

> And Lebanon is not sufficient to burn, nor the beasts thereof sufficient for a burnt offering (Isa. 40:16).

Remember, Lebanon was the country with great cedar trees. Cedar wood was commonly used for the fires on the altar. The prophet is saying here that if that mighty cedar forest of Lebanon were made into one big altar fire it would not be big enough to do honor to God. How does He compare with the forces we know in this world? They are like nothing compared to Him. Pagan idols are not worthy of comparison. Any human conception is inadequate.

> The workman melteth a graven image, and the goldsmith spreadeth it over with gold, and casteth silver chains. He that is so impoverished that he hath no oblation chooseth a tree that will not rot; he seeketh unto him a cunning workman to prepare a graven image, that shall not be moved (Isa. 40:19,20).

When some start explaining what God is like, they often give a human version with a human idea of God. This is just like a workman making God out of wood or gold and silver. We have people who make "God" out of ideas and then they will tell how great God is by trying to picture Him from a human point of view.

> Have ye not known? have ye not heard? hath it not been told you from the beginning? have ye not understood from the foundations of the earth? It is he that sitteth upon the circle of the earth, and the inhabitants thereof are as grasshoppers (Isa. 40:21,22).

I believe this circle of the earth refers to the horizon, as far as one can see; and God is there. What is being brought to believers' hearts and minds is the fact that no human being and no human idea is worthy of comparison with God. The prophet speaks also of the sovereignty of God: "That bringeth the princes to nothing," and again, "Lift up your eyes on high, and behold who hath created these things." God made every glimmer of light they could see in the heavens. As limitless as the heavens are, as immense as that expanse is, Almighty God is greater. "Not one faileth." These stars move in their courses. Almighty God controls all things of the universe by His great power.

> Hast thou not known? hast thou not heard, that the everlasting God, the Lord, the Creator of the ends of the earth, fainteth not, neither is weary? there is no searching of his understanding. He giveth power to the faint; and to them that have no might he increaseth strength (Isa. 40:28,29).

Any explanation of human experiences must never stop at the point that God has given up or that He is unable to help. No! God is almighty. God does not faint. If any person in his earthly experience is in a situation where the heart grows faint and he feels defeated, he should remember that God gives power to the faint.

> Even the youths shall faint and be weary, and the young men shall utterly fall: but they that wait upon the Lord shall renew their strength; they shall mount up with wings as eagles; they shall run, and not be weary; and they shall walk, and not faint (Isa. 40:30,31).

A person could start out with walking, then begin running, after which he would try to fly. That would be the human way of doing it. But here there is a difference. God will make a person fly like an eagle; He will make him run and not be weary; He will make him walk and not faint. This last is the hardest of all. It is not too hard to fly when a person is up there and everything is coming his way, as when he has been lifted in some spiritual experience. Perhaps he has been to a church service, or he has been in prayer, or with believing friends. A believer could come out of that fellowship and just fly. Wonderful! After awhile he will hit the ground and start running, but he will tire from that and then he will just walk. He has not been to church for some time. He has failed to read his Bible. He is now just barely walking. But the promise is that he will walk and not faint. This is the marvelous consequence of having his God with him. This is the message the prophet brings in beginning to comfort His people. "Comfort ye, comfort ye my people." How? Lift up your voice and call to them: "Behold your God!"

Look up at God. Who is He? Almighty Creator, sovereign, Ruler, Keeper, wise, powerful, almighty, gentle: He will keep them. They can put their trust in Him. And if they are weary and they faint, they should come to Him; He will strengthen them.

What a marvelous message Isaiah has given to us! This is the beginning of comfort to God's people.

Chapter 28

THE LIVING GOD

In studying the Book of Isaiah, we need to keep in mind that this book is a collection of sermons by a prophet who is like a preacher. It is very much as though this is a compendium of ideas or a collection of notes of a preacher. One might say these are the sermon notes of this prophet of Israel. We should also remind ourselves that the prophet seeks to interpret to the people the mind of God.

For us to know God's mind about our daily life would be helpful to a certain extent. We might have a fairly good idea about living as we face life naturally; we do not need anyone to tell us it is wrong to steal or kill; we do not need a revelation from God to tell us it is wrong to lie. The Bible and the books of the prophets, in interpreting to us the mind of God, do not spend much time arguing about conduct. Is it all right to charge interest on your money? Should you take pay for doing kindness to people? Those are not the things that are discussed. In general, so far as relationships between people are concerned, Almighty God is interested in the way men treat men, and what is revealed is not so much that a certain way of acting is unkind as that when you are unkind, God sees it and God judges men.

Human beings must live in this world and are confronted with problems in living. Many times they are not sure what they should do, or that they could have help to determine not only what they should do, but that they should do it. Suppose you have the opportunity to be kind to someone who has done you harm. A prophet would tell you God would approve that, and further he would point out if you are kind to this person who is not kind to you, God will be with you and He will bless you. At the same time, the prophet would remind you that if you fail to do what you should do, God will not only withhold His blessing but He will judge you.

That is the general Old Testament law that the prophet would preach. In addition, he would proclaim that even if you have done wrong, if you turn to God, He will receive you. One of the first promises we read in Isaiah is:

> Though your sins be as scarlet, they shall be as white as snow; though they be red like crimson, they shall be as wool (Isa. 1:18).

Some will stop at that point but they should read the next two verses:

> If ye be willing and obedient, ye shall eat the good of the land: but if ye refuse and rebel, ye shall be devoured with the sword (Isa. 1:19,20).

That was a warning. The prophets preached in that fashion.

The first thirty-nine chapters of this book set forth an examination of God's relation to His people and to the world round about. In that portion is largely a report of God dealing with several groups of His own people. Isaiah wrote to some people whom we would call a worldly group of believers. There are people who understand the gospel well enough to know that not only has Christ Jesus reconciled them to God and opened the way for them to come to God, and so united them with God, but that the Lord Jesus Christ is available for daily living. They wish they knew more about His help. Every time they attend church they hope they will learn something about it. We think of these as being spiritually minded people. In the same church there are those who believe in God up to a certain point. They make a profession of faith, they believe in the Lord Jesus Christ and receive Him as their Savior. They are trusting Him to save their souls. But a great many people stop at that point. We think of those people as worldly believers. In the same church there will be both groups of people. You will recall in the time of the twelve apostles there were three — Peter, James, and John — who were oftentimes closer to the Lord while the other nine were not so close. That situation is often true in any group.

I have felt that in the first chapters of the Book of Isaiah we have in Judah a type of people who tried to live close to God.

Wherever Judah is referred to, we can interpret a message that God would give to those people who seek to do His will. Israel was a type of those people who claim to belong to God but do not follow Him closely. They were the people in the northern kingdom, the larger group. We took note that Syria was a neighbor who knew about Israel and Judah and wanted what they had, but who did not want any relationship with God. We can think of Syria as being a type of people who know about the Christian gospel and want its benefits, but are not willing to give any credit to the name of the Lord Jesus Christ. They want the peace of God that passes all understanding, but they do not want the faith of God that will give the peace that passes all understanding. Instead, such persons will go to a psychiatrist to get a psychological adjustment, hoping thereby to arrive at the same kind of peace the Christians have. They want things the Christians have, but without Christian faith. I give that interpretation to Syria, because they wanted land that belonged to Judah but they did not want to belong to God.

Also in these opening thirty-nine chapters there is reference to another group of people: the nation of Assyria. These were arrogant strangers who did not know anything about Israel or God and were ready to wipe out all of God's people. They were the pagans. Throughout these chapters messages were given to Judah, Israel, Syria, and Assyria. There were repeated references to what was called the remnant — a small group who hungered and thirsted for a closer relationship with God. Judah as a nation tried to be right in God's sight but not everyone earnestly and humbly sought God's daily presence. Even in Israel, casual and worldly as they were, there were some who wanted to be close to God. God knew who these sincere believers were and He called them "the remnant."

The last twenty-seven chapters of Isaiah seem to be messages that are beamed directly to these people who really want to know God, viz., the remnant. It is the remnant who will be brought into focus. They are the ones who will be addressed. This section begins with a message "to Jerusalem" — probably those people who actually seek the will of God. When one commits self to God and earnestly seeks His favor, struggle and strife soon come to an end and iniquity is pardoned. God does not deal with such people on the basis of sin, but in grace. If I humble myself and confess my sin to God, He will forgive my sin, cleanse me from all unrighteousness, cast all my sins behind His back, and remove them as far from me as the east is from the west, and they shall no more be called to mind. Certainly I will have shortcomings and will fall into things I do not want to do, but God knows that deep down in my heart I do not want to do such things. He knows my frame. "Like as a father pitieth his children, so the Lord pitieth them that fear him" (Ps. 103:13).

To such people the Word of God begins in chapter 40. Following "Speak ye comfortably to Jerusalem, and cry unto her, that her warfare is accomplished, that her iniquity is pardoned . . . " is the description of the forerunner of the King, the herald of God's Messiah. This was fulfilled by John the Baptist, the voice of one crying in the wilderness. In that short passage at the beginning of chapter 40, the principal emphasis is on the eternal, unshakable Word of God. "The grass withereth, the flower fadeth: but the word of our God shall stand for ever" (Isa. 40:8).

In the ninth verse is proclaimed the theme of all the remainder of the Book of Isaiah. It is this single call: "Behold your God!" That points to the very beginning of the spiritual experience of people who are committed to God. "Look into His face."

Isaiah 40 presents the outstanding truth about God. He is set forth as the Creator Almighty, the One in whom we can trust, and the One who will keep His own. This same theme is carried through chapters 41, 44, and 45: it is always "Behold your God!" In Isaiah 41 another aspect of the truth of God is brought out: He is the overruling sovereign: the One who is in control.

> Keep silence before me, O islands; and let the people renew their strength: let them come near; then let them speak: let us come near together to judgment (Isa. 41:1).

This is a call to come in close and hear what the prophet is going to say.

> Who raised up the righteous man from the east, called him to his foot, gave the nations before him, and made him rule over kings? he gave them as the dust to his sword, and as driven

stubble to his bow. He pursued them, and passed safely; even by the way that he had not gone with his feet. Who hath wrought and done it, calling the generations from the beginning? I the Lord, the first, and with the last; I am he (Isa. 41:2-4).

In those verses God presents Himself not only as the Creator of all the universe and the Keeper of those who put their trust in Him, but as the Ruler, the One who raises men up and directs and controls them. The prophet then points out that when man is confronted with the problem of who is in control, the pagan people seek out their idols. Ordinarily we think of idols as grotesque images. An idol is any object of adoration and worship other than God.

Human beings constantly come into situations where they are confronted with the unknown. In their minds men project answers to every unknown question. In such projections of their answers to unknown questions, they also project God. God is not what everybody thinks He is; God is what He has revealed to people in Jesus Christ. He is in Himself what He is. Any sinful man can imagine what God is like, or what he thinks God is like; one only needs to look at the idols of the world to see what grotesque images men can conceive when they imagine what God is like. Some people make images of wood and of stone, others make them of sticks. And there are some people who do not make them outwardly, but conceive them inwardly. All people have some idea of God as the Creator of the world. Even on college campuses students have ideas as to how this world came to pass. If their idea includes the thought that some vague unknown force made it, that is their God. Whatever they think is the most powerful force in the universe is their God.

Some people today may think of God as electric energy. We laugh at those in ancient times who thought the sun was God. That was actually solar energy. Those in olden times who worshiped the sun are of the same piece of cloth as the modern people who worship electrical or electronic energy, as if electric dynamic energy makes this world operate. That is their way of seeing God. How does one man get to be so great and to have so much power, and then lose it? Who decides about these things? Some people explain these matters according to whatever God they have in mind. This is what Isaiah describes when he speaks of people who made a god out of wood or other material.

> They helped every one his neighbour; and every one said to his brother, Be of good courage (Isa. 41:6).

Human beings were seen trying to comfort and to encourage each other.

> So the carpenter encouraged the goldsmith, and he that smootheth with the hammer him that smote the anvil, saying, It is ready for the soldering: and he fastened it with nails, that it should not be moved (Isa. 41:7).

This again was a description of the building of an idol. There are people today, gathering together and trying to figure out what makes the universe go and how things operate. It is the same kind of thing.

Isaiah reported what God has to say about this futile search of mankind:

> But thou, Israel, art my servant, Jacob whom I have chosen, the seed of Abraham my friend. Thou whom I have taken from the ends of the earth, and called thee from the chief men thereof, and said unto thee, Thou art my servant; I have chosen thee, and not cast thee away (Isa. 41:8,9).

This is the message Isaiah wants to get across to people who really seek the face of God. He speaks to their hearts this comforting word: you do not have to make images of God. He is the One who chose you, the One who will keep you. That is your God.

In reading further, we come now to one of the most wonderful verses in the Bible.

> Fear thou not: For I am with thee: be not dismayed; for I am thy God: I will strengthen thee; yea, I will help thee; yea, I will uphold thee with the right hand of my righteousness (Isa. 41:10).

What a marvelous promise! When others who do not know God are trying to figure out answers, God sends word to His own people:

> Behold, all they that were incensed against thee shall be ashamed and confounded: they shall be as nothing; and they that strive with thee shall perish (Isa. 41:11).

This reminds us of the promise to Abraham: "Cursed be every

one that curseth thee, and blessed be he that blesseth thee"
(Gen. 27:29). So here we read:

> For I the Lord thy God will hold thy right hand, saying unto
> thee, Fear not; I will help thee (Isa. 41:13).

These are marvelous words of promise, spoken to those who
seek the face of God. The believer does not need to imagine
Him; he does not need to explain Him. All he needs to do is
come to Him and trust Him. God will take the believer by his
right hand and will never let him go. And He will help the
believer according to His own promise.

Chapter 29

THE IDEAL SERVANT

God has a personal interest in those who seek His face, and in that personal interest He promises to bless. One is reminded of the covenant with Abraham in which God said, "Cursed be every one that curseth thee, and blessed be he that blesseth thee" (Gen. 27:29). This portion of our study contains verse after verse of God's promises. In chapter 41 we read:

> Behold, all they that were incensed against thee shall be ashamed and confounded: they shall be as nothing; and they that strive with thee shall perish. Thou shalt seek them, and shalt not find them, even them that contended with thee: they that war against thee shall be as nothing, and as a thing of nought. For I the Lord thy God will hold thy right hand, saying unto thee, Fear not; I will help thee (Isa. 41:11-13).

Some years ago a young woman asked me to preach a sermon on her special text, Isaiah 41:13. To this day, every time I repeat that verse something stirs in my bones, and everything I know about God encourages me to say it is true just exactly as it reads. The marvelous blessing of God is not something we earn, or something we achieve. We cannot run fast enough to win it or climb high enough to get it. "I will help thee"; a person can live and die with that — the blessing of those people, the remnant, who seek the face of God. He is on our side; we do not have to be afraid. Wonderful words! We have victory ahead, though it may never come in this world, which is only a temporary place. God will give us the inner understanding to know that though everything around may fall to pieces, He will keep us and take us to Himself. God reveals His promise in these wonderful words:

When the poor and needy seek water, and there is none, and their tongue faileth for thirst, I the Lord will hear them, I the God of Israel will not forsake them. I will open rivers in high places, and fountains in the midst of the valleys: I will make the wilderness a pool of water, and the dry land springs of water. I will plant in the wilderness the cedar, the shittah tree, and the myrtle, and the oil tree; I will set in the desert the fir tree, and the pine, and the box tree together: that they may see, and know, and consider, and understand together, that the hand of the Lord hath done this, and the Holy One of Israel hath created it (Isa. 41:17-20).

Almighty God makes it clear that by all the power He possesses He will, if necessary, reverse every natural process. This is reflected in the words of the apostle Paul when he wrote that God will "quicken our mortal bodies" by the power with which He raised up Jesus Christ from the dead. Almighty God will move in when natural processes have failed and will actually raise up believers and transform them by His grace and mercy. Note once more the words "That they may see, and know, and consider, and understand together." God does not want anyone to misunderstand — four different ways of saying it are expressed here.

Isaiah gives an invitation to consider what is called comparative religion.

Produce your cause, saith the Lord; bring forth your strong reasons, saith the King of Jacob. Let them bring them forth, and show us what shall happen: let them show the former things what they be, that we may consider them, and know the latter end of them; or declare us things for to come (Isa. 41:21,22).

God challenges the idols to do something if they think they are God. He challenges the remnant to ask those idols what is going to happen and how it can control the future.

Behold, ye are of nothing, and your work of nought: an abomination is he that chooseth you. I have raised up one from the north, and he shall come: from the rising of the sun shall he call upon my name: and he shall come upon princes as upon mortar, and as the potter treadeth clay (Isa. 41:24,25).

Isaiah is probably intimating the coming of the king of Assyria because what happened to Israel was under the hand of God.

> For I beheld, and there was no man; even among them, and
> there was no counselor, that, when I asked of them, could
> answer a word. Behold, they are all vanity; their works are
> nothing: their molten images are wind and confusion (Isa.
> 41:28,29).

What can a person expect if he prays to a post or a stone image?
Or what can he have if he worships some eternal principle,
some cause? There is no personal relationship in such practice.
Even in our day those who are not believers in Christ find the
world an empty place.

Isaiah now presents a sharp contrast:

> Behold my servant, whom I uphold; mine elect, in whom my
> soul delighteth; I have put my spirit upon him: he shall bring
> forth judgment to the Gentiles. He shall not cry, nor lift up, nor
> cause his voice to be heard in the street. A bruised reed shall he
> not break, and the smoking flax shall he not quench: he shall
> bring forth judgment unto truth. He shall not fail nor be dis-
> couraged, till he have set judgment in the earth: and the isles
> shall wait for his law (Isa. 42:1-4).

These verses are taken in the New Testament to refer to Christ
Jesus. What was the meaning in Isaiah's day? This Scripture
calls on the pagans to bring their gods and to tell what can be
done for anybody. What can they say to a broken heart, a
crushed spirit? By way of contrast, God says, "Look at My
Servant." Then God reveals His Messiah, the One who is
known as the Lord Jesus Christ. "A bruised reed shall he not
break." Reeds were used for various purposes, and one would
be inclined to throw away a reed that was bruised or broken,
but the Messiah will not do that. He will not throw away one
person, as humble and weak and broken as that one person may
be. The soul that feels broken and useless can put his trust in
the Lord Jesus Christ. Flax was used for fire, and any kind of
straw fire that does not burn well smokes badly. In a case like
that, the Messiah would not pour water on it, saying it was not
any good; He would get that fire to burn, and He would keep it
burning. That is a figurative way of saying that the least person
is precious in the sight of Christ. "He shall bring forth judgment unto truth. He shall not fail nor be discouraged, till he
have set judgment in the earth: and the isles shall wait for his
law." This is a promise to take to your own heart. There have

been times in my spiritual experience when that sentence has been a lifesaver. Jesus Christ will actually bring His will to pass in my soul; He will accomplish that which He has set Himself to do.

Believers do not worship a post, a picture, or some marble statue. They worship a living Being, One whose heart is more tender than a woman's heart, who really cares for them. Believers are "graven" on the palms of His hands. He knows where they are and who they are and He will never leave them nor forsake them. This is the glorious word Isaiah continues to write:

> Thus saith God the Lord, he that created the heavens, and stretched them out; he that spread forth the earth, and that which cometh out of it; he that giveth breath unto the people upon it, and spirit to them that walk therein: I the Lord have called thee in righteousness, and will hold thine hand, and will keep thee, and give thee for a covenant of the people, for a light of the Gentiles; to open the blind eyes, to bring out the prisoners from the prison, and them that sit in darkness out of the prison house (Isa. 42:5-7).

In this manner Almighty God speaks of His Messiah, His Servant. And Christ will succeed with me, my salvation is assured, because on my side are God the Father, God the Son, and God the Holy Spirit. I can praise His name now because of what He will accomplish.

In the opening part of his prophecy, Isaiah had to show many times the judgment of God upon wickedness. Isaiah wrote that God would resist those who were proud and that He would smash those who opposed Him. Now Isaiah can write these gracious words for the remnant:

> I am the Lord: that is my name: and my glory will I not give to another, neither my praise to graven images (Isa. 42:8).

And again:

> Sing unto the Lord a new song, and his praise from the end of the earth, ye that go down to the sea, and all that is therein; the isles, and the inhabitants thereof (Isa. 42:10).

The prophet now describes in a glorious song of triumph the marvelous assurance that God will keep the remnant:

> I have long time holden my peace; I have been still, and refrained myself: now will I cry like a travailing woman; I will

destroy and devour at once. I will make waste mountains and hills and dry up all their herbs; and I will make the rivers islands, and I will dry up the pools. And I will bring the blind by a way that they knew not; I will lead them in paths that they have not known: I will make darkness light before them, and crooked things straight. These things will I do unto them, and not forsake them (Isa. 42:14-16).

God makes all these promises concerning what He will do through His Messiah, whom we understand to be His Servant, Christ Jesus. Isaiah reveals in this statement how God esteems His Servant:

The Lord is well pleased for his righteousness' sake; he will magnify the law, and make it honourable (Isa. 42:21).

Isaiah then goes on to say:

Who among you will give ear to this? who will hearken and hear for the time to come? Who gave Jacob for a spoil, and Israel to the robbers? did not the Lord, he against whom we have sinned? for they would not walk in his ways, neither were they obedient unto his law. Therefore he hath poured upon him the fury of his anger, and the strength of battle: and it hath set him on fire round about, yet he knew not; and it burned him, yet he laid it not to heart (Isa. 42:23-25).

In these words the prophet indicates that the chastening of Israel was brought on because of the wrong they had done; but God was now pouring out upon them His great favor and His great grace, in providing for the salvation of the remnant through His own Servant, the Messiah.

Chapter 30

THE REDEEMER

Isaiah 40–66 seems to be particularly directed to believing people of his day, the remnant, who sought to know the Lord. When sin is abroad in the land, and doubt, fear, and confusing ideas are abroad in the hearts and minds of many people, the message spoken to God's people is this: "Behold your God! Lift up your eyes and look at Him."

In chapter 43 Isaiah reveals God to be the Redeemer.

> But now thus saith the Lord that created thee, O Jacob, and he that formed thee, O Israel, Fear not: for I have redeemed thee, I have called thee by thy name; thou art mine (Isa. 43:1).

The truth is that a person may not feel that God has redeemed him, but it could still be true. Personal feelings are not a good guide. If anyone should for any reason whatever be down-hearted and discouraged, he should look into the Word of God. What is God planning to do? A person should not be governed by his feelings: he should be guided by the Word of God. Isaiah revealed what God had done quite apart from any act on the part of the remnant.

This truth is revealed again and again in Scripture. In the beginning when Adam, having become conscious of his own disobedience to God and being aware of his sin, hid and was in hiding when God called, "Adam, where art thou?" When Hagar had run away from Sarah and the harsh treatment she was receiving, she heard this truth in the voice of God: "Hagar, Hagar, what aileth thee?" This is the word that came to Moses when in the wilderness he saw the bush burning but somehow not consumed; it was then he received God's call. Perhaps the best-known such incident occurred when Saul, the Pharisee, on the road to Damascus suddenly saw a light brighter than the noonday sun and heard, "Saul, Saul, why persecutest thou me?" At no time will a revelation from God be so powerful as when your own name is called. That is the most basic and at the same time, most moving truth in a believer's experience, when God says, "Thou art mine."

> When thou passest through the waters, I will be with thee; and through the rivers, they shall not overflow thee: when thou walkest through the fire, thou shalt not be burned; neither shall the flame kindle upon thee. For I am the Lord thy God, the Holy One of Israel, thy Saviour: I gave Egypt for thy ransom, Ethiopia and Seba for thee. Since thou wast precious in my sight, thou hast been honourable, and I have loved thee: therefore will I give men for thee, and people for thy life. Fear not: for I am with thee: I will bring thy seed from the east, and gather thee from the west; I will say to the north, Give up; and to the south, Keep not back: bring my sons from far, and my daughters from the ends of the earth; even every one that is called by my name: for I have created him for my glory, I have formed him; yea, I have made him (Isa. 43:2-7).

This is the word of Almighty God. What a word to speak to one's heart in a day of confusion, a day of shattering desolation, when everything seems contrary! When the believer goes through the deep waters, God will go with him. When he is in trouble, God will not suddenly take him out of it; He will take him by the hand and lead him through it. God will never leave nor forsake the believer. The Lord Jesus Christ, who was perfect, walked on this earth with a heavy heart. He was a man of sorrows, acquainted with grief. The day came, just before He was arrested and taken before the court to be condemned to death, when He could say to His disciples: "My soul is exceeding sorrowful unto death" (Mark 14:34). Believers, too, can be "in heaviness through manifold temptations"; they can be face to face with impossible situations, but never will God forsake them.

There were those in Isaiah's time who claimed that other gods had meaning, too. Certainly, there was Jehovah who was the Lord God of Israel; but there were others: the gods of the Babylonians, the gods of the Assyrians, and the various gods of the Canaanites. This meant there were various ideas abroad in the land, other than the truth that was in the Lord God of Israel. Isaiah admonished the people, challenging them to bring forth evidence that somebody was actually helped by their pagan ideas.

> I, even I, am the Lord; and beside me there is no saviour (Isa. 43:11).

This is the message Isaiah brought to these people: Redeemed people are to testify to the world that they have been redeemed.

Isaiah then reveals what God will do in order to redeem His people:

> Thus saith the Lord, your redeemer, the Holy One of Israel; For your sake I have sent to Babylon, and have brought down all their nobles, and the Chaldeans, whose cry is in the ships. I am the Lord your Holy One, the creator of Israel, your King (Isa. 43:14,15).

God is reminding Israel that in order to redeem them He destroyed the oppressor.

If one would ask what God has destroyed for believers in Christ Jesus, it can be seen right at the very outset that, among other things, God has destroyed death. The Lord Jesus Christ died and rose from the dead; death has lost its sting and the grave has lost its victory. The great enemy of the souls of believers has been robbed of his prey, because God will raise believers from the dead. As long as a believer lives in the flesh, Satan may tempt and entice him, but if he reckons himself to be dead and if he accepts the crucifixion of his flesh and denies himself, then he is delivered and free from the temptations.

Isaiah goes on to reveal that to achieve redemption God will do a new thing:

> Remember ye not the former things, neither consider the things of old. Behold, I will do a new thing; now it shall spring forth; shall ye not know it? I will even make a way in the wilderness, and rivers in the desert. . . . I give waters in the wilderness, and rivers in the desert, to give drink to my people, my chosen. This people have I formed for myself; they shall show forth my praise (Isa. 43:18-21).

Isaiah is talking about giving life where there was death, quickening mortal bodies that were dead in trespasses and sins. This is a startling promise! Do you know someone whose heart seems actually barren? Do you really believe that God can make water spring out of a desert? God will do a new thing in the believer. God will move him from death to life.

In Isaiah 43:22-28 Isaiah reveals that in spite of God's purpose to redeem Israel, Israel would not turn to Him. But now the prophet proclaims here an aspect of redemption that needs to be recognized.

> But thou hast not called upon me, O Jacob; but thou hast been weary of me, O Israel. Thou hast not brought me the small cattle of thy burnt offerings; neither hast thou honoured me with thy sacrifices. I have not caused thee to serve with an offering, nor wearied thee with incense (Isa. 43:22,23).

Israel did not worship God. They did not praise Him. In the remainder of the chapter and in the chapter that follows, Isaiah reveals God's intention to save and redeem His people even though they have not been faithful to Him. This is one of the most wonderful aspects of the gospel. God will redeem believers even when they are not worthy. Paul writes about this amazing love in these words:

> For scarcely for a righteous man will one die: yet peradventure for a good man some would even dare to die. But God commendeth his love toward us, in that, while we were yet sinners, Christ died for us (Rom. 5:7,8).

Chapter 31

THE ONLY GOD

God as Redeemer is particularly emphasized in chapters 43 and 44. What is meant when it is said that something is redeemed? *Redeemed* is more or less an economic term. If you should buy some object in a store that you had not finished paying for and it was being held until you had completely paid for it, when you completed the payment you would "redeem" it. Most of us are more accustomed to the term in connection with mortgages on property. When a piece of property is mortgaged, the owner owes certain money on it. Then there are limitations to what can be done with the property. It can be sold only with permission. If someone else should pay off the mortgage, that person is said to have redeemed the property for the owner.

The concept of redemption is based on the idea that the individual or object to be redeemed has something against him or it. There is a debt, or an obligation; and if that debt is not satisfied, it might mean the loss of that piece of property. But if someone will pay the debt, the property goes free. And that is the way it is with us. "The soul that sinneth, it shall die" (Ezek. 18:4) and so every human being is potentially under the sentence of death. When the Lord Jesus Christ saves a person, He redeems him from this sentence of death. He does it by offering His life for that person and dying in his stead. It is the joy of the believer to remember that because the blood of the Lord Jesus Christ was shed for him, he is free.

What God has been setting forth through the prophet in chapters 43 to 44 to His people in Israel is that He is the Redeemer. But in the latter part of chapter 43 there is a note of something that is not happy. It is not easy to read. It appears that even though God was doing all for Israel, Israel did not seem to appreciate it. We are thinking of those whom God will save. We are reminded again that "God commendeth his love toward us, in that, while we were yet sinners, Christ died for us" (Rom. 5:8). Each of us at some point along the way has some record of disobeying God. Yet He died for us.

> But thou hast not called upon me, O Jacob; but thou hast been weary of me, O Israel. Thou hast not brought me the small cattle of thy burnt offerings; neither hast thou honoured me with thy sacrifices. I have not caused thee to serve with an offering, nor wearied thee with incense (Isa. 43:22,23).

The small cattle are the lambs and the calves commonly brought for the sacrifices. God's requirements are not stringent, but Israel had not offered praise to Him with a sacrifice of a sweet smell.

Here is the wonderful truth of the grace of God: He gave His Son to die for me, and even though I could be wayward and turn away, yet He would save me.

> I, even I, am he that blotteth out thy transgressions for mine own sake, and will not remember thy sins (Isa. 43:25).

He will blot out our sins not because we deserve it but because He has it in His mind to do us good. Why is this emphasized? Because when we understand this, it puts a floor under our feet to walk on. If I think my relationship with God depends on my being good, I am worried all the time for fear I won't be good, and I know right well I won't be. But when I understand His kindness and grace and mercy, I have assurance.

The phrase "put me in remembrance" is found in verse 26. That means when you pray, remember your own unworthiness and that it is by His grace that you are able to come to Him. Declare to God the memory of His grace and mercy. It follows, however, that if I become disobedient to Him, He will chasten me. "For whom the Lord loveth he chasteneth, and scourgeth every son whom he receiveth" (Heb. 12:6).

In verses 26 and 27 Isaiah explains to the godly minded people of Israel why the country suffered, why God let calamity come upon them. It was to chasten them, to call them back from their waywardness. Remember, God is not dealing with them in punishment; to interpret it as such would fill them with resentment. He hoes the weeds out of our garden and He prunes the branches in our vines for our benefit. He wants us to draw nearer to Him. He lets us know sorrow and grief so that we will seek His face more and more, so that we can say, like Paul: "Yea, we glory in tribulation." Paul was not morbid, but he is saying, "When I hurt I am glad to know that God is working out something in my life; and when trouble and distress come, I am absolutely certain God is working out something good in me."

> Yet now hear, O Jacob my servant; and Israel, whom I have chosen: Thus saith the Lord that made thee, and formed thee from the womb, which will help thee; Fear not, O Jacob, my servant; and thou, Jesurun, whom I have chosen. For I will pour water upon him that is thirsty, and floods upon the dry ground: I will pour my spirit upon thy seed, and my blessing upon thine offspring: and they shall spring up as among the grass, as willows by the water courses (Isa. 44:1-4).

This is a marvelous promise. Despite the chastening, God has not given up His purpose to redeem. He will accomplish this by pouring out His spirit into Israel. God's promises require on the believer's part a certain response: he should be faithful and obedient to God. But the human heart is such that a person can neglect Him and disobey Him. Because that was the case with Israel, God had to lead them through suffering experiences. However, through the work of the Holy Spirit, who lives in our hearts when we receive Jesus Christ, we are led to want to be well pleasing in the sight of God. This is the marvelous blessing of the New Testament. If He had left it up to us, we would have failed. But He makes us grow up like willows by the water courses and our spiritual life like a tree growing by the rivers, plentifully watered by the grace of God. We respond to Him because He works in us "to will and to do of his good pleasure" (Phil. 2:13).

> One shall say, I am the Lord's; and another shall call himself by the name of Jacob; and another shall subscribe with his hand unto the Lord, and surname himself by the name of Israel (Isa. 44:5).

That will be the disposition of the people. God will so affect them that they will be glad to say they belong to Him.

> Thus saith the Lord the King of Israel, and his redeemer the Lord of hosts: I am the first, and I am the last; and beside me

> there is no God. And who, as I, shall call, and shall declare it, and set it in order for me, since I appointed the ancient people? and the things that are coming, and shall come, let them show unto them. Fear ye not, neither be afraid: have not I told thee from that time, and have declared it? ye are even my witnesses. Is there a God beside me? yea, there is no God; I know not any (Isa. 44:6-8).

The Lord God is the only One who can save us.

There is a prolonged contrast in verses 7 to 20 in which Isaiah points out the inadequacy of any other god: the graven images cannot save. There were many people in Israel in those days who believed in other gods. Isaiah reminds them that none of those gods had the power to transform the people who were worshiping them. There are many people whose religion is like that. They attend church; they sing and read and pray and plan. When they stop thinking and reading and planning, all is silent. They do not have it in their hearts to go through with it, so they quit. That is not the gospel of God. There are those who put their trust in Him and call upon Him; then in weakness they may fall away and forget. But He does not. He then starts working in them "to will and to do of His good pleasure." They will find that their whole spiritual experience is the result of God working in them. They no longer need to climb; they are lifted. They no longer need to try to do; all is being done for them. They no longer need to try to earn; all is being given as a gift. They no longer hope to qualify; they already are accepted, and that changes the whole outlook. Isaiah would say, "Look around you and you will see nothing else like it anywhere in the world."

> Remember these, O Jacob and Israel; for thou art my servant: I have formed thee. . . . I have blotted out, as a thick cloud, thy transgressions, and as a cloud, thy sins: return unto me; for I have redeemed thee. . . . I am the Lord that maketh all things; that stretcheth forth the heavens alone; that spreadeth abroad the earth by myself; that frustrateth the tokens of the liars, and maketh diviners mad; that turneth wise men backward, and maketh their knowledge foolish . . . even saying to Jerusalem, Thou shalt be built; and to the temple, Thy foundation shall be laid (Isa. 44:21-28).

We are dealing with an almighty, powerful, living God; and we are to remember that at all times. We do not need to climb; He will carry us. We do not need to run; He will take us in His arms. We do not need to work for it; He will give it to us. All He wants from you and me is willing acceptance of Him. This was the great truth the prophet urged upon his people: that they should believe in Almighty God, the Redeemer of Israel. And He is our Redeemer, our Savior.

Chapter 32

THE SOVEREIGN GOD

In the course of Isaiah's ministry there were some persons who earnestly sought the mind of God and His blessing. Isaiah reiterated that while others would be destroyed, those people would be spared and God would bless them. Such people were called "the remnant." As previously stated, we are inclined to think that the latter chapters in the book are messages sent to this remnant. In the time of Isaiah the people who wanted to do God's will were having an experience of great confusion. When, in your own heart, you are kindly disposed toward others, willing to give them the benefit of every doubt, it is disturbing when they do not turn to God and walk with Him. You can be tempted to doubt in your own heart, though you do not want to doubt. This is often the way sincere people feel at a time of widespread sin in the land.

Isaiah brings a special message to such people, trying to bolster their faith. It bears repeating that the gist of his message in chapter 40 and following is epitomized in the words "Behold your God!" If believers are in a situation where things are not going according to the will of God, they can never know peace of mind by looking at the world around them. Things often happen in a way that would incline one to think there is no God at all, and no amount of painting it over will change it. But the Holy Spirit lifts the heart to look into the face of God. The believer may never see how things will work out, but when he looks at God there will come into his heart a certain quietness and confidence, and in this is his strength. In some way, God will always glorify Himself. There will be final victory.

Isaiah is preaching to these people about God, arguing as if

God were revealing Himself over and over to them. What the prophet stresses in the first eight verses of chapter 45 is the sovereignty of God. God brought in a man who did not know Him but who was to do what God wanted done.

> Thus saith the Lord to his anointed, to Cyrus, whose right hand I have holden, to subdue nations before him; and I will loose the loins of kings, to open before him the two leaved gates; and the gates shall not be shut; I will go before thee, and make the crooked places straight: I will break in pieces the gates of brass, and cut in sunder the bars of iron: and I will give thee the treasures of darkness, and hidden riches of secret places, that thou mayest know that I, the Lord, which call thee by thy name, am the God of Israel (Isa. 45:1-3).

The people of Israel heard Isaiah preach in this fashion and were given to understand that God had raised this pagan king up to prosper. He would let Cyrus work out His will, thereby benefiting Israel and Judah.

> That they may know from the rising of the sun, and from the west, that there is none beside me. I am the Lord, and there is none else. I form the light, and create darkness: I make peace, and create evil: I the Lord do all these things (Isa. 45:6,7).

Let us bear in mind that God created evil as the result of sin. Here He bluntly proclaims through His prophet: "When good occurs I do it, and when evil happens I am responsible for letting it happen." In the case of Judas, for instance, many people have wondered if Judas was compelled to do what he did, because God used him for that purpose. Some wonder if Jesus of Nazareth would have gone to the cross if Judas had not betrayed him. It is best to remember that each soul is responsible for his own actions (Ezek. 18). God is able to overrule in such a way that He can turn around what people intend to do wrong and advance what He wants to have done. When a baby sickens and dies, it does not mean God is doing something in an arbitrary fashion, but we should be assured that Almighty God has in hand everything that happens anywhere, any time.

I do not know any way in which we can satisfy the human heart about the question of why God allows evil in the world. I am not that wise, and the Scriptures do not specifically illumine our thinking about this, but Isaiah 45:7 comes as close as any in Scripture to explaining to us that God allows evil because He can use the evil for bringing good to pass in His overall plan.

> Drop down, ye heavens, from above, and let the skies pour down righteousness: let the earth open, and let them bring forth salvation, and let righteousness spring up together; I the Lord have created it (Isa. 45:8).

He may create darkness, but heaven is light. He may create evil, but Christ Jesus brings peace. While they are in this world, believers shall have tribulation, but they can be of good cheer: the Lord Jesus Christ overcame the world. In Him the believer can look forward to perfect peace.

In Isaiah 45:1-8 it is revealed that God takes the responsibility for everything that happens and declares that He works all things together for good. With this in mind, we can understand why the impudent person is warned against complaining against God. Paul, in Romans 9, sounds the same warning. Elsewhere Isaiah quotes God as saying, "To whom then will ye liken me?" The answer is that we cannot liken Him to anybody, and here woe is pronounced upon that man who impudently challenges God's motives (Isa. 45:9,10). God is not bound to explain Himself, and this is something to remember.

> Verily thou art a God that hidest thyself, O God of Israel, the Saviour (Isa. 45:15).

In writing about this, Paul says the ways of God are past finding out. When a human being tries to understand the hand of God in his affairs, he can be completely baffled. But the revelation goes further: the purposes of God were never obscured.

> But Israel shall be saved in the Lord with an everlasting salvation: ye shall not be ashamed nor confounded world without end (Isa. 45:17).

We should let that word ring out in our souls. We can absolutely trust Him. Isaiah reveals further:

> I have not spoken in secret, in a dark place of the earth: I said not unto the seed of Jacob, Seek ye me in vain: I the Lord speak righteousness, I declare things that are right. Assemble your-

> selves and come; draw near together, ye that are escaped of the
> nations: they have no knowledge that set up the wood of their
> graven image, and pray unto a god that cannot save (Isa.
> 45:19,20).

This refers to the remnant, those who did not go along with the crowd. They were wise in turning away from people who had a religion that did nothing for them. We cannot know what God will do by looking at events, but God can tell what He will do in His Word. Looking into the face of Jesus Christ, we can get a promise that will absolutely be carried out.

> Look unto me, and be ye saved, all the ends of the earth: for I am
> God, and there is none else. I have sworn by myself, the word is
> gone out of my mouth in righteousness, and shall not return,
> That unto me every knee shall bow, every tongue shall swear
> (Isaiah 45:22,23).

This was repeated by Paul in his Epistle to the Philippians as referring to the Lord Jesus Christ. God has "given him a name which is above every name: that at the name of Jesus every knee should bow, of things in heaven, and things in earth, and things under the earth; and that every tongue should confess that Jesus Christ is Lord, to the glory of God the Father" (Phil. 2:9-11).

> Surely, shall one say, in the Lord have I righteousness and
> strength: even to him shall men come; and all that are incensed
> against him shall be ashamed. In the Lord shall all the seed of
> Israel be justified, and shall glory (Isa. 45:24,25).

Thus did Isaiah proclaim the triumphant message to the people. This chapter began by emphasizing the sovereignty of God, making the bold claim that God is on the throne, overruling all things. Isaiah plainly preached that everything happens under the command of God. Some things will be good and some things will be bad, but God will overrule all and bring His will to pass. The "good" and the "bad" are relative terms; some things are obviously good for us, and some things seem to be bad for us, but in the hand of Almighty God we remember Romans 8:28: "All things work together for good to them that love God, to them who are the called according to his purpose."

After God has made this great claim that He is over all,

there is the warning that man should not be impudent. Although God is in charge of all things, one could study the course of history in vain to try and find the mind of God. The ways of God are past finding out, but we can read His Word. We can look into the face of Jesus Christ, and when we do, we will get a promise that God will save us. "Look unto me all ye ends of the earth and be ye saved." Because God does intend to give salvation to all who look to Him, we should have full confidence in Him. He is able to perform that which He has promised.

Chapter 33

GOD WILL ACCOMPLISH HIS PLAN

God is entitled to utmost consideration in the hearts and minds of human beings, and anyone who gives consideration to any other than God has an idol. What we mean by an idol is something being worshiped in the place of God. Living in this world presents problems, and one can live in such a way as to get hurt, to lose out, and to be defeated. On the other hand, one can live in such a way as to be blessed, to have a harvest both fruitful and helpful. A person is naturally going to seek help; he will try in some way to arrange to make sure he wins the victory. The particular principle in which you put your trust, the particular idea that you follow with confidence, is your god. In trying to help the people get the picture clearly before them, Isaiah brings out the difference between the true God and all other kinds of religious belief.

He begins chapter 46 by stressing the fact that idols have to be carried:

> Bel boweth down, Nebo stoopeth, their idols were upon the beasts, and upon the cattle: your carriages were heavy loaden; they are a burden to the weary beast (Isa. 46:1).

That is the kind of religion that has to be pushed to make it any good; the moment you stop pushing it, nothing happens.

> Hearken unto me, O house of Jacob, and all the remnant of the house of Israel, which are borne by me from the belly, which are carried from the womb: and even to your old age I am he; and even to hoar hairs will I carry you: I have made, and I will bear; even I will carry, and will deliver you (Isa. 46:3,4).

That is the true religion. To what kind of religion are you entrusting yourself? Are you trusting your church attendance for your soul's salvation? Then you had best attend regularly to say the least, because if you ever quit, you lose your soul. Do you think your religion is just what you give to the poor? Then if you stop giving to the poor, you will not have any — is that it? Is your religion just what you do for people? Suppose some day you become paralyzed and cannot be kind to people, then what? Will you lose your religion? That is the way Isaiah would talk to you. Mind you, I have mentioned only good things because when those pagan people worshiped their idols, they meant only good things.

By way of contrast, do you know enough about the Lord Jesus Christ to know that He will carry you? Have you learned that you can cast your burden on the Lord because He cares for you? And do you really know that "underneath are the everlasting arms"? (Deut. 33:27). That is what Isaiah is bringing out.

> To whom will ye liken me, and make me equal, and compare me, that we may be like? They lavish gold out of the bag, and weigh silver in the balance, and hire a goldsmith; and he maketh it a god: they fall down, yea, they worship. They bear him upon the shoulder, they carry him, and set him in his place, and he standeth; from his place shall he not remove: yea, one shall cry unto him, yet can he not answer, nor save him out of his trouble. Remember this, and show yourselves men: bring it again to mind, O ye transgressors (Isa. 46:5-8).

Isaiah urges them to be mature, to act grown up, and to use good sense.

Isaiah 46:9-13 presents a reaffirmation of the sovereignty of God.

> Remember the former things of old: for I am God, and there is none else; I am God, and there is none like me. . . . My counsel shall stand, and I will do all my pleasure. . . . I bring near my righteousness; it shall not be far off, and my salvation shall not tarry: and I will place salvation in Zion for Israel my glory (Isa. 46:9-13).

It makes good sense to put your trust in God: He will carry you.

In Isaiah 47 a message is revealed to Babylon, the nation that had enslaved God's people because they had failed to do what God wanted them to do. But God had His eye on His people.

> Come down, and sit in the dust, O virgin daughter of Babylon, sit on the ground: there is no throne, O daughter of the Chaldeans: for thou shalt no more be called tender and delicate. Take the millstones, and grind meal: uncover thy locks, make bare the leg, uncover the thigh, pass over the rivers. Thy nakedness shall be uncovered, yea, thy shame shall be seen: I will take vengeance, and I will not meet thee as a man (Isa. 47:1-3).

The prophet is warning them they will be put into slavery. Their fine clothes will be stripped off them and they will have to wear working clothes. Remember when those people invaded the land they hurt God's people; they destroyed the city. God allowed them to do that because it served His purpose; but now He is going to settle with them.

Isaiah continues:

> As for our Redeemer, the Lord of Hosts is his name, the Holy One of Israel. Sit thou silent, and get thee into darkness, O daughter of the Chaldeans: for thou shalt no more be called, The lady of kingdoms. I was wroth with my people, I have polluted mine inheritance, and given them into thine hand: thou didst show them no mercy; upon the ancient hast thou very heavily laid thy yoke (Isa. 47:4-6).

God would not hold them responsible because they did not know the promises to Abraham, but He would hold them responsible as human beings, and that is true all through the Bible, right down to this present day. There are many things God will overlook, but unkindness to the point of cruelty in its rougher form God will not tolerate. Here are expressions of conceit back in those days:

> And thou saidst, I shall be a lady forever: so that thou didst not lay these things to thy heart, neither didst remember the latter end of it (Isa. 47:7).

They did everything in a proud, vain fashion.

> Therefore hear now this, thou that art given to pleasures, that dwellest carelessly, that sayest in thine heart, I am, and none else beside me; I shall not sit as a widow, neither shall I know the loss of children: but these two things shall come to thee in a moment in one day, the loss of children, and widowhood: they shall come upon thee in their perfection for the multitude of thy sorceries, and for the great abundance of thine enchantments (Isa. 47:8,9).

In their spiritual experience the people did not seek God.

They suffered from egotistic pride, and God was to judge them.

> Therefore shall evil come upon thee; thou shalt not know from whence it riseth: and mischief shall fall upon thee; thou shalt not be able to put it off: and desolation shall come upon thee suddenly, which thou shalt not know (Isa. 47:11).

Then God says in a challenging way:

> Stand now with thine enchantments, and with the multitude of thy sorceries, wherein thou hast laboured from thy youth; if so be thou shalt be able to profit, if so be thou mayest prevail (Isa. 47:12).

See if your false religion will do you any good now is the challenge Isaiah expresses in the concluding verses in that chapter:

> Thou art wearied in the multitude of thy counsels. Let now the astrologers, the stargazers, the monthly prognosticators, stand up, and save thee from these things that shall come upon thee. Behold, they shall be as stubble; the fire shall burn them; they shall not deliver themselves from the power of the flame: there shall not be a coal to warm at, nor fire to sit before it. Thus shall they be unto thee with whom thou hast laboured, even thy merchants, from thy youth: they shall wander every one to his quarter; none shall save thee (Isa. 47:13-15).

This is the word of doom that is spoken to a pagan people who, for the time being, reigned in power. They came in with their might and under God's providence they conquered the whole country. But God had them in mind and He watched them as they moved; He saw their sinfulness and was prepared to judge them.

In Isaiah 48 we shall see again that because of Israel's waywardness, God would chasten them.

> Hear ye this, O house of Jacob, which are called by the name of Israel, and are come forth out of the waters of Judah, which swear by the name of the Lord, and make mention of the God of Israel, but not in truth, nor in righteousness. For they call themselves of the holy city, and stay themselves upon the God of Israel; The Lord of hosts is his name (Isa. 48:1,2).

This is a message leveled especially at people who profess to know God but who fail to "play the game." Then Isaiah reveals the mind of God about Himself:

> I have declared the former things from the beginning; and they
> went forth out of my mouth, and I showed them; I did them
> suddenly, and they came to pass (Isa. 48:3).

God gave Israel evidence of His living reality. He predicted what He would do and then did as He predicted. God knew Israel was disposed to be sinful.

> Because I knew that thou art obstinate, and thy neck is an iron
> sinew, and thy brow brass; I have even from the beginning
> declared it to thee; before it came to pass I showed it thee: lest
> thou shouldest say, Mine idol hath done them, and my graven
> image, and my molten image, hath commanded them (Isa.
> 48:4,5).

The same thought is continued as Isaiah reveals that God knew all about their unbelief:

> For I knew that thou wouldest deal very treacherously, and wast
> called a transgressor from the womb (Isa. 48:8).

The Scripture records that is how Jacob received his name. "Jacob" means a person who will take another person's place, as in fact he took Esau's place. God reveals that He will restrain His anger for His own reason.

> For my name's sake will I defer mine anger, and for my praise
> will I refrain for thee, that I cut thee not off (Isa. 48:9).

Because of the way Israel acted, God would have been justified in cutting them off. But He had given His promise to Abraham. Remember, Moses prayed about that. God told Moses he would have to stay with the people and take them through to Canaan, otherwise people would say God started something and did not finish it. How could God be faithful to a disobedient people? Because God is holy. There was only one way He could do it: He would have to chasten them, and that is what God did in Isaiah's time.

This line of thought is continued as Isaiah reveals the Word of God:

> Hearken unto me, O Jacob and Israel, my called; I am he; I am
> the first, I also am the last. Mine hand also hath laid the founda-
> tion of the earth, and my right hand hath spanned the heavens:
> when I call unto them, they stand up together. All ye, assemble
> yourselves, and hear; which among them hath declared these
> things? The Lord hath loved him: he will do His pleasure on

Babylon, and his arm shall be on the Chaldeans (Isa. 48:12-14).

The patience of God is shown as Isaiah reveals the heart of God:

> Come ye near unto me, hear ye this; I have not spoken in secret from the beginning; from the time that it was, there am I: and now the Lord God, and his spirit, hath sent me. Thus saith the Lord, thy Redeemer, the Holy One of Israel; I am the Lord thy God which teacheth thee to profit, which leadeth thee by the way that thou shouldest go. O that thou hadst hearkened to my commandments! then had thy peace been as a river, and thy righteousness as the waves of the sea (Isa. 48:16-18).

The mind of God toward His people is this: "If you had only done what I wanted you to do; I could have done so much for you!"

We remember Jesus of Nazareth sitting outside Jerusalem upon the hilltop, weeping: "O Jerusalem, Jerusalem, thou that killest the prophets, and stonest them which are sent unto thee, how often would I have gathered thy children together, even as a hen gathereth her chickens under her wings, and ye would not!" (Matt. 23:37). God is lamenting the fact that Israel would not have had so much trouble if they had only stayed close to Him.

> Thy seed also had been as the sand, and the offspring of thy bowels like the gravel thereof; his name should not have been cut off nor destroyed from before me (Isa. 48:19).

Isaiah revealed the Word of God to the house of Jacob and has been reminding them of the suffering they have had and now he has told them the reason why. God had to bring in the Assyrians, then the Chaldeans, and afterward the Persians, because His own people were a treacherous people.

> Go ye forth of Babylon, flee ye from the Chaldeans, with a voice of singing declare ye, tell this, utter it even to the end of the earth; say ye, The Lord hath redeemed his servant Jacob (Isa. 48:20).

We should note this wonderful thought: In spite of their misery, their defeat, and their enslavement, God will redeem His people. He will destroy the enemy and now He will set His people free, and they will sing out, "The Lord hath redeemed his servant Jacob." Isaiah presents a marvelous description of redemption:

And they thirsted not when he led them through the deserts: he caused the waters to flow out of the rock for them: he clave the rock also, and the waters gushed out (Isa. 48:21).

When God saves, He refreshes and He satisfies, even in this world. Despite the desert, God will supply water for His people to drink. By way of contrast, Isaiah utters this word:

There is no peace, saith the Lord, unto the wicked (Isa. 48:22).

But there is rest and peace for His people who are redeemed. This is how God shows Himself in a dark, frustrating day of defeat among His people. They should look up into the face of God: He will work out His will on their behalf. God will, in due time, judge every evil thing, and He will keep those who put their trust in Him, because He is Almighty God.

Chapter 34

MESSIAH WILL PERFORM GOD'S WILL

In the Old Testament the Chosen One, the Anointed One, is the Messiah. There was a promise all through the Old Testament that one day God would send His chosen Servant, who would deliver His people from their enemies. In time it became more obvious that this Messiah would deliver them from their sins and would bring them into the presence of God. He would present them before God, acceptable to Him. This promise had been given to God's people, Israel.

The Jewish nation in Isaiah's time was in danger of equating their national existence with that of the ancient people of God, Israel. The Jews began to apply to themselves nationally the promises made to Israel. They interpreted these gracious promises of God to refer to this world's affairs. It is true that God had done that for a time, and when He blessed them, He gave them good crops and good health, and He spared them from famine and drought. He kept from them the insects that would have destroyed their crops and the mildew that would have destroyed their grain. In this way God favored them. Also, when God favored them, He gave them victory over their military enemies.

In understanding Israel's experience in the Old Testament here on earth, we can remember the tabernacle and the temple. The tabernacle was an outward symbol of the real truth; and the temple of God, made of wood and stone and built in the time of Solomon, was also an outward symbol of the truth — the truth being that God dwells in human hearts. This points to the meaning of verses like this in the Scriptures: "Sacrifice and offering thou didst not desire" (Ps. 40:6). Yet God had indicated He wanted them to bring sacrifices; He indicated He wanted them to bring the blood of bulls and of goats and lambs for the remission of sins. But those things were not even mentioned in the Book of Hebrews as being important. The Scripture tells us that the blood of those animals can never make a person right before God; they were symbols of the fact that one day One would die for them, One whose blood would cleanse them from sin — the Messiah.

The Jewish nation applied those promises of God to themselves nationally, as though God were interested in the geographic situation, Palestine. To them, it was as if He were interested in preserving a physical people, the sons of Abraham, who would be called the children of Israel. God used the case of Israel as a nation the way He used the tabernacle, the temple, and the sacrifices there. Christ Jesus died for us and that is the end of the animal sacrifices. We have no temple made with hands, because the church is the temple of the living God; God dwells in the hearts of His people. The words of the Old Testament fit that truth, although in those times Israel did not see it clearly. The Old Testament prophets led the people in their teaching, opening new ideas to them and preparing them for a salvation that would one day be revealed. At that time it would be seen that the great truth of God is spiritual rather than material.

Isaiah 49 reveals that the fulfillment of the promise to Israel may mean shifting the grace of God from Jacob to the Gentiles.

> Listen, O isles, unto me; and hearken, ye people, from far; The Lord hath called me from the womb; from the bowels of my mother hath he made mention of my name. And he hath made my mouth like a sharp sword; in the shadow of his hand hath he hid me, and made me a polished shaft; in his quiver hath he hid me; and said unto me, Thou art my servant, O Israel, in whom I will be glorified (Isa. 49:1-3).

I think that is figurative language by which the Messiah would say to the whole world: "God has chosen me to use me." I have no objection to taking the first two verses as referring to Israel as a nation, but I think as we look at every such promise made that way, we will see that all of the promises of God are "yea and amen" in Christ Jesus. Let us look further at verse 4:

> Then I said, I have laboured in vain, I have spent my strength for
> nought, and in vain: yet surely my judgment is with the Lord,
> and my work with my God (Isa. 49:4).

Who would say, "If Israel is the servant of God in whom God
will be glorified, then I have labored in vain"? It seems strange
that if anyone would have thought it would be the Jews who
would fulfill God's glory, then he would have labored in vain. If
the word "Israel" refers to the Jews, then you can say "I have
labored in vain. I have spent my strength for nought," because
the Jews had failed Him; Judah had failed Him.

> And now, saith the Lord that formed me from the womb to be
> his servant, to bring Jacob again to him . . . (Isa. 49:5).

One should not take this to refer only to Israel. The statement
seems to fit the Messiah very clearly. He was brought into this
world distinctly to be the Servant of His Father; and certainly
Messiah's call was to bring God's people back to Him.

> Though Israel be not gathered, yet shall I be glorious in the eyes
> of the Lord, and my God shall be my strength (Isa. 49:5).

How will this be done?

> And he said, It is a light thing that thou shouldest be my servant
> to raise up the tribes of Jacob, and to restore the preserved of
> Israel: I will also give thee for a light to the Gentiles, that thou
> mayest be my salvation unto the end of the earth (Isa. 49:6).

In these words the prophet reveals that the Messiah will save
not only the remnant, but many Gentiles also.
    God the Father is revealed as speaking to the Messiah:

> Thus saith the Lord, the Redeemer of Israel, and his Holy One,
> to him whom man despiseth, to him whom the nation abhor-
> reth, to a servant of rulers, Kings shall see and arise, princes also
> shall worship, because of the Lord that is faithful, and the Holy
> One of Israel, and he shall choose thee (Isa. 49:7).

Bringing those Jewish people back to the city of Jerusalem
would have been a relatively small thing. All men will be
called, not only the flesh descendants of Jacob, but Gentiles
as well.
    The Lord God is revealed as saying to His servant:

> Thus saith the Lord, In an acceptable time have I heard thee,
> and in a day of salvation have I helped thee: and I will preserve

thee, and give thee for a covenant of the people, to establish the
earth, to cause to inherit the desolate heritages; that thou
mayest say to the prisoners, Go forth; to them that are in
darkness, Show yourselves. They shall feed in the ways, and
their pastures shall be in all high places. They shall not hunger
nor thirst; neither shall the heat nor sun smite them: for he that
hath mercy on them shall lead them, even by the springs of
water shall he guide them (Isa. 49:8-10).

This described the blessing of the gospel. If the Jews, those
children of Israel who were the flesh descendants of Israel,
should fail to respond to the gospel, God would raise up His
own people from among the Gentiles.

John the Baptist told the Jews that if they would not turn to
the Lord Jesus Christ, "God is able of these stones to raise up
children unto Abraham" (Matt. 3:9). This is a remarkable truth:
When God makes certain promises that He will glorify the
name of the Lord Jesus Christ, He does not tie His promises up
with any individual person or group or place on earth. I am
reminded of the words spoken to Esther by Mordecai, that if
she did not go forward to serve God, help would come to the
people of God from another quarter. God has in mind to give to
the Lord Jesus Christ saved souls. The call went out to the Jews
first; if they would not come, God would give His Son saved
souls by going to the Gentiles.

There is a parable in the Book of Luke that tells this story: A
certain man made a marriage feast for his son and when it was
ready, word was sent to all who should have been bidden,
those to whom one would expect the invitation to go. But they
offered various excuses. One said he had bought a piece of land
and needed to check up on it; another said he had bought
several oxen and it was necessary to complete the deal; still
another said he had married a wife and was not free to come.
We may smile at these feeble excuses, but doesn't this come
close to home? God wants all people to realize that He is most
important and that His blessing is more important than anything else.

The Bible tells us that when the servants reported these
excuses to the Lord of that feast, he told them, in effect, to go
out and invite others to come. They were to invite persons who
ordinarily would not have been invited. And when the servants
returned, they said there was still room. The master of the feast

then said, "Go out into the highways and hedges, and compel them to come in, that my house may be filled" (Luke 14:16-24). The fact that the Lord Jesus told that parable should sober each of us. God's program is not tied up with any person, with any church, or with any nation; He will never let His program be hindered by the weakness of mankind. His call goes out to all men. It comes to some people first — those whose parents and grandparents were godly. But God will then call people who otherwise would not have been called; He will bring in others who ordinarily would not even want to come. All who come will be brought in by His grace and by His mercy.

I think back on my own experience and consider how God reached out and took me, a person who in himself had no disposition to believe. He gave me a faith that is precious, that I might share it with others. God will have the name of the Lord Jesus Christ honored, and if I should not honor Him, He will call another person in my place to honor Him.

Isaiah revealed the thought of a witness who had not succeeded in bringing Israel to God:

> Though Israel be not gathered, yet shall I be glorious in the eyes of the Lord, and my God shall be my strength (Isa. 49:5).

There is a gracious description of the promises of the gospel to the Gentiles who will be called to God through the Messiah:

> They shall not hunger nor thirst; neither shall the heat nor sun smite them: for he that hath mercy on them shall lead them, even by the springs of water shall he guide them. . . . Sing, O heavens; and be joyful, O earth; and break forth into singing, O mountains: for the Lord hath comforted his people, and will have mercy upon his afflicted. But Zion said, The Lord hath forsaken me, and my Lord hath forgotten me (Isa. 49:10, 13,14).

It is always important to remember God has not identified Himself with any group. If the people who have the opportunity to come to God do not take it, God will bring others in, and they will be His people. But this is not meant to imply that God will ever forsake His own.

> Can a woman forget her sucking child, that she should not have

compassion on the son of her womb? yea, they may forget, yet
will I not forget thee (Isa. 49:15).

God will be faithful to His people, who need not be identified by any physical name or biological inheritance. His
people will be those who put their trust in Him and who
respond to Him when He calls.

Behold, I have graven thee upon the palms of my hands; thy
walls are continually before me (Isa. 49:16).

When God gave His promises to Jerusalem, He was not
identifying any particular families in that place. He was revealing this idea of His people who, in response to His call, would
glorify the name of His Son, the Lord Jesus Christ, who would
give His life for them. They were the ones to whom the
promise was made, promises that are being fulfilled even to
this day among those who believe in Him.

God continues to reveal promises all through chapter 49.

The children which thou shalt have, after thou hast lost the
other, shall say again in thine ears, The place is too strait for me:
give place to me that I may dwell (Isa. 49:20).

There will be those who had the opportunity, and they will love
it, and in themselves they will cherish it. Here Isaiah is telling
them and warning them of the things that will happen. Paul
interpreted this truth in his preaching, "saying none other
things than those which the prophets and Moses did say should
come" (Acts 26:22) when he testified of this salvation.

Then shalt thou say in thine heart, Who hath begotten me these,
seeing I have lost my children, and am desolate, a captive, and
removing to and fro? and who hath brought up these? Behold, I
was left alone; these, where had they been? Thus saith the Lord
God, Behold, I will lift up mine hand to the Gentiles, and set up
my standard to the people: and they shall bring thy sons in their
arms, and thy daughters shall be carried upon their shoulders
(Isa. 49:21,22).

God will call in the Gentiles when His own people refuse to
obey Him. In this chapter we have this amazing insight into
spiritual truths set out in Old Testament days, when the
prophet was warning the children of Israel that God was not
tied up with the physical fortunes of any biological group of

people, such as the national group of people called Israel, or the Jews. God made a certain promise to Abraham, a promise that He would carry out to those who believed like Abraham: and His promise is not conditional on the flesh. The grace of God is for those who respond to Him and believe in Him. And that is where you and I come in: we are among those people. Back in the Old Testament days when my forefathers were worshiping trees and spirits in rocks and streams, worshiping the sun, moon, and stars, anyone could have wondered how in the world a descendant of such people would ever come to know God. But Isaiah revealed the Word of God:

Behold, I will lift up mine hand to the Gentiles . . . (Isa. 49:22).

Because there would be people who had the opportunity to believe and then let it go unheeded, God planned to reach out and bring in someone like myself and to show the truth to him. This would complete the company and fulfill His plan in seeing to it that the marriage feast has the full quota of those who belong to Him.

It is amazing that all of this was set out in the Old Testament in this chapter, which ends by saying:

All flesh shall know that I the Lord am thy Saviour and thy Redeemer, the mighty One of Jacob (Isa. 49:26).

The world is going to know that Almighty God, the Father of our Lord Jesus Christ, is really the Savior of mankind.

Chapter 35

GOD WILL VINDICATE HIS PEOPLE

In Isaiah's time there were people who believed the promises of God, but, being members of the Jewish nation, they
could not understand how God's promises to keep His people
would be fulfilled when the nation of Israel was being destroyed. God made certain promises to Israel — that is, to
Jacob — that seemed to apply to the twelve tribes of Israel,
promises that would include all the descendants of Israel. But
now the ten northern tribes had been carried away captive.
They had not been blotted out, but they had lost their political
identity and were no longer considered Israel, having been
absorbed into other nations.

What about the promises of God? Did this mean God's
program was not at an end because these people failed Him?
The prophets preached to show the people that was not true.
When God made His promise to Abraham and said, "In thy
seed shall the nations of the earth be blessed," that seed would
not be biological; they would be the spiritual progeny. Those
who believe in God in the way Abraham believed in God are
the children of Abraham. The Gentiles who believe in the Lord
Jesus Christ understand that. They share in the promises to
Abraham and are counted the children of Abraham, just as they
are counted children of God. God is no respecter of persons.
Peter said to Cornelius:

> But in every nation he that feareth him, and worketh righteous-
> ness, is accepted with him (Acts 10:35).

These people who are so accepted belong in the group to whom
the promise was made.

> And in thy seed shall all the nations of the earth be blessed (Gen.
> 22:18).

But the seed would not be limited to the flesh descendants because, as the Bible is careful to point out, Abraham had children in the flesh who were not even included in the group. Ishmael was a child of Abraham, but he was not included in the people of Israel. Even so far as Israel is concerned, Paul said in the Book of Romans:

> For they are not all Israel, which are of Israel (Rom. 9:6).

They do not belong in the Israel of promise; and how well we know that in our day and time.

Often the children of Christian parents may be very neglectful of their opportunities. What is God going to do? Is He then going to let the whole church suffer because some children have been disobedient? We find over and over again that God will call to Himself people with no background at all in spiritual matters and will raise them for His use. The children of godly parents are greatly favored, because God can work with them from their childhood on, but we need to keep in mind that the promises of God are not limited by the frailties of mankind; a human being can actually disqualify himself from participation in the blessing of God simply by failure to respond and obey.

This seems to be the general truth of the gospel as pictured here in chapter 50. The first three verses seem to imply that God's people may wonder why they have been chastened, defeated in battle. Why have the people been carried away captive if they are the people of God?

> Thus saith the Lord, Where is the bill of your mother's divorcement, whom I have put away? or which of my creditors is it to whom I have sold you? Behold, for your iniquities have ye sold yourselves, and for your transgressions is your mother put away. Wherefore, when I came, was there no man? when I called, was there none to answer? Is my hand shortened at all, that it cannot redeem? or have I no power to deliver? behold, at my rebuke I dry up the sea, I make the rivers a wilderness: their fish stinketh, because there is no water, and dieth for thirst. I clothe the heavens with blackness, and I make sackcloth their covering (Isa. 50:1-3).

God is saying, "I am Almighty God. Do you think that I could not have done something about your distress? If you had called on me, wouldn't I have helped you?"

> The Lord God hath given me the tongue of the learned, that I should know how to speak a word in season to him that is weary: he wakeneth morning by morning, he wakeneth mine ear to hear as the learned. The Lord God hath opened mine ear, and I was not rebellious, neither turned away back. I gave my back to the smiters, and my cheeks to them that plucked off the hair: I hid not my face from shame and spitting. For the Lord God will help me; therefore shall I not be confounded: therefore have I set my face like a flint, and I know that I shall not be ashamed. . . . Behold, the Lord God will help me; who is he that shall condemn me? lo, they all shall wax old as a garment; the moth shall eat them up (Isa. 50:4-7,9).

The point in the discussion here, the basic trust and confidence of the Messiah despite His suffering, is summed up in these words: "The Lord God will help me." I believe the first verses in chapter 50 deal with the question Has God unrighteously abandoned His people? Or did He let His people suffer because He could not help them? The answer is "No, they suffered because of their sins." Verses 4 to 11 can be taken as referring to the Messiah Himself, who describes His own suffering. Christ was allowed to suffer because He identified Himself with the people of God to bring them back to God; but God would help Him.

In chapters 51 and 52 the call is to God's people to hope, for God will save His people in spite of the experiences they have had.

> Hearken to me, ye that follow after righteousness, ye that seek the Lord: look unto the rock whence ye are hewn, and to the hole of the pit whence ye are digged. Look unto Abraham your father, and unto Sarah that bare you: for I called him alone, and blessed him, and increased him. For the Lord shall comfort Zion: he will comfort all her waste places; and he will make her wilderness like Eden, and her desert like the garden of the Lord; joy and gladness shall be found therein, thanksgiving, and the voice of melody (Isa. 51:1-3).

When God called His people to comfort them, He said, "Think back. Consider what I have done." I think of myself. For generation after generation my forefathers lived in darkness. But God called some ahead of me, even as He called me and brought me to Himself. This is what He says to these people: "If you will just think how God has helped you, it will encourage you." In the words of verse 3, "He will comfort all her waste places." This is spoken to a people who have been ruined. If you who are reading these words are sensitive to spiritual matters, you must many times have a heavy heart when you see among church people you know, and in the churches, evidence of widespread disobedience and neglect. There is widespread worldliness, and in many ways overt sin is being commonly practiced. It is our privilege, on the basis of the Scripture we are studying here, to lift up our faces and to look into the face of God. Believers can lay hold of His promises and know that God will bring to Himself those who will glorify His name.

> My righteousness is near; my salvation is gone forth, and mine arms shall judge the people; the isles shall wait upon me, and on mine arm shall they trust. Lift up your eyes to the heavens, and look upon the earth beneath: for the heavens shall vanish away like smoke, and the earth shall wax old like a garment, and they that dwell therein shall die in like manner: but my salvation shall be forever, and my righteousness shall not be abolished. Hearken unto me, ye that know righteousness, the people in whose heart is my law; fear ye not the reproach of men, neither be ye afraid of their revilings. . . . Awake, awake, put on strength, O arm of the Lord; awake, as in the ancient days, in the generations of old. Art thou not it that hath cut Rahab, and wounded the dragon (Isa. 51:5-7,9)?

These are all calls to God's people to arouse themselves, to open their hearts to God, and to lay hold of His promises.

Isaiah then leads on to the thought that the chastening will actually be taken away.

> Thus saith thy Lord the Lord, and thy God that pleadeth the cause of his people, Behold, I have taken out of thine hand the cup of trembling, even the dregs of the cup of my fury; thou shalt no more drink it again: but I will put it into the hand of them that afflict thee; which have said to thy soul, Bow down, that we may go over: and thou hast laid thy body as the ground, and as the street, to them that went over (Isa. 51:22,23).

He will let them suffer the consequences of their sinfulness, but the time will come when He will redeem and deliver them. He will take the chastening and put it on those who have done His people harm.

Isaiah follows the same thought in chapter 52.

> Awake, awake; put on thy strength, O Zion; put on thy beautiful
> garments, O Jerusalem, the holy city: for henceforth there shall
> no more come into thee the uncircumcised and the unclean (Isa.
> 52:1).

This is the repeated call to His people from the Lord. They
should believe the promises and rejoice in the eternal purpose
of God, putting their trust in Him. Should there be any who
have a feeling of unworthiness, unfruitfulness, and emptiness,
the message is this: "Lift up your eyes. Carry such thoughts as
this in your mind: since Christ Jesus has died for you, your sins
will be forgiven, and you will be spared judgment. Inasmuch as
He has been raised from the dead, you will also be lifted up into
the presence of God. Since the Lord Jesus Christ has poured
out His Holy Spirit into your heart, you can have the presence
of God in you. As surely as you are conscious of the presence of
God, the load will be lifted and you will be strengthened. This
is your hope; this is your heritage. Claim it for yourself."
Something like this seems to be the revelation in this portion of
Scripture.

If someone should say to you, "You are just like a tree in the
wintertime. There is not a leaf on you," and you could say about
yourself, "My daily life is like a barren stick," this passage of
Scripture would teach you to not let your eyes remain focused
on yourself. You should focus your eyes on God and believe His
promises.

The prophet continues:

> For thus saith the Lord God, My people went down aforetime
> into Egypt to sojourn there; and the Assyrian oppressed them
> without cause. Now therefore, what have I here, saith the Lord,
> that my people is taken away for nought? they that rule over
> them make them to howl, saith the Lord; and my name continu-
> ally every day is blasphemed. Therefore my people shall know
> my name: therefore they shall know in that day that I am he that
> doth speak: behold, it is I (Isa. 52:4-6).

God is promising that they will be delivered.

> How beautiful upon the mountains are the feet of him that
> bringeth good tidings, that publisheth peace; that bringeth good
> tidings of good, that publisheth salvation; that saith unto Zion,
> Thy God reigneth! (Isa. 52:7).

The hope of the remnant is in God. Those who have had reason to be discouraged and even to despair, because when they looked about them they saw nothing but barren emptiness, now are turned by the Word of God. The Lord's arm is not shortened that He cannot save. Suppose the remnant has had the feeling that they are not what they should be in spite of every effort. They are called to lift up their eyes and to believe the promises of God.

> Break forth into joy, sing together, ye waste places of Jerusalem: for the Lord hath comforted his people, he hath redeemed Jerusalem. . . . Depart ye, depart ye, go ye out from thence, touch no unclean thing; go ye out of the midst of her; be ye clean, that bear the vessels of the Lord. For ye shall not go out with haste, nor go by flight: for the Lord will go before you; and the God of Israel will be your rereward [rear guard, NIV] (Isa. 52:9,11,12).

All of this will be possible because God gave His Servant, His Son, to deliver them.

Chapter 36

CHRIST OUR SUBSTITUTE

As we continue our study of the prophet Isaiah, we have in mind that the Old Testament contains the messages of God through His servants to His people. There were also messages sent to unbelieving people from God, mostly to the effect that if such people would come to God, He would save them. The message was always the same: "Look unto me and be ye saved all the ends of the earth" (Isa. 45:22). Why does God have more to say to those who have become believers? Because having turned to God and started walking with Him, these people can now learn the ways of God to more blessing.

Walking with God is a matter of one's understanding. The New Testament speaks of being alienated from the life of God through the ignorance that is in man. Actually, it is knowing God that is life eternal. If a person does not know God, he cannot put his trust in Him: "How shall they believe in him of whom they have not heard?" (Rom. 10:14). There is this great general principle for all believers to recognize: If they have started walking with the Lord and putting their trust in Him, it is very important for them to study His Word to find out more of what is available, that they might find out more of the resources of the grace of God on their behalf. We learned earlier that there were messages in this book to unbelieving people. Usually the messages were short, with the theme much the same: All men are in danger of destruction if they continue in their unbelief. They were invited to turn to God and be saved.

Now in Israel's case the story is much more profound, more elaborate. They were being taught how they could be blessed more and more. However, people who believe in God sometimes tend to become careless and are tempted to follow their own ideas. They are like children who, even though they have parents whom they may trust, do not obey; their experience can be one of distress and chastening. Israel's experience was something like this. God would not destroy them but He would chasten them. He would lead them through suffering experiences in which they would learn to turn to Him. In the course of Isaiah's preaching to his people, he set forth the idea that God would redeem His people. Those who sincerely sought His face would certainly be saved. He would be their Deliverer: "I will hold thee by thy right hand. . . . I will not leave thee nor forsake thee."

All the promises of God in the Old Testament days seemed to be grouped together for actual realization through the ministry of one Person whom God would send, who would bring God's will to pass. The Old Testament called Him the Messiah; the New Testament calls Him the Christ. In this portion He is called the Servant.

> Behold, my servant shall deal prudently, he shall be exalted and extolled, and be very high (Isa. 52:13).

This One who will come to do the will of God and activate it on earth will have a great name. He will be lifted up and greatly reverenced and appreciated.

> As many were astonished at thee; his visage was so marred more than any man, and his form more than the sons of men (Isa. 52:14).

This seems to be the only description in Scripture that we have of the face of Jesus Christ. There is no New Testament description of Jesus. Most artists, in painting a picture of Him, generally try to achieve a look of nobility, something of the high quality of character they assume He possessed.

> So shall he sprinkle many nations; the kings shall shut their mouths at him: for that which had not been told them shall they see; and that which they had not heard shall they consider (Isa. 52:15).

A number of years ago a high school student came to me in my church in Texas and asked me if the word "sprinkle" was ever used in the Bible. I had this passage in mind and was able to point it out to him. We find this idea later in chapter 55, verses 10 and 11.

> Who hath believed our report? and to whom is the arm of the Lord revealed? For he shall grow up before him as a tender plant, and as a root out of a dry ground: he hath no form nor comeliness; and when we shall see him, there is no beauty that we should desire him (Isa. 53:1,2).

I am not sure one should interpret this to mean that His face was ugly, but the language is such we have no reason to think He was handsome. To me a passage like this simply means He looked ordinary. In the New Testament, when strangers would come to see Him, no one identified Him by His description. When Judas planned to betray Him, he said to the soldiers, "Whomsoever I shall kiss, that same is he: hold him fast" (Matt. 26:48). Apparently there was nothing notable about His appearance.

> He is despised and rejected of men; a man of sorrows, and acquainted with grief: and we hid as it were our faces from him; he was despised, and we esteemed him not (Isa. 53:3).

It is possible that when Peter denied the Lord, he was not different from the other disciples. Jesus of Nazareth had said they would all forsake Him. We should have in mind that when the Lord Jesus was here on earth, there were no churches and there was no literature about Him. A somewhat comparable situation today would occur when a special preacher receives little acclaim. This man did wonderful things, but no one paid any particular attention to Him.

> Surely he hath borne our griefs, and carried our sorrows: yet we did esteem him stricken, smitten of God, and afflicted (Isa. 53:4).

The personal experiences He had here on earth were of such a nature that the religious people thought He must have done something wrong and offended God to have received that kind of treatment. But the truth is quite different:

> He was wounded for our transgressions, he was bruised for our iniquities: the chastisement of our peace was upon him; and with his stripes we are healed (Isa. 53:5).

We know that could refer to the experience He had when brought into Pilate's court, but we have no reason to think that was the only time he was abused in His thirty years as Jesus of Nazareth. He probably was abused many times.

> All we like sheep have gone astray; we have turned every one to his own way; and the Lord hath laid on him the iniquity of us all (Isa. 53:6).

The matter of going astray like a sheep brings to our mind what happens when sheep are sent out to pasture. They scatter and each one goes his own way hunting his food. That is what we do. The word *iniquity* means the "deviousness" of which we are all guilty; it means "crookedness."

> He was oppressed, and he was afflicted, yet he opened not his mouth: he is brought as a lamb to the slaughter, and as a sheep before her shearers is dumb, so he openeth not his mouth. He was taken from prison and from judgment: and who shall declare his generation? for he was cut off out of the land of the living: for the transgression of my people was he stricken. And he made his grave with the wicked, and with the rich in his death; because he had done no violence, neither was any deceit in his mouth. Yet it pleased the Lord to bruise him; he hath put him to grief (Isa. 53:7-10).

Now in my mind, this is one of the most amazing promises of Scripture:

> When thou shalt make his soul an offering for sin, he shall see his seed, he shall prolong his days, and the pleasure of the Lord shall prosper in his hand. He shall see of the travail of his soul, and shall be satisfied: by his knowledge shall my righteous servant justify many; for he shall bear their iniquities. Therefore will I divide him a portion with the great, and he shall divide the spoil with the strong; because he hath poured out his soul unto death: and he was numbered with the transgressors; and he bare the sin of many, and made intercession for the transgressors (Isa. 53:10-12).

This is the most famous passage in the Bible predicting the death of the Suffering Servant of God — the Messiah who would bear our sins and die in our place. Much precious blessing has been derived from this passage of Scripture. In the New Testament we read concerning this passage: "Then Philip opened his mouth, and began at the same scripture, and preached unto him Jesus (Acts 8:35).

Chapter 37

GOD'S GRACIOUS CALL

After the stirring study concerning the Messiah in chapter 53, there is revealed a message intended more directly for the people of God, the believers. Certain promises are urged upon them. These are people who do not know for sure whether to trust in God — people who have suffered and are inclined to be discouraged and fearful. They are not sure whether they can believe the promises of God or not. We will see in chapters 54 and 55 that God graciously speaks to these people about what He will do. We read:

> Sing, O barren, thou that didst not bear; break forth into singing, and cry aloud, thou that didst not travail with child: for more are the children of the desolate than the children of the married wife, saith the Lord (Isa. 54:1).

This is an unusual way of stressing the fact that those who felt themselves barren and that everything they had done was useless are to take courage and understand that by the grace of God more will be done for them than for the other people who seem to be more prosperous. At the time Isaiah was preaching, there were people who had a superficial way of doing things and were benefited by popular approval and popular consensus. They seemed to get along very well. But there were also the people who sincerely wanted to do the will of God but who had the experience of being persecuted and of being shunted to the sidelines. They had the experience of being chastened and having their hopes shattered. Isaiah now reveals that they were to receive more benefits in life than the other people who seemed to be more prosperous. This urges those whose normal experience was discouragement and depression to put their trust in the Lord. They would have more reason to be happy than those who seemed to be more fortunate.

Isaiah prophesies that those who walk humbly before God and who seem to suffer the loss of all earthly advantage would actually prosper under God and gain more benefits than they expected. Figurative, poetic language is used to assure those who feel humble and empty. This brings to mind the Beatitudes: "Blessed are the poor in spirit: for theirs is the kingdom of heaven" and "Blessed are they that mourn: for they shall be comforted" (Matt. 5:3,4). Those who walk with God will experience suffering and loss, but they should take courage: God will bless fully and richly.

> For thy Maker is thine husband; the Lord of hosts is his name; and thy Redeemer the Holy One of Israel; The God of the whole earth shall he be called. For the Lord hath called thee as a woman forsaken and grieved in spirit, and a wife of youth, when thou wast refused, saith thy God. For a small moment have I forsaken thee; but with great mercies will I gather thee (Isa. 54:5-7).

This marvelous promise was made to people who had suffered chastening. When God let His will be felt by Israel so that the whole nation suffered under His judgment, the sincere people who really wanted to do the will of God suffered with the others. It was a shattering experience. They trusted in God but things went against them. But now a word of comfort is spoken to them:

> For a small moment have I forsaken thee; but with great mercies will I gather thee. In a little wrath I hid my face from thee for a moment; but with everlasting kindness will I have mercy on thee, saith the Lord thy Redeemer (Isa. 54:7,8).

The enemy came in and Jerusalem was destroyed. The temple was burned.

The expression "for a small moment" is used several different times in Scripture. In 2 Corinthians 4:17 Paul speaks of this small moment: "For our light affliction, which is but for a moment, worketh for us a far more exceeding and eternal weight of glory."

We read in the record of Scripture what Paul's "light affliction" was: he was stoned and left for dead; he was falsely accused and imprisoned; he was beaten and shipwrecked. But he summed it up when he called it "our light affliction, which is but for a moment." Thirty or forty years are like nothing, compared to eternity. After affliction is over, and as we look back, it seems like a small time; however, when we are going through it, we may remember the psalmist who repeatedly said, "O Lord, how long?" (Pss. 6:3; 74:10; 90:13). All the suffering these people knew was to be counted as just a little thing, for the blessing that He would bestow upon them would be great by comparison.

> For this is as the waters of Noah unto me: for as I have sworn that the waters of Noah should no more go over the earth; so have I sworn that I would not be wroth with thee, nor rebuke thee (Isa. 54:9).

Notice how Isaiah refers to the oath God made after the flood, that the world would never again be destroyed by water. That same God said about those who come to Him: "I will never leave thee nor forsake thee" (Heb. 13:5; cf. Deut. 31:6,8; Josh. 1:5).

> For the mountains shall depart, and the hills be removed; but my kindness shall not depart from thee, neither shall the covenant of my peace be removed, saith the Lord that hath mercy on thee (Isa. 54:10).

The New Testament records that the Lord Jesus said, "Heaven and earth shall pass away: but my words shall not pass away" (Luke 21:33). The promises of God will be kept, and this is what the prophet is telling these people.

> O thou afflicted, tossed with tempest, and not comforted, behold, I will lay thy stones with fair colours, and lay thy foundations with sapphires. And I will make thy windows of agates, and thy gates of carbuncles, and all thy borders of pleasant stones. And all thy children shall be taught of the Lord; and great shall be the peace of thy children. In righteousness shalt thou be established: thou shalt be far from oppression; for thou shalt not fear: and from terror; for it shall not come near thee (Isa. 54:11-14).

Isaiah then reveals one of the most wonderful promises in the Bible:

> No weapon that is formed against thee shall prosper; and every tongue that shall rise against thee in judgment thou shalt condemn. This is the heritage of the servants of the Lord, and their righteousness is of me, saith the Lord (Isa. 54:17).

That is a promise that Almighty God will keep forever.

This brings to mind that Job said, "Thou he slay me, yet will I trust him" (Job 13:15), and this is the kind of faith all of God's people must have. This entire chapter is intended to bring confidence and comfort to people who have suffered persecution and loss. God allowed them to have trouble, but now He speaks to them in this gracious way. Any one of these verses of Scripture may be something a believer needs in a particular personal experience. It may be something entirely different from anything else he may have ever heard. If the time should come that any believer feels he is being ill-used, he should commit himself to the Lord; He will defend him.

David suffered the humiliating experience of fleeing from his own son Absalom, who was trying to take the throne away from him and trying to kill him. One of Saul's sympathizers, Shimei, ran along on the top of the hill above the canyon where David was walking. He shouted curses on David, rolling rocks down on him. One of David's soldiers wanted to go up and silence Shimei, but David said, "So let him curse, because the Lord hath said unto him, Curse David" (2 Sam. 16:10). Many times I have thought about that. We do not need to judge; we can leave that to God. Should any believer at any time be unjustly accused or suffer at the hands of his fellowman, this is the verse for him. It is my verse that I share with you; it has provided for me a floor to walk on, a couch to rest on. There can be no greater assurance than that found in Isaiah 54:17. The Lord Jesus said to His disciples: "Nothing shall by any means hurt you" (Luke 10:19). This is the marvelous promise that God gives to His people who put their trust in Him. "This is the heritage of the servants of the Lord, and their righteousness is of me, saith the Lord." God says, "I will take care of you."

Chapter 38

GOD'S GRACE IS FREE

Isaiah points out in his prophecy that God's people were disobedient to the point where it was necessary for God not only to chastise them, but actually to bring such judgment to bear upon them that the whole nation would be carried away captive. Thus, a number of those who had counted themselves as being among God's people were repudiated and destroyed. After all of the people had been carried away captive, the opportunity was given to those who really believed to return. It was a natural situation: after the people had been seventy years in the new land, those who had no special interest in the things of God probably stayed in Babylon where they had made new friends and new connections, but those who believed in God came back to Judah to rebuild their country and to live a life of believing in God.

These people are spoken of as the remnant. They represent a minority of all the people. Today also, among those who have heard the name of God and call themselves by His name, a great many do not in their hearts really trust in God. They claim God's promises but they do not seek His face nor have fellowship with Him. God deals with them in His own way. But for those who seek the face of God, who want to have His blessing, and who want to fellowship with God, God has something special. What Isaiah is stressing in chapter 55 is that the grace of God is free. The prophet writes thus:

> Ho, every one that thirsteth, come ye to the waters, and he that hath no money; come ye, buy, and eat; yea, come, buy wine and milk without money and without price. Wherefore do ye spend

> money for that which is not bread? and your labour for that
> which satisfieth not? hearken diligently unto me, and eat ye that
> which is good, and let your soul delight itself in fatness (Isa.
> 55:1,2).

Anybody who wanted the blessing of God was to come. Apparently the only prerequisite was that such persons hunger and thirst. The prophet has in mind that everyone who thirsts comes to the waters; every hungry person comes to get food. At the same time the prophet raised this question:

> Wherefore do ye spend money for that which is not bread? and
> your labour for that which satisfieth not? hearken diligently unto
> me, and eat ye that which is good, and let your soul delight itself
> in fatness (Isa. 55:2).

Why worry and burden yourself and put yourself under strain and exertion for that which does not satisfy the soul? This is the call that goes out. All who want the blessing of God may come. This is something that will strengthen them.

Here we can see the steps that are outlined for coming to the Lord:

> Incline your ear, and come unto me: hear, and your soul shall
> live; and I will make an everlasting covenant with you, even the
> sure mercies of David (Isa. 55:3).

"Incline your ear" means "listen." When you listen, you are putting your mind to it; noises may attract your attention for a moment, but if they are not significant, you shut them out as soon as you can. You listen for particular sounds: the things you want to hear. The same is true of conversation. There are certain persons you like to hear from and for those persons you incline your ears. God is saying, "Incline your ear; bend over to listen to me."

The second step is "and come unto me." You come a little closer to Him. The third step is "hear." Now you actually pay attention to that which is said. The fourth step is "and your soul shall live." Finally, God says, "I will make an everlasting covenant with you, even the sure mercies of David," which goes beyond the fact that your soul shall live. You will live in blessing. The sure mercies of David are, I believe, sketched in the next two verses:

> Behold, I have given him for a witness to the people, a leader
> and commander to the people. Behold, thou shalt call a nation
> that thou knowest not, and nations that knew not thee shall run
> unto thee because of the Lord thy God, and for the Holy One of
> Israel; for he hath glorified thee (Isa. 55:4,5).

This I believe to be a statement of the promise that had been made to David himself. God is now saying He has given David to be a leader and a commander to the people, not only the people of God but to strangers known as Gentiles. When this promise was made to David, it did not necessarily focus attention on just that one who was king of Judah, the son of Jesse. When Isaiah wrote, "I will make an everlasting covenant with you, even the sure mercies of David. Behold, I have given him for a witness to the people," he was probably referring to the son of David — the Messiah. The Lord Jesus Christ, as the son of David, naturally inherited the sure mercies of David, which God had promised David.

In His covenant with David, God had promised that one of his seed would sit on the throne forever, that his kingdom would be an everlasting one, and that all the nations should belong to it. God would do that in mercy to David. The sure mercies of David are the covenanted promises God had given to David: He would take of the seed of David and set this One up as a leader and commander to the people, and to Him the Gentiles would come. One of the most wonderful promises in the Scriptures is to be found in this chapter:

> Seek ye the Lord while he may be found, call ye upon him while
> he is near: let the wicked forsake his way, and the unrighteous
> man his thoughts: and let him return unto the Lord, and he will
> have mercy upon him; and to our God, for he will abundantly
> pardon (Isa. 55:6,7).

This is another way of extending the invitation found in verse 1 and also in verse 3. This matter of seeking the Lord while He may be found and calling upon Him while He is near makes one wonder if the Lord is not near at all times. In the ordinary course of spiritual experience, it does not work out that the believer is as open-hearted to God at one time as at another. Believers are not always alert to the things of God; especially is this true for some careless persons who may perhaps live at times for days, or even months, with no thought of God entering into their hearts. Under certain circumstances, they may have a sense that God is near. They should turn to God at that time when they feel His presence. This could be true for any of us.

Even if we do believe in God, is it not true, with the routines of life, that we do not think of God equally at all times? At times we feel nearer to God, often when we are alone. Perhaps we open our Bibles to read and we feel that we are moving into the presence of God. Maybe it is our time of prayer. That is the time to turn to Him.

"Let the wicked forsake his way." I always thought of the wicked as someone who did something extremely vicious or vulgar. A wicked person was an awful person, and in my most pessimistic moments I would not have thought of wicked people being in church. But this verse did not really open up to me until after I was in the ministry and I found out that I could even be a preacher and be wicked. To be "wicked" in this sense does not refer to such a sin as taking the family money and gambling it away. The Hebrew word translated "wicked" describes a person who has deviated, a person who has forsaken a straight road. A good translation of the Hebrew word into English would be "crooked" — something that is not straight.

Can you agree that our tendency is to deviate? Even when we get a new home and we start out having everything where it should be, is it not true that after a while the chances are that we deviate considerably? When you began a new job, do you remember how you planned to work perhaps extra hours, to arrive early and to stay late, but it did not work out that way? Have you ever had the experience of deviating from your good intentions with reference to spiritual matters? Whether you realize it or not, you are still very human, and in your human nature you easily become a little crooked; you are not quite straight about things. The Hebrew language would call you "wicked."

When a person is wicked in morals, he becomes immoral; when he is wicked in honesty he becomes dishonest. This happens any time a person deviates from the will of God. This Scripture says, Let the deviating person forsake his deviations. Let him not go that way any more. "Let the wicked forsake his way." I used to quote this passage with all the bad people in mind. But then why does it say, "Let us return unto the Lord?" Many ungodly persons have never known the Lord; they could not return to Him. One day when I was studying this passage, I suddenly found that the shoe fit on my foot. I put the other one on, and it fit, too. After I recovered from the shock of learning I was the person this was written for, I found a wonderful truth: Let the person who is deviating from what he knows he should be doing quit his deviation, and let the unrighteous person who is thinking of things that are not right in the sight of God, return to the Lord. Let him come back again to the Lord, and it will be the way it was when he received Christ as his Savior — the way it was when he took Jesus Christ as his Lord and Master. The call is "Come back and He will have mercy on you; He will abundantly pardon."

In Isaiah 55 this great truth is being set out: The grace of God is free and it is free for all who come to Him. We have to hunger and thirst but we do not need to pay. We just need to come, and if we will incline our ear, listen, and come near to the Lord, our soul will live.

God reveals more wonderful words in the latter part of the chapter:

> For my thoughts are not your thoughts, neither are your ways
> my ways, saith the Lord (Isa. 55:8).

Do you know what that means? Do you know what most of us would do if somebody was not playing fair with us, and because they were not playing fair with us, they got into trouble? We would be inclined to say they got what was coming to them. But God is not like that. When a person turns away from God, He lovingly calls that person back to Himself. God will not easily let anyone go if he has known God and put his hand in His. He has given you His word and He will keep His word.

The remaining five verses should be particularly noticed as they are so familiar; and each is meaningful:

> For as the heavens are higher than the earth, so are my ways
> higher than your ways, and my thoughts than your thoughts.
> For as the rain cometh down, and the snow from heaven, and
> returneth not thither, but watereth the earth, and maketh it
> bring forth and bud, that it may give seed to the sower, and
> bread to the eater: so shall my word be that goeth forth out of my

mouth: it shall not return unto me void, but it shall accomplish that which I please, and it shall prosper in the thing whereto I sent it. For ye shall go out with joy, and be led forth with peace: the mountains and the hills shall break forth before you into singing, and all the trees of the field shall clap their hands. Instead of the thorn shall come up the fir tree, and instead of the brier shall come up the myrtle tree: and it shall be to the Lord for a name, for an everlasting sign that shall not be cut off (Isa. 55:9-13).

Surely the sheer beauty of those words is unsurpassed.

Chapter 39

THE CALL TO REPENTANCE AND FAITH

In this portion of Isaiah's prophecy there is a line of truth that was emphasized by John the Baptist. Bear in mind that John the Baptist preached to the people of his day, "Repent and believe, for the kingdom of heaven is at hand." Here Isaiah preaches:

> Thus saith the Lord, Keep ye judgment, and do justice: for my salvation is near to come, and my righteousness to be revealed. Blessed is the man that doeth this, and the son of man that layeth hold on it; that keepeth the sabbath from polluting it, and keepeth his hand from doing any evil (Isa. 56:1,2).

The prophet seems to be using "Sabbath keeping" as an illustration of obeying the law, and "keeping his hand from doing any evil" as an indication that he was doing that which is righteous in the sight of God.

Isaiah continues to amplify his message:

> Neither let the son of the stranger, that hath joined himself to the Lord, speak, saying, The Lord hath utterly separated me from his people: neither let the eunuch say, Behold, I am a dry tree (Isa. 56:3).

When strangers came in among them, the people of Israel would not accept them; thus, it was easy for strangers to feel shut out. The prophet urged Israel not to let the son of the stranger, the person who feels like a stepchild, if he has joined himself to the Lord, have reason to say:

> The Lord hath utterly separated me from his people: neither let the eunuch say, Behold, I am a dry tree. For thus saith the Lord unto the eunuchs that keep my sabbaths, and choose the things that please me, and take hold of my covenant; even unto them will I give in mine house and within my walls a place and a name

219

> better than of sons and of daughters: I will give them an everlasting name, that shall not be cut off. Also the sons of the stranger, that join themselves to the Lord, to serve him, and to love the name of the Lord, to be his servants, every one that keepeth the sabbath from polluting it, and taketh hold of my covenant; even them will I bring to my holy mountain, and make them joyful in my house of prayer: their burnt offerings and their sacrifices shall be accepted upon mine altar; for mine house shall be called a house of prayer for all people (Isa. 56:3-7).

This is an amazing promise. The Lord is saying that all people should judge themselves, put their trust in Him, and expect to be received and to be blessed.

Isaiah then specifically points out that if there should be some person feeling in himself a sense of despair, thinking there will never be anything good for himself, the Lord is saying that if he has put his trust in God, he should never feel defeated. The great call of God in the time of Isaiah was for all the children of Israel to come to God. Many had turned away, but a remnant came — in addition to Jews, others who were not Jews. In applying that to our day, we could think of something like this: A family that has been established in the home as believers in Christ had grandparents who believed in God, and parents who brought them up in the nurture and admonition of the Lord, but the children have become wayward, and the grandchildren have also become wayward. The call of God is that they should come back and turn to Him. Now in any such family there could be some who would actually come back to God. God would bless them, but He would also call others who do not have believing parents, who had never been baptized in infancy nor dedicated to God as children; and these also He will bless.

The concluding verses in chapter 56 are rather stern words to indicate that there is to be a general falling away. People who should know Him would not be faithful to Him.

> All ye beasts of the field, come to devour, yea, all ye beasts in the forest. His watchmen are blind: they are all ignorant, they are all dumb dogs, they cannot bark; sleeping, lying down, loving to slumber (Isa. 56:9,10).

The picture here is one of a people in danger of losing something through carelessness. That actually does occur among the people of God. As distressing as it is, we find people neglecting spiritual matters for their own selfish pleasure and profit.

> Come ye, say they, I will fetch wine, and we will fill ourselves with strong drink; and tomorrow shall be as this day, and much more abundant (Isa. 56:12).

These people seem to be thinking, "Everything is just fine; we are successful in business and we are going to have more days like this all the time." It is common to know people whose interest is personal, who are scheming how to get things for themselves. Isaiah would say this is the time for us to realize it is as though the watchdogs were all asleep. The gate has been left open and the enemy can come and go at will. But God sees all those things and will not pass them by.

Chapter 40

WARNING TO THE UNREPENTANT

It is important to keep in mind that in the Book of Isaiah we have messages that have been preached by a prophet of Israel. Generally speaking, I think there is a notion that preachers are people who talk to anybody who will listen to them about those things they feel are important. So people listen, or don't listen, as they please. That may be the way it works out with a great many people, but that is not really the idea. The same may be true, I should say, with trying to understand the prophet. I would not be surprised if there are people who imagine that the prophets were just men who had some bright idea about life and who had a burden on their hearts to tell people, and so they preached. I suspect some think that all the prophets did was to complain about how the people were doing and how they should do better. If you wanted to listen you could, if you didn't want to listen, you didn't. And because their ideas were considered good, they were called prophets.

But that is not quite the way it was. Before there were any prophets, there were human beings on earth in trouble, not able to face the issues of life. It has been that way from the beginning, and it is that way now all over the world. It is easy for human beings to have the feeling that life just isn't worth living. There can be on the part of a great many a feeling of resentment that "if there is a God, He must have it in for me or He would never let the world treat me like this." But, revealed through His Word comes the great truth that the Creator of the world, the One who is the Judge of mankind, has compassion for man in his trouble. This Almighty God who made the heavens and the earth actually is interested in the welfare and the experience of human beings. He wants to give them a way of life that will enable them to live in this world satisfactorily and to look forward to greater things in the world to come.

The Creator of this world is also the God of the other world. God made man with a capacity for spiritual things in his soul, so that in his relationships man could have relationship to another world that is invisible — the world of God. Thus God prepared for mankind a way of living, in which man could yield himself to God and so get the help of God for living in this world adequately and satisfactorily. People will never be able to make this world good or pleasant; it was not intended to be like that. God has set up a situation in this world where man is to have a choice, so that he can turn from this world to God.

God started this in the Old Testament times with Abraham. God called him and laid a simple principle before him, promising that if he would obey, God would give him a land to possess. God would keep him and make him His own, so that He would be with Abraham. By the time of Isaiah there was in the world a group of people called "Israel," distinguished from all others in one way: they were committed to live as well as they knew how in obedience to the will of God. But human beings are such that even after they undertake to do something in a certain way, they may not carry it out. Israel did not go through with their commitment; they did not keep the rules given to them by God. God is slow to anger and plenteous in mercy; He trains His people in various ways. God sent prophets who taught the people His ways. Thus it has been through the years.

By the time Isaiah was preaching, Israel was a nation of some history and had established themselves in their land. They had built the city of Jerusalem with the temple in which to worship. God had marked them with favor from time to time. Yet, although God had blessed them, they faltered. Their hearts became enamored of worldly things. In Isaiah's time these people approached God with their lips but their hearts were far away from Him. So God sent prophets to warn the people. In the latter part of the Book of Isaiah there is a series of messages the prophet preached to people who really wanted to do the will of God, those who were called the remnant. These were people who believed God had special plans for them. Isaiah preached to them in order to show them the way to God.

The world as a whole thinks that what a preacher does is to tell what should be done. Actually, preachers should be telling people what God will do. Preachers should show people how they can relate themselves to God and how they can yield themselves to Him.

In Isaiah 57 there is a big contrast. There are two parts: first, a stern warning again to people who claim to believe in God but who really do not obey Him; and second, a gracious promise to humble people who do believe in God. The warning is given in the first twelve verses. This passage occurs in the context of gospel pronouncement. Much has been said in chapters 53 through 56 about the fullness of God's mercy and the riches of His grace, but here is the warning to keep the record clear. As gracious as God is toward sincere hearts, He will not countenance insincere, unfaithful hearts. He uses as a figure of unfaithfulness such words as *harlot* and *adultery* because that is the way God refers to people who are supposed to belong to Him but who really do not.

One of the unique features about the Scripture is that it uses illustrations that mean something where human beings live. This is what it has done here:

> But draw near hither, ye sons of the sorceress, the seed of the adulterer and the whore. Against whom do ye sport yourselves? against whom make ye a wide mouth, and draw out the tongue? are ye not children of transgression, a seed of falsehood? (Isa. 57:3,4).

This is an ugly description of an ugly thing. God exposes hearts that are not sincere. Some of the figures used are obscure to us, but many of them are very plain in what they say. God challenges them as much as to say, "Do you think you will get away with your tricky way of doing things?"

> Behind the doors also and the posts hast thou set up thy remembrance: for thou hast discovered thyself to another than me, and art gone up; thou hast enlarged thy bed, and made thee a covenant with them; thou lovedst their bed where thou sawest it. And thou wentest to the king with ointment, and didst increase thy perfumes, and didst send thy messengers far off, and didst debase thyself even unto hell (Isa. 57:8,9).

This is the picture of a woman who, in order to advance herself, actually gave herself over to illicit relationships with prominent people. That is the ugly story of Israel and that is what God thinks of any person who claims to be walking with Him when his heart is concerned with the pleasures of this world.

This is not a broadside against faltering people, nor a wholesale condemnation of anybody who might do wrong. This is an exposure of people who claim to be doing the things of the Lord but are secretly trying to do something else in order to gain an advantage of some kind.

> Thou art wearied in the greatness of thy way; yet saidst thou not, There is no hope: thou hast found the life of thine hand; there-fore thou wast not grieved. And of whom hast thou been afraid or feared, that thou hast lied, and hast not remembered me, nor laid it to thy heart? have not I held my peace even of old, and thou fearest me not? I will declare thy righteousness, and thy works; for they shall not profit thee. When thou criest, let thy companies deliver thee; but the wind shall carry them all away; vanity shall take them: but he that putteth his trust in me shall possess the land, and shall inherit my holy mountain (Isa. 57:10-13).

No questions are asked; absolutely no conditions are given. All He asks of any human being is that that person trust in Him, but the context implies that He looks for sincerity.

The expression "possess the land" refers to the promised land; we would say today the promises of God.

> And shall say, Cast ye up, cast ye up, prepare the way, take up the stumbling block out of the way of my people. For thus saith the high and lofty One that inhabiteth eternity, whose name is Holy; I dwell in the high and holy place, with him also that is of a contrite and humble spirit, to revive the spirit of the humble, and to revive the heart of the contrite ones. For I will not contend for ever, neither will I be always wroth: for the spirit should fail before me, and the souls which I have made (Isa. 57:14-16).

The children of Israel had done wrong. Because of this God had punished them, or rather judged them:

> For the iniquity of his covetousness was I wroth, and smote him: I hid me, and was wroth, and he went on frowardly in the way of his heart. I have seen his ways, and will heal him: I will lead him also, and restore comforts unto him and to his mourners (Isa. 57:17,18).

The conditions, then, under which believers can qualify for God's gracious healing are these: they are to be humble and contrite, genuine and sincere, before God.

> I create the fruit of the lips; Peace, peace to him that is far off, and to him that is near, saith the Lord; and I will heal him. But the wicked are like the troubled sea, when it cannot rest, whose waters cast up mire and dirt. There is no peace, saith my God, to the wicked (Isa. 57:19-21).

Remember, when the word "wicked" is used in the Hebrew language, it refers to someone who is out of the way, on the wrong road. If he stays on the wrong road, he will come to grief; and if he stays there long enough, he will become vulgar and vicious. The moment one deviates from the will of God, *at that time* (in the Hebrew language) wickedness sets in. Only when we are walking in the will of God can we have this peace that God provides.

Chapter 41

TRUE REPENTANCE

Isaiah 58 sets out a clear description of what real revival, turning to God, looks like. The prophet is being commanded by God:

> Cry aloud, spare not, lift up thy voice like a trumpet, and show
> my people their transgression, and the house of Jacob their sins
> (Isa. 58:1).

God will save such as come to Him and trust in Him. The one point being emphasized is that the human being is to yield to God. But there are many willing to yield who do not know how, and that is where the prophet comes in; he tells them how. Here the prophet is dealing with God's people about their sins. We should have in mind that a person coming to the Lord to be saved is like a patient going to the hospital to be cured. The doctors and nurses will minister to the patient and, according to the limits of their ability, they will alleviate the illness, but it may take time to effect a cure. So when the soul comes to God, the results may not happen in a moment. If I receive God into my heart, I will not at that moment be completely transformed. My attitude may be changed; I may have turned from going in one direction to go in another. I may be completely different: whereas I used to walk away from God, now I walk toward Him. Many things I had been doing wrong will need to be relearned. Often, before I learn the new things, I need to see what is wrong in the old things. So the prophet begins by opening to the believing people the nature of their own hearts.

When people listen to a true minister of the Word of God, they feel time and time again that they are sinners, which is the truth. When sin becomes obvious, it is hoped the preacher will also show that Christ is the Savior. When the sinfulness of the heart is revealed and the graciousness of God shown, the preacher seeks to induce the person to turn to the Lord. The New Testament expresses this positively: "Deny yourself and turn to the Lord." In order to deny themselves, people first need to see that there is something about them that is not what it should be. Many people are not willing to let go of themselves as long as they think there is anything good in them. All need to say with the apostle Paul:

> For I know that in me (that is, in my flesh,) dwelleth no good thing: for to will is present with me; but how to perform that which is good I find not (Rom. 7:18).

To induce this attitude and to help people accept this truth, the prophet preaches and teaches.

> Yet they seek me daily, and delight to know my ways, as a nation that did righteousness, and forsook not the ordinance of their God: they ask of me the ordinances of justice; they take delight in approaching to God (Isa. 58:2).

What really upsets a parent is for a child who has done wrong to want to be treated as though he has done right; and that is the way God feels.

> Wherefore have we fasted, say they, and thou seest not? (Isa. 58:3).

We know the word "fasting" is in the Bible and, generally speaking, we know little more about it. Actually, fasting is far more than going without a meal and this chapter will make that clear. These people had fasted once or twice a week before God but they were not blessed and they blamed God for the lack of blessing.

> Wherefore have we fasted, say they, and thou seest not? wherefore have we afflicted our soul, and thou takest no knowledge? Behold, in the day of your fast ye find pleasure, and exact all your labours (Isa. 58:3).

They ask why it is that when they have acted religiously and have afflicted their souls, mourned and prayed about their sins, and have gone through heart-searching experiences, God did not seem to change His attitude. But here is the answer: "Behold, in the day of your fast ye find pleasure, and exact all your labors." Consider this: they were not to do the ordinary things that they did for pleasure or for profit. Even among us there are those today who make a practice of attending an early church service on Sunday morning so that the rest of that day they may do as they please, whether it be for pleasure or for business. God notices this, and He does not accept that as genuine.

> Behold, ye fast for strife and debate, and to smite with the fist of wickedness: ye shall not fast as ye do this day, to make your voice to be heard on high (Isa. 58:4).

Apparently there is such a thing as a person going to church in a way that is an affliction to the soul:

> Is it such a fast that I have chosen? a day for a man to afflict his soul? is it to bow down his head as a bulrush, and to spread sackcloth and ashes under him? wilt thou call this a fast, and an acceptable day to the Lord? (Isa. 58:5).

I believe fasting generally includes the idea that worshipers should deny themselves something. They fast from food when they do not eat the usual food, and they fast from their labors when they do not do the usual labor. Some people avoid going to certain places of amusement because they think those amusements are too worldly, and they are thus fasting. Jesus of Nazareth talked about this. He said that when believers fast, they are not to let their faces be long and sad so that everybody else would know they were suffering a great loss.

> Is not this the fast that I have chosen? to loose the bands of wickedness, to undo the heavy burdens, and to let the oppressed go free, and that ye break every yoke? (Isa. 58:6).

Wherever we see people who are turning away from God, we should try to win them back. In our country there is not so much physical hunger as spiritual hunger, and oftentimes there is social hunger.

> Is it not to deal thy bread to the hungry, and that thou bring the poor that are cast out to thy house? when thou seest the naked, that thou cover him; and that thou hide not thyself from thine own flesh? (Isa. 58:7).

If we hear of someone in real trouble, will we visit that person and let her feel our human sympathy? God is pleased with that. That is what He looks for.

And the Lord shall guide thee continually, and satisfy thy soul in drought, and make fat thy bones: and thou shalt be like a watered garden, and like a spring of water, whose waters fail not. And they that shall be of thee shall build the old waste places: thou shalt raise up the foundations of many generations; and thou shalt be called, The repairer of the breach, The restorer of paths to dwell in (Isa. 58:11,12).

I realize more and more that is what God is looking for.

There are those who carry heavy burdens because of the sins of some for whom they care; and the Lord knows about that. The Lord Jesus said, "My soul is exceeding sorrowful even unto death," but when He looked into the face of God, there was joy. That is not cheap but there is an inward sense of well-being when we realize that God is on our side; He will take care of us, and we will rejoice. Paul said, "Rejoice in the Lord alway, and again, I say, rejoice" (Phil. 4:4). God is gracious and merciful. We can turn to Him and be blessed.

Chapter 42

THE SINS OF GOD'S PEOPLE

After Isaiah had described the simple procedure by which any person could come to God and had emphasized again the gracious promises of God to save whosoever would come, in chapter 59 he gives a description of the sins of God's people.

It seems that Israel had been inclined to question the power of God in that the land had not experienced the favor of God. There had not been that victory over their enemies that tradition had encouraged them to expect, but Isaiah bluntly points out the real reason.

> Behold, the Lord's hand is not shortened, that it cannot save; neither his ear heavy, that it cannot hear: but your iniquities have separated between you and your God, and your sins have hid his face from you, that he will not hear. For your hands are defiled with blood, and your fingers with iniquity; your lips have spoken lies, your tongue hath muttered perverseness (Isa. 59:1-3).

This brings clearly to mind the fact that the grace of God is available to those who have repented and confessed their sins. Unconfessed sin disqualifies the sinner from receiving God's salvation.

Isaiah goes on to point out that these people have deliberately followed a course of ungodly thinking and doing. They have not sought justice in dealing with other people, nor have they sought truth in thinking about God. They have actually promoted that which led them to evil.

> The way of peace they know not; and there is no judgment in their goings: they have made them crooked paths: whosoever goeth therein shall not know peace (Isa. 59:8).

231

Because of such ungodly conduct the people of Israel were doomed to distress and darkness. They had the normal desires to achieve security and satisfaction, but, being without God, they had no prospect of salvation. Their plight was indeed desperate.

> Therefore is judgment far from us, neither doth justice overtake us: we wait for light, but behold obscurity; for brightness, but we walk in darkness. We grope for the wall like the blind, and we grope as if we had no eyes: we stumble at noon day as in the night; we are in desolate places as dead men. We roar all like bears, and mourn sore like doves: we look for judgment, but there is none; for salvation, but it is far off from us (Isa. 59: 9-11).

Isaiah acknowledges to God the transgressions and the sins of the people that shut them away from God. There is an unwillingness to face the truth, causing lying toward God and injustice toward man.

> And judgment is turned away backward, and justice standeth afar off: for truth is fallen in the street, and equity cannot enter. Yea, truth faileth; and he that departeth from evil maketh himself a prey: and the Lord saw it, and it displeased him that there was no judgment (Isa. 59:14,15).

The prophet reveals that God saw that His people were helpless, and that no one was interceding for them, so He took action to help them. He sent the Messiah to enter the situation as their Defender; and He will engage in battle with the enemies of God's people.

> So shall they fear the name of the Lord from the west, and his glory from the rising of the sun. When the enemy shall come in like a flood, the spirit of the Lord shall lift up a standard against him (Isa. 59:19).

In spite of the record of apostasy in Israel and the widespread prevalence of sin and unbelief, God will in grace send the Messiah.

> And the Redeemer shall come to Zion, and unto them that turn from transgression in Jacob, saith the Lord (Isa. 59:20).

And then Isaiah reveals the gracious plan of God to permanently deliver those who believe in Him by putting His Spirit and His word in them forever.

As for me, this is my covenant with them, saith the Lord; My spirit that is upon thee, and my words which I have put in thy mouth, shall not depart out of thy mouth, nor out of the mouth of thy seed, nor out of the mouth of thy seed's seed, saith the Lord, from henceforth and for ever (Isa. 59:21).

Chapter 43

A SONG OF TRIUMPH

Isaiah 60 is almost like pulling the curtains aside on a bright day to let the sun shine in.

> Arise, shine; for thy light is come, and the glory of the Lord is risen upon thee (Isa. 60:1).

The enduring emphasis throughout this chapter is that the glory of the Lord has come to shine upon His people. "Arise" is a call to attention, to stand up and face the world, as it were — to be ready to take part in things. Someone might very well wonder how we can shine. There are various ways. Suppose you had in mind bringing light into the consciousness of others. Instead of just thinking that the light is in you, think of it as if it were a part of yourself. Suppose you think of yourself as a reflector (the Old Testament use of the word). Perhaps you remember that as a child you held a mirror and threw sunlight at a certain spot. You had to bring the mirror into such relationship with the sun that the sun came full on it, then you could turn the mirror so that it reflected the light.

So if you are going to shine, you will have to bring your heart into such a relationship with God that the light of His countenance will shine directly into your heart. If you do that, it will reflect light wherever you are. It was that way with Moses. You remember he spent forty days on Mt. Sinai in the presence of God and when he came down and moved among the people, his face shone so brightly they could not look at it. He had to take a veil and cover his face to be able to move among the people, and he did not even realize the glow. Jesus of Nazareth had something to say about this:

> Let your light so shine before men, that they may see your good works, and glorify your Father which is in heaven (Matt. 5:16).

234

He also said:

> Neither do men light a candle, and put it under a bushel, but on
> a candlestick; and it giveth light unto all that are in the house
> (Matt. 5:15).

In the Sermon on the Mount we learn that the shining forth is
done in good works. Nothing in the world will bring so much
light into the hearts of others as kindness. I once read that
kindness is the universal language.

> For, behold, the darkness shall cover the earth, and gross
> darkness the people: but the Lord shall arise upon thee, and his
> glory shall be seen upon thee (Isa. 60:2).

I sometimes get discouraged about the world these days, until I
remember that I am not figuring on the world getting anywhere, anyway; then I am no longer discouraged. No one
knows what a day will bring forth, but remember this: "The
Lord shall arise upon thee, and his glory shall be seen upon
thee."

> And the Gentiles shall come to thy light, and kings to the
> brightness of thy rising. Lift up thine eyes round about, and see:
> all they gather themselves together, they come to thee: thy sons
> shall come from far, and thy daughters shall be nursed at thy
> side. Then thou shalt see, and flow together, and thine heart
> shall fear, and be enlarged; because the abundance of the sea
> shall be converted unto thee, the forces of the Gentiles shall
> come unto thee (Isa. 60:3-5).

This is a way of saying there will be a response from all over
the world to the things of God. The Lord will raise up a
standard, and people will respond to Him. From verse 6 the
remainder of the chapter contains a poetic and detailed description of that day and time. As we read it, we can fill in our
own day and time. Various values and treasures will come.

> The multitude of camels shall cover thee, the dromedaries of
> Midian and Ephah; all they from Sheba shall come: they shall
> bring gold and incense; and they shall show forth the praises of
> the Lord (Isa. 60:6).

Those who put their trust in God will be enriched.

> And the sons of strangers shall build up thy walls, and their kings
> shall minister unto thee: for in my wrath I smote thee, but in my
> favour have I had mercy on thee (Isa. 60:10).

An amazing statement! This is the word spoken to people who had suffered the judgment of God, but after they repented, His mercy was rich and full. We are reminded of the promise to Abraham: "I will bless them that bless thee, and curse him that curseth thee" (Gen. 12:3).

> Therefore thy gates shall be open continually; they shall not be shut day nor night; that men may bring unto thee the forces of the Gentiles, and that their kings may be brought. For the nation and kingdom that will not serve thee shall perish; yea, those nations shall be utterly wasted (Isa. 60:11,12).

God's blessing will bring together much that is good to those who put their trust in Him. This idea is continued in succeeding verses.

> The sons also of them that afflicted thee shall come bending unto thee; and all they that despised thee shall bow themselves down at the soles of thy feet; and they shall call thee, The city of the Lord, The Zion of the Holy One of Israel. Whereas thou hast been forsaken and hated, so that no man went through thee, I will make thee an eternal excellency, a joy of many generations (Isa. 60:14,15).

This is wonderful, triumphant victory for those who put their trust in God. Once they were wayward and God dealt with them in judgment, but they repented and cast themselves upon the grace of God. Then God moved all the forces of heaven and earth to bring blessing upon these people. Outstanding in all of this will be that God is the Redeemer, the Savior.

> Violence shall no more be heard in thy land, wasting nor destruction within thy borders; but thou shalt call thy walls Salvation, and thy gates Praise (Isa. 60:18).

This is the blessed glory that will come upon those who sincerely turn to God. Salvation is of God; over and over we are reminded believers do not have to earn it.

> The sun shall be no more thy light by day; neither for brightness shall the moon give light unto thee: but the Lord shall be unto thee an everlasting light, and thy God thy glory (Isa. 60:19).

Here Isaiah looks forward to the eternal day, a description of which is found in the closing chapters of Revelation. One of the things about heaven is that there is no night there. Another thing is that there is no need for the sun because the Lord will be the light of heaven.

> Thy sun shall no more go down; neither shall thy moon withdraw itself: for the Lord shall be thine everlasting light, and the days of thy mourning shall be ended. Thy people also shall be all righteous: they shall inherit the land for ever, the branch of my planting, the work of my hands, that I may be glorified. A little one shall become a thousand, and a small one a strong nation: I the Lord will hasten it in his time (Isa. 60:20-22).

The entire sixtieth chapter is one tremendous presentation of a glorious, lasting light that will shine from the presence of God upon those who put their trust in Him. This is altogether beyond the natural. God will pour out blessings that will be wonderful, rich, full, free, eternal.

Chapter 44

THE REMNANT SHALL BE BLESSED

> The spirit of the Lord God is upon me; because the Lord hath anointed me to preach good tidings unto the meek; he hath sent me to bind up the broken-hearted, to proclaim liberty to the captives, and the opening of the prison to them that are bound; to proclaim the acceptable year of the Lord, and the day of vengeance of our God; to comfort all that mourn; to appoint unto them that mourn in Zion, to give unto them beauty for ashes, the oil of joy for mourning, the garment of praise for the spirit of heaviness; that they might be called trees of righteousness, the planting of the Lord, that he might be glorified (Isa. 61:1-3).

Jesus of Nazareth went into the synagogue in Nazareth on the Sabbath day as He was accustomed to do; and the man who was in charge handed Him the scroll and asked Him to read. The scroll He read was the book of the prophet Isaiah. We are told that when He finished reading, He sat down (it was the custom that when a man lectured, he would sit) and He taught them. We read in Luke 4 how He stopped in the middle of Isaiah 61:2; perhaps because His first coming was to bring good news, not judgment. "And he began to say unto them, This day is this scripture fulfilled in your ears" (Luke 4:21). When He was through, the Book of Luke records that they marvelled at all the gracious words that He uttered. I would like to preach the gospel in such a way that people would say, "That just can't be true; that's just too good." Then I would know I was probably telling the truth.

In human experience, when we commit ourselves to something and start moving in that direction, we sometimes get queer notions about things and we need to be straightened out from time to time. Our appropriation of the things of God is prolonged. We move along step by step, and our progress is not steady. Oftentimes we make a start, then we relax our intentions. But God is faithful; He knows our hearts and He will deal with us in such a way that we will not remain indifferent.

The events that created the situation in which Isaiah preached were actual events in history. The people of Israel had been called by God to serve Him, but they had been unfaithful to Him. They had become wayward and God had sent men to warn them, teaching them that they were not doing what they were supposed to do. He sent severe judgment on them, which first destroyed the northern nation of Israel and then, several generations later, the southern nation of Judah so that the people were carried away captive. During those experiences, God worked on the people in a way of letting them feel the reality of His dealing with them. While God was dealing with them in judgment, some responded to Him. Those were the ones with whom God was going to deal in a special way.

In the message of the Book of Isaiah, God's people are called on to seek His face sincerely. He promises them something new: the new covenant. This is a promise to those who turn to Him. He will come Himself and change them and He will live His life in them. The remnant will be blessed through the Messiah, the chosen One. The first judgment will be shattering, but those who in judgment turn to Him will be greatly blessed, and will glorify God in service.

> And they shall build the old wastes, they shall raise up the former desolations, and they shall repair the waste cities, the desolations of many generations (Isa. 61:4).

These believers will be used in an amazing achievement of works of salvation.

> And strangers shall stand and feed your flocks, and the sons of the alien shall be your plowmen and your vinedressers. But ye shall be named the Priests of the Lord: men shall call you the Ministers of our God: ye shall eat the riches of the Gentiles, and in their glory shall ye boast yourselves (Isa. 61:5,6).

Every good thing will come to these people. Because of His grace God will work this new thing in them.

Would the affect of their testimony mean they would restore certain social practices? I would say yes, but also spiritual practices. The language is that of the earthly nature of the kingdom of Israel: the language of cities and of waste places; but it also has spiritual significance. Every distress they endured under God's chastening hand will be abundantly compensated in blessing.

> For your shame ye shall have double; and for confusion they shall rejoice in their portion: therefore in their land they shall possess the double: everlasting joy shall be unto them. For I the Lord love judgment, I hate robbery for burnt offering; and I will direct their work in truth, and I will make an everlasting covenant with them (Isa. 61:7,8).

In the new covenant God will produce results:

> I will greatly rejoice in the Lord, my soul shall be joyful in my God; for he hath clothed me with the garments of salvation, he hath covered me with the robe of righteousness, as a bridegroom decketh himself with ornaments, and as a bride adorneth herself with her jewels. For as the earth bringeth forth her bud, and as the garden causeth the things that are sown in it to spring forth; so the Lord God will cause righteousness and praise to spring forth before all the nations (Isa. 61:10,11).

God will work in you and produce joy, salvation, and righteousness the way He makes grass grow and flowers bloom. In the new covenant God will work in us to will and to do of His good pleasure, and if we have the right attitude toward Him and a right relationship with Him, we do not need to work to produce righteous living: it will happen in us.

Under the old covenant, "Blessed is the man that doeth these things," but in the new covenant, "Blessed is the man in whom God works out His will."

Chapter 62 is a prolonged description of the promise of glory to God's people. Verse after verse tells what God will do for His people.

> For Zion's sake will I not hold my peace, and for Jerusalem's sake I will not rest, until the righteousness thereof go forth as brightness, and the salvation thereof as a lamp that burneth (Isa. 62:1).

Bear in mind that every promise God makes to Zion, to His people, He makes to all who believe in the Lord Jesus Christ. What He promises here in this prophecy, He is doing now in the believer in Christ. God will not rest until He accomplishes in every sincere believing person what He has in mind to do. Paul was persuaded "that He which hath begun a good work in you will perform it" (Phil. 1:6) and in Isaiah we read this prophecy concerning the Lord Jesus Christ: "He shall not fail nor be discouraged" (Isa. 42:4).

> And the Gentiles shall see thy righteousness, and all kings thy glory: and thou shalt be called by a new name, which the mouth of the Lord shall name (Isa. 62:2).

In Old Testament days this work of God was called "a new name"; in the New Testament we are told we "must be born again" (John 3:7).

> Thou shalt also be a crown of glory in the hand of the Lord, and a royal diadem in the hand of thy God (Isa. 62:3).

God will produce in us that which will be a crown of glory in His hand. We are coming to a description of that normal spiritual experience that includes our starting out with the Lord, then our having a shattering experience in which our waywardness leads us away from Him. When He brings chastening experiences, we feel as though God has completely forsaken us, but there is a gracious promise.

> Thou shalt no more be termed Forsaken; neither shall thy land any more be termed Desolate: but thou shalt be called Hephzibah, and thy land Beulah: for the Lord delighteth in thee, and thy land shall be married (Isa. 62:4).

Believers will be fortunate enough to be considered members of the bride of Christ. He will rejoice in us as if it were a marriage, and this will happen to all those who believe.

> For as a young man marrieth a virgin, so shall thy sons marry thee: and as the bridegroom rejoiceth over the bride, so shall thy God rejoice over thee (Isa. 62:5).

The Lord will not rest until His people are fully saved into glory.

> I have set watchmen upon thy walls, O Jerusalem, which shall never hold their peace day nor night: ye that make mention of the Lord, keep not silence, and give him no rest, till he establish, and till he make Jerusalem a praise in the earth (Isa. 62:6,7).

God inspires intercessory prayer on our behalf; we are moved to want to pray for others and this disposition to pray for others is from God. I ask myself if, as a watchman, I have been as faithful as I could have been. May each of us respond to the inward urge to pray for other people; that is part of God's plan.

When believers pray constantly, that is one of the ways God gets things done.

> The Lord hath sworn by his right hand, and by the arm of his strength, Surely I will no more give thy corn to be meat for thine enemies; and the sons of the stranger shall not drink thy wine, for the which thou hast laboured: but they that have gathered it shall eat it, and praise the Lord; and they that have brought it together shall drink it in the courts of my holiness (Isa. 62:8,9).

Believers will prosper and be kept from harm because in this new covenant prayer is being offered. While you and I share in this praying, we should keep in mind that we have a faithful One praying who never slumbers nor sleeps — the Lord Jesus Himself. This is the basis for the confidence we have that God will accomplish His purpose.

We read further that all of this will be done in the Messiah.

> Go through, go through the gates; prepare ye the way of the people; cast up, cast up the highway; gather out the stones; lift up a standard for the people. Behold, the Lord hath proclaimed unto the end of the world, Say ye to the daughter of Zion, Behold, thy salvation cometh (Isa. 62:10,11).

We have learned to feel that this message could apply to Jesus of Nazareth riding into Jerusalem on the colt of a donkey to offer Himself as the blessed One of God, and that the idea of preparing the highway could refer to the ministry of John the Baptist, who was the forerunner of Jesus Christ.

> Behold, his reward is with him, and his work before him. And they shall call them, The holy people, The redeemed of the Lord: and thou shalt be called, Sought out, A city not forsaken (Isa. 62:11,12).

What a marvelous thing it is to belong to Him! It is so simple! The believer sincerely and humbly receives God's word. He honestly and truly is straightforward with God and confesses his sins, throwing himself upon the mercy and the grace of God. Intercessory prayer will be involved. It is a common thing for us to pray in calamity; let us also learn to pray for growth and for fruitfulness, so that good people may be strengthened. We should not overlook the importance of praying for one another at all times.

Chapter 45

THE REMNANT WILL BELIEVE

When interpreting a book like Isaiah, it is well to keep in mind that it was not written so that it would follow a logical order — A, B, C — all the way through. It is not written in consecutive fashion so that everything in chapter 11 follows everything in the first ten chapters, and so on. It is as though there were certain great truths Isaiah had in heart and mind that he spoke of at various times in various ways. In the field of music there is a composition that we call a symphony where a musical theme is played over and over — one time at a high level, another time at a lower level — sometimes accenting certain notes. When one listens to it attentively, he senses the same theme repeated over and over until it makes a profound impression on him.

It is best to think of the Book of Isaiah like that — a certain truth being played over and over. The same idea will be repeated many times. God will bring His people to judgment; He will bring them to distress. Some will turn to Him, and He will by His Messiah save them. When He does, He will gloriously bless them. Chapter 62 described the glorious blessing that will come upon His people; chapter 63 starts again from the beginning. The first six verses introduce the Messiah.

> Who is this that cometh from Edom, with dyed garments from Bozrah? this that is glorious in his apparel, traveling in the greatness of his strength? I that speak in righteousness, mighty to save. Wherefore art thou red in thine apparel, and thy garments like him that treadeth in the winevat? I have trodden the winepress alone; and of the people there was none with me: for I will tread them in mine anger, and trample them in my fury; and their blood shall be sprinkled upon my garments, and I will stain all my raiment. For the day of vengeance is in mine heart, and the year of my redeemed is come (Isa. 63:1-4).

Stern words! They refer to the Messiah. Oftentimes when I hear people speak of the Lord Jesus Christ, I can appreciate the truth of what they say as far as it goes, but then I become uneasy because it is so often overstated: His kindness, His gentleness, His sweetness. All this is wonderfully true and comforting to the humble and to the contrite heart; but there is nothing kind or gentle or sweet in Christ for the rebellious ones, of whom there are many. This is an aspect of Christ that in our gospel preaching today is largely omitted. Christ will smite the nations with a rod of iron; He is coming in judgment; He will judge the people with fire. This is Bible language. In the Book of Revelation we find Him like the mighty Warrior, riding on His white horse — the King of Kings, with "the Word of God" emblazoned upon Him. God will not be mocked by anyone. When the human heart persists in being incorrigible and one hardens himself against Almighty God, God will not treat him in soft fashion.

This seems to be in sharp contrast with what we have just heard: the gracious, sweet words that God speaks to the humble and the contrite heart, whom the Lord will not despise. Paul says in 1 Thessalonians 1:8 that Jesus Christ is coming "in flaming fire, taking vengeance on them that know not God."

> And I looked, and there was none to help; I wondered that there was none to uphold: therefore mine own arm brought salvation unto me; and my fury, it upheld me. And I will tread down the people in mine anger, and make them drunk in my fury, and I will bring down their strength to the earth (Isa. 63:5,6).

Messiah will come in zealous judgment; He will tread down in anger those who oppose God. He looked "and there was none to help." People did not care about helping the poor. Since none among God's own people would lead into true righteousness, He took it upon Himself to do so, moving in judgment.

Following this, with this judgment coming, there is a resumé of spiritual experience as it is seen in the history of Israel:

> I will mention the lovingkindness of the Lord, and the praises of the Lord, according to all that the Lord hath bestowed on us, and the great goodness toward the house of Israel, which he hath

bestowed on them according to his mercies, and according to the multitude of his lovingkindnesses. For he said, Surely they are my people, children that will not lie: so he was their Saviour. In all their affliction he was afflicted, and the angel of his presence saved them: in his love and in his pity he redeemed them; and he bare them, and carried them all the days of old (Isa. 63:7-9).

God began His gracious dealing in kindness. "In all their affliction he was afflicted." I know of no more wonderful words about God than those. When we have trouble, He has trouble; when we have sorrow, He has sorrow. "He bare them, and carried them all the days of old." This could well be a description of the way He brought Israel out of the land of Egypt, carrying them on His wings.

But they rebelled, and vexed his holy spirit: therefore he was turned to be their enemy, and he fought against them (Isa. 63:10).

The language here implies that God turned against them in judgment and chastening. There is only that one verse, no long description of what happened.

Then he remembered the days of old, Moses, and his people, saying, Where is he that brought them up out of the sea with the shepherd of his flock? where is he that put his holy spirit within him? that led them by the right hand of Moses with his glorious arm, dividing the water before them, to make himself an everlasting name? (Isa. 63:11,12).

When God deals with people in judgment and chastening, leading them through suffering experiences, they cry out and ask, "Where is God? this God who brought us out of the land of Egypt?" But now Isaiah records their repentant prayer:

Look down from heaven, and behold from the habitation of thy holiness and of thy glory: where is thy zeal and thy strength, the sounding of thy bowels and of thy mercies toward me? are they restrained? Doubtless thou art our father, though Abraham be ignorant of us, and Israel acknowledge us not: thou, O Lord, art our father, our redeemer; thy name is from everlasting (Isa. 63:15,16).

This is the prayer of a believer who is being chastened — one who believes in the Lord but wanders away from Him and then is brought up sharply by God's chastening, as Israel had been. This is the remnant who, in chastening, do not become bitter. They cry out to God. They are in distress and they cry out to God. Their prayer can serve as a basis for repentant prayer. The believer should start laying hold on the name of God. This is where his greatest hope is. God is faithful. The believer's greatest expectation is that God is his Father. They cling to Him and call for Him:

> O Lord, why hast thou made us to err from thy ways, and hardened our heart from thy fear? Return for thy servants' sake, the tribes of thine inheritance. The people of thy holiness have possessed it but a little while: our adversaries have trodden down thy sanctuary. We are thine: thou never barest rule over them; they were not called by thy name. Oh that thou wouldest rend the heavens, that thou wouldest come down, that the mountains might flow down at thy presence, as when the melting fire burneth, the fire causeth the waters to boil, to make thy name known to thine adversaries, that the nations may tremble at thy presence! (Isa. 63:17-19; 64:1,2).

This is the cry of repentant people: that the Lord God should come and show Himself and take a hand in this matter. They freely confess they are as nothing, but God is everything. This is the essence of repentant prayer: laying hold on God. We are reminded of Jacob at Peniel on the occasion when he met the angel and they wrestled until the breaking of day. The one thing Jacob wanted was blessing from God: "I will not let thee go except thou bless me."

> When thou didst terrible things which we looked not for, thou camest down, the mountains flowed down at thy presence. For since the beginning of the world men have not heard, nor perceived by the ear, neither hath the eye seen, O God, beside thee, what he hath prepared for him that waiteth for him (Isa. 64:3,4).

In 1 Corinthians 2:9 Paul repeats this passage.

> Thou meetest him that rejoiceth and worketh righteousness, those that remember thee in thy ways: behold, thou art wroth; for we have sinned: in those is continuance, and we shall be saved (Isa. 64:5).

This is confession. They admitted their sins. They did not blame God for dealing with them in judgment but they did not want to be cut off.

> But we are all as an unclean thing, and all our righteousness are as filthy rags; and we all do fade as a leaf; and our iniquities, like the wind, have taken us away. And there is none that calleth upon thy name, that stirreth up himself to take hold of thee: for thou hast hid thy face from us, and hast consumed us, because of our iniquities (Isa. 64:6,7).

It is important to me to have this insight, that even though I am a sinner, and even if my record does not amount to anything, God is mine. He invited me to come and I came; He belongs to me and I belong to Him.

> But now, O Lord, thou art our father; we are the clay, and thou our potter; and we all are the work of thy hand (Isa. 64:8).

This is the essence of repentant prayer. In this praying, notice again that not only do they say, "There is none that calleth upon thy name, that stirreth up himself to take hold of thee" but they acknowledge He has hid His face from them. Let us pause for a moment and answer a question we sometimes ask one another: Should we pray even when we do not feel like it? or should we pray only when we feel like it? It is a mark of spiritual vitality when we stir ourselves to pray. Human nature does not want to take the time for prayer. The disposition to pray is a little like the sugar in the bottom of the cup. If we leave the disposition to pray alone, it will sink to the bottom of the cup, so to speak, and we will not taste it. We should stir up our sense of the possibility in prayer. We should stir up our confidence in praying until we pray about anything we are concerned about.

> Be not wroth very sore, O Lord, neither remember iniquity for ever: behold, see, we beseech thee, we are all thy people. Thy holy cities are a wilderness, Zion is a wilderness, Jerusalem a desolation (Isa. 64:9,10).

In this they admit they are unclean but they are God's people. They ask Him not to leave them now. Their spiritual experience has been devastated. They are miserable.

> Our holy and our beautiful house, where our fathers praised thee, is burned up with fire: and all our pleasant things are laid waste. Wilt thou refrain thyself for these things, O Lord? wilt thou hold thy peace, and afflict us very sore? (Isa. 64:11,12).

That is the end of that prayer. It might be they did not seem to get anywhere, but they were there all the time. They were casting themselves on the mercy of Almighty God.

In chapters 63 and 64 we have a description of the course of spiritual experience. This is the way it started, with the lovingkindness of God doing great things for His people. And that was wonderful: "In all their afflictions He was afflicted." But they rebelled and vexed His Holy Spirit. Then came the chastening, the judgment. When everything went to pieces, the people started thinking. Then they came to Him personally. First with prayer, and then with confession. This is what sinning believers should do: cast themselves on the mercy of Almighty God, calling on Him to glorify Himself and save them.

Chapter 46

BLESSING FOR THE REDEEMED

In a very striking way, in these last two chapters, it is as though Isaiah summarized the main thrust of his message. The particular function of the prophet was to speak to God's people. The people in the Old Testament — Abraham, Isaac, and Jacob, and afterwards the children of Israel — and those who in the New Testament are spoken of as the believers in the Lord Jesus Christ, commonly known as the church, constitute a group of people who have a special relationship with God. They are related to Him through His promises in Christ Jesus.

Here is something that might escape us as we approach these things: to these — God's people — much of the Scripture is addressed. Nearly all of the prophets dealt with God's people, and all of the Épistles in the New Testament are written to God's people. God has a message for the world as a whole, a very simple one. But that is not primarily what the prophets came to do. Isaiah did have a message to other nations, and the focus and attention of God's interest is to the ends of the earth, but His interest in those people to the ends of the earth is through His plan of salvation.

As Creator, He made all men, and as the God of nature and Judge of all the earth, He deals with all men.

> The heavens declare the glory of God; and the firmament showeth his handiwork. Day unto day uttereth speech, and night unto night showeth knowledge. There is no speech nor language, where their voice is not heard (Ps. 19:1-3).

Everyone can know something of God from the light of nature, and every man born in this world who has a conscience has a light from God shining in his heart. Every man who has had any kind of experience at all knows of the hand of providence in his affairs, whether he can call God by name or not. The graciousness of God in nature is one thing, but grace in Christ Jesus is much greater. God does something in His plan of salvation that is not a natural process; it is a process of grace. In the natural processes in the world, the principle that prevails seems to be "whatsoever a man soweth, that shall he also reap." The wages of sin is death for man by himself. But God sent His Son into the world that whosoever among these human beings would believe in Him should not perish but have everlasting life.

These people who believe in Him, who now have started walking with Him, are called the people of God. And as they bring up their children in the faith, the children also are among those whom we call the people of God. The persons to whom the prophet preached and to whom the apostles wrote the Epistles are the believers. What is God's great message to these people? It is that they are wayward and rebellious. God's people tend to be wayward and therefore they do not always have fellowship with God. The Lord Jesus said that the master of the household sent word to bring in other people who had not been invited, and yet there was room. The master was angry that these people who were called first did not come when they were invited. Then he said, "Go out into the highways and byways and find the blind and the lame and the halt. Compel them to come in. My house will be filled with guests."

Even at the coming of the Lord there are the wise and the foolish virgins. The foolish ones are people who understand in their minds the plan of God, but their hearts are far from it. The Old Testament prophets ministered to such people and warned them that God looks on the heart. They warned them that if they were willing and obedient, they would eat the good of the land, but if they refused and rebelled, they would be "devoured with the sword" (Isa. 1:18,19). In Isaiah 65 we have this word from God that refers to the Gentiles in the New Testament:

> I am sought of them that asked not for me; I am found of them
> that sought me not: I said, Behold me, behold me, unto a nation
> that was not called by my name (Isa. 65:1).

This brings out the amazing truth that God will turn to out-
siders and call them to Himself when His own people will not
walk with Him.

There follows a description that is quoted in the New Testament as definitely referring to God's people:

> I have spread out my hands all the day unto a rebellious people,
> which walketh in a way that was not good, after their own
> thoughts; a people that provoketh me to anger continually to my
> face; that sacrificeth in gardens, and burneth incense upon altars
> of brick; which remain among the graves, and lodge in the
> monuments, which eat swine's flesh, and broth of abominable
> things is in their vessels; which say, Stand by thyself, come not
> near to me; for I am holier than thou. These are a smoke in my
> nose, a fire that burneth all the day. Behold, it is written before
> me: I will not keep silence, but will recompense, even recom-
> pense into their bosom, your iniquities, and the iniquities of
> your fathers together, saith the Lord, which have burned in-
> cense upon the mountains, and blasphemed me upon the hills:
> therefore will I measure their former work into their bosom (Isa.
> 65:2-7).

Isaiah brings out again and again the truth that God is moved
to judgment because people whom He had blessed took the
liberty of associating with His enemies. It was this that moved
Him to judge them. But in judgment He will always watch for
those who are real believers.

> Thus saith the Lord, As the new wine is found in the cluster, and
> one saith, Destroy it not; for a blessing is in it: so will I do for my
> servants' sakes, that I may not destroy them all. And I will bring
> forth a seed out of Jacob, and out of Judah an inheritor of my
> mountains: and mine elect shall inherit it, and my servants shall
> dwell there (Isa. 65:8,9).

There is in every generation a remnant who have not bowed
to Baal. They are the ones whom God will call to Himself.

> But ye are they that forsake the Lord, that forget my holy
> mountain, that prepare a table for that troop, and that furnish
> the drink offering unto that number. Therefore will I number
> you to the sword, and ye shall all bow down to the slaughter:
> because when I called, ye did not answer; when I spake, ye did
> not hear; but did evil before mine eyes, and did choose that
> wherein I delighted not (Isa. 65:11,12).

One trembles to think that there are among us those who

know about God and who teach in Sunday school, yet who seldom read God's Word to find out what God has to say. This is what God says to them:

> Therefore thus saith the Lord God, Behold, my servants shall eat, but ye shall be hungry: behold, my servants shall drink, but ye shall be thirsty: behold, my servants shall rejoice, but ye shall be ashamed: Behold, my servants shall sing for joy of heart, but ye shall cry for sorrow of heart, and shall howl for vexation of spirit (Isa. 65:13,14).

There is more of this stern warning in these closing words of Isaiah. His major ministry was a warning to the people that God would not be satisfied with anything superficial. But God would do gracious things for those who believed:

> For, behold, I create new heavens and a new earth: and the former shall not be remembered, nor come into mind. But be ye glad and rejoice for ever in that which I create: for, behold, I create Jerusalem a rejoicing, and her people a joy. And I will rejoice in Jerusalem, and joy in my people: and the voice of weeping shall be no more heard in her, nor the voice of crying. There shall be no more thence an infant of days, nor an old man that hath not filled his days: for the child shall die a hundred years old; but the sinner being a hundred years old shall be accursed. And they shall build houses, and inhabit them; and they shall plant vineyards, and eat the fruit of them. They shall not build, and another inhabit; they shall not plant, and another eat: for as the days of a tree are the days of my people, and mine elect shall long enjoy the work of their hands (Isa. 65:17-22).

Some of the gracious things God will do are also told in verses 23-25:

> They shall not labour in vain, nor bring forth for trouble; for they are the seed of the blessed of the Lord, and their offspring with them. And it shall come to pass, that before they call, I will answer; and while they are yet speaking, I will hear. The wolf and the lamb shall feed together, and the lion shall eat straw like the bullock: and dust shall be the serpent's meat. They shall not hurt nor destroy in all my holy mountain, saith the Lord (Isa. 65:23-25).

God knows who are His. He knows those who seek His face. In the next chapter this is even more plainly expressed.

> Thus saith the Lord, The heaven is my throne, and the earth is my footstool: where is the house that ye build unto me? and where is the place of my rest? For all those things hath mine

hand made, and all those things have been, saith the Lord: but
to this man will I look, even to him that is poor and of a contrite
spirit, and trembleth at my word (Isa. 66:1,2).

More gracious words could not be spoken. Almighty God will
actually look to the one who is poor in spirit, the one who takes
God seriously. God will move heaven for that person.

They have chosen their own ways, and their soul delighteth in
their abominations. I also will choose their delusions, and will
bring their fears upon them; because when I called, none did
answer; when I spake, they did not hear: but they did evil before
mine eyes, and chose that in which I delighted not (Isa. 66:3,4).

This is the second time Isaiah says this. On such people comes
the judgment of God. In Isaiah 66:5 the prophet speaks to
God's remnant. They are deeply impressed and affected by his
word. They are amazed that God will bless them and freely
receive them when they come to Him. And so the prophet talks
more about it, and all through this chapter he describes word
for word God's plans for them.

As one whom his mother comforteth, so will I comfort you; and
ye shall be comforted in Jerusalem. And when ye see this, your
heart shall rejoice, and your bones shall flourish like an herb:
and the hand of the Lord shall be known toward his servants,
and his indignation toward his enemies. For, behold, the Lord
will come with fire, and with his chariots like a whirlwind, to
render his anger with fury, and his rebuke with flames of fire
(Isa. 66:13-15).

This truth is all through the Bible: God comes with flaming fire
to take vengeance on them that do not know Him, and He
comes with sweet tenderness to gather into His arms those who
put their trust in Him. He is at one time the Judge that will
destroy that which is wicked and the tenderhearted Father
who will gather the little ones to Him and keep them.

For by fire and by his sword will the Lord plead with all flesh:
and the slain of the Lord shall be many. They that sanctify
themselves, and purify themselves in the gardens behind one
tree in the midst, eating swine's flesh, and the abomination, and
the mouse, shall be consumed together, saith the Lord. For I
know their works and their thoughts: it shall come, that I will
gather all nations and tongues; and they shall come, and see my
glory (Isa. 66:16-18).

Then Isaiah speaks again about what God will do with those who put their trust in Him:

> And I will set a sign among them, and I will send those that escape of them unto the nations . . . and they shall declare my glory among the Gentiles (Isa. 66:19).

Many of us see in this a promise of the foreign missionary enterprise of the church because that will go on. Those who humbly seek His face will be blessed and through them He will take His message to the Gentiles, to people who have not heard.

I am of the opinion that so far as the flesh descendants of Israel and Syria and Judah and the Gentiles are concerned, it is not significant when it comes to interpreting Scripture. I am satisfied that the Israelites represent the people who have had the Word of God, the opportunity to worship God. Judah represents the minority group who really seeks to worship God, and in the temple they really try to know Him. So far as Syria is concerned, they represent the neighbors who know about the people of God, but do not want to worship God. Yet they covet the territory that God's people have. Assyria, Babylon, the desert, Arabia, and all these other places represent the world outside, those that have never heard the truth. I am not sure it is important that we should find their flesh descendants at this time; it is the spiritual descendants who count. When we read here, "They shall declare my glory among the Gentiles," I believe this is the idea: God will bless the ministry that takes His gospel to people who have never heard it. Here is a sober and solemn truth that is found all through the gospel. People can be so close to the gospel and so involved in church life that spiritual matters become familiar to them and they fail to see the Lord in whose name they have been baptized.

Who do they think God is, after all? Isaiah describes them as those who draw near to God with their mouths, but whose hearts are far from Him (Isa. 29:13). Isaiah reveals that God is provoked with that. God will do this: He will turn to people who have not heard of Him and He will call those from afar. Many times we wonder if it is not true that the gospel shines brighter in evangelistic activity than it does in the routine activity of church programs, and if it is not true that when a man who is a great evangelist stands before the world and declares the grace of the Lord Jesus Christ and promises people they can be saved, many come to God then who would not come under ordinary circumstances. Our missionaries in the foreign field often see more instances of people coming to God in a vivid and dramatic way than we often find at home. It was that way in the Scriptures, as seen in the prophets.

It was Isaiah's task to speak to a wayward people who claimed to know God. He was told when he was called that when he preached, the people would stop their ears and would not listen; they would shut their eyes and would not look; they would close their hearts so they would not hear, lest they could hear with their hearts and see with their eyes and actually be converted. So they would turn away. You remember Isaiah asked God how long that would be, and he was told to go on and preach until the cities were without inhabitants because it was his call to preach to a people who were drifting away. It was at the same time Isaiah's privilege in the course of his preaching to have this marvelous truth come out that when God saw His people failing to come near to Him, He laid bare His right arm. That is, God undertook something different: in the new covenant He would put His law in the hearts of those who were humble. He would put His Spirit within the heart of those who yielded themselves to Him and He would save to Himself a people who would be different in that they would seek the face of the Lord at all times, calling upon Him, because His Spirit would be in them, moving them that way. That was the remnant who would glorify God and to whom He would give all the promises.

This was Isaiah's great ministry in the course of all the years he preached. Isaiah further says to these people:

> And they shall bring all your brethren for an offering unto the Lord out of all nations upon horses, and in chariots, and in litters, and upon mules, and upon swift beasts, to my holy mountain Jerusalem (Isa. 66:20).

There will be a great gathering together of people out of all the nations because of this message that will go out from those who will declare His glory to the Gentiles.

> For as the new heavens and the new earth, which I will make, shall remain before me, saith the Lord, so shall your seed and your name remain. And it shall come to pass, that from one new moon to another, and from one sabbath to another, shall all flesh come to worship before me, saith the Lord (Isa. 66:22,23).

This applies to those who put their trust in Him and who walk with Him. So it was Isaiah's privilege in his lifetime to warn the people that God would judge waywardness, promising them what God would do in grace and mercy for those who would humbly seek His face. That is the great message of the book that will continue with us for all time.